THE ATLANTIC COAST

THE

ATLANTIC COAST

BY

DANIEL AMMEN

REAR ADMIRAL U. S. NAVY

NEW YORK

CHARLES SCRIBNER'S SONS

Λ

Facsimile Reprint Edition from
the original edition of 1881-1883
by The Archive Society, 1992.
Address all inquiries to:

The Archive Society
130 Locust Street
Harrisburg, PA 17101

PREFACE.

In acceding to a request to write the following pages, the writer had to regret that a brother officer had not undertaken the task, in the belief that the result would have more fully met the expectations of the public. With the view of presenting the facts as clearly as possible, the writer has not spared himself in the examination of whatever was within his reach, and trusts he may thus escape the just criticism of the intelligent reader, the more, too, as these sheets have received in advance of publication the criticism of several of the more prominent actors in the scenes.

The writer is indebted to an able friend for the criticism that these pages are largely made up of quotations, which is certainly the fact. This method has been adopted to give occurrences from every point of view obtainable where the quotation is apposite and not designed to be deceptive or meretricious. They sometimes differ considerably and honestly; each, however, is intended to present the occurrence from a given point of view. To these have been added such comment, narration, or connection as seemed pertinent and likely to afford the reader as clear an insight of the occurrence as may be possible. The writer would have gladly substituted a written detail and referred to his authorities had he supposed that it would be equally interesting and profitable to the reader, as compared with diverse statements honestly made and from as many points of view as there were intelligent observers to be found. Official reports have been carefully examined, and, indeed, form almost wholly the basis of what is presented.

It is desired to avoid exaggeration and adulation, as far as possible, leaving as it were to the reader to put on the gloss, or enthusiastic appreciation, with his own hand, and to present the facts without prejudice to friend or foe. It is for the reader to assign the merit of the men engaged, sometimes under trying difficulties, whether it be in victory, in lack of actual success, or in defeat. The public can of course more readily appreciate brilliant success than a lack of it, yet oftentimes a less measure of success does not measure a less degree of professional skill or of courage.

The publishers purpose presenting the naval operations during our civil war in three volumes. The first would naturally comprise events precedent and immediate, and as many of these transpired within the Capes of Virginia, they and matters of primary interest, and matters relating to blockaders and blockade-runners, will be found in the volume written by Professor Soley, U. S. Navy. This volume, which may be regarded as the second, treats of naval operations from Cape Hatteras to Cape Florida, along the coasts, and within the sounds, rivers, and harbors of this watershed.

As an actuality, two centres of operations existed : the one at Port Royal, the dépôt of supplies and usual headquarters of the South Atlantic Blockading Squadron ; the other within the sounds, and on the coast of North Carolina, over which the North Atlantic Blockading Squadron held watch. In order to avoid confusion, the events of each section are treated separately.

It may be added that the writer commanded a vessel in the battle of Port Royal and in subsequent operations along that coast until May, 1863, and was also present in the two bombardments of Fort Fisher. He is under many obligations to the Navy Department, to the Chiefs of Bureau of Ordnance and Construction, and to Colonel Robert N. Scott, U. S. Army, for much valuable information not otherwise attainable, and also to several friends versed in naval and military affairs, for their kindly assistance.

WASHINGTON, May, 1883.

CONTENTS.

CHAPTER VI.

CHAPTER VII.

CHAPTER VIII.

CHAPTER IX.

CHAPTER X.

CHAPTER XI.

LIST OF MAPS.

THE ATLANTIC COAST.

CHAPTER I.

CONDITION OF THE NAVY AT THE BEGINNING OF THE WAR.

POLITICAL events of great gravity occurring in Kansas, which grew out of the repeal of the "Missouri Compromise," and later, the "John Brown raid" at Harper's Ferry in October, 1860, had familiarized the people of the United States with sectional hostility and bloodshed. The centres of direction of aggressive action were in the South, and of defence against them in the North. South Carolina had vauntingly sent her uniformed company "to defend her rights" far away from her own soil, and the North had sent arms and men to resist force by force.

The violent unquiet element of the South had fully determined that the election of Mr. Lincoln to the Presidency was in itself a cause of war, and it had so organized and armed its forces as to bear down any reasonable consideration of the differences between the two sections ; nay, more, it had, aided by the demagogues of that section, constrained the men of thought and of character to accept the action of these men as embodying their own ideas. In coming centuries the remarkable address of Alexander H. Stephens at

II.—1

Milledgeville, Ga., on the 14th of November, 1860, will be read as a clear exposition of the actual political differences that were magnified by demagogues into what were urged as monstrous wrongs, and abuses that war only could terminate.

After the election of Mr. Lincoln, Mr. Buchanan, in his last message to Congress, favored, as far as he could, the attempted separation of the States, by denying "the right of coercion" to the general Government. During the remainder of his administration the heads of the Departments generally so disposed the officers, war material, and the naval vessels in commission, as to best serve the Confederates when hostilities became an actuality.

The unhappy days rolled on, and at length Mr. Lincoln was inaugurated. State after State passed acts of secession, and others that were actually prepared to follow, cried "no coercion" or, "neutrality" as the price of remaining in the Union.

At Cummings Point, the nearest land to Fort Sumter at the entrance to Charleston harbor, a battery had been erected during February and March, for the avowed purpose of reducing that work. When the attack was made, or rather after Fort Sumter had fallen, on the 13th of April, 1861, the President called on the different States to furnish 75,000 men for a period of three months. This was met by scorn and derision in all the bordering slave States, and Virginia at once passed her act of secession. Then it was, that the mask that had not concealed, and yet had been respected by the general Government, was thrown off by the conspirators. A prominent Navy officer then on duty at Washington said to those under him, even before this event, "The Government is virtually dissolved; there is the semblance of one, nothing more. Disorder reigns everywhere, except in the South, where a stable Government is already established, which will ere long receive acquisitions of membership in the States to which you belong. Mr. Lincoln will hardly attempt coercion, it would be *unconstitutional.* Would you meanly serve another people when your States have gone, even though no war grows out of the separation, or would you be base enough, for your selfish ends to do so, were there a war against the people from whom you have sprung, to whom you are allied, and whom you can now serve so well ? "

For days and even weeks the Government at Washington gave no sign nor token, and when at last it did, insidious speciousness of presentation had done sad work. Many able and unselfish officers, without a thought of treason, or without desire to do wrong or to do violence to the Government, found themselves, rather unwittingly than venally, in the toils of the enemy. These conditions prevailed at Washington and Southward, both in the army and the navy. Those officers who were deemed most likely to be influenced to suit the ends of the conspirators, had been placed, as said before, within favoring districts.

On the 4th of March, 1861, Isaac Toucey of Connecticut, who had been Secretary of the Navy for the four previous years, was succeeded by Gideon Welles, of the same State. He remained in that position for the eight years following. At that date the chiefs of Bureaus were as follows : Of Yards and Docks, Captain Joseph Smith ; of Construction, John Lenthal ; of Provisions and Clothing, Horatio Bridge ; of Ordnance and Hydrography, Captain George W. Magruder ; of Medicine, Surgeon William Whelan. These officers had been incumbents for years, and remained throughout the Civil War, with the exception of Captain Magruder, a

Virginian, who remained in office, loyally serving the purposes of the inchoate Confederacy, until the seizure of the Norfolk Navy Yard, when he tendered his resignation, and was dismissed by the President as a recognition of unfaithful service.

Within a few days after the attack on Fort Sumter, of the 78 captains on the active list, 12 resigned or were dismissed; of 114 commanders, 39; of 321 lieutenants, 73.[1]

The Confederates had been organizing their forces for months, and menaced Washington, Fortress Monroe, and Norfolk Navy Yard. It was absolutely a matter of doubt under the actual circumstances whether they might not accomplish the possession of all of these places. It was of the utmost importance to the inchoate Confederacy to get possession of the Norfolk Navy Yard and secure the large amount of ordnance stored there and to establish a good line of defence.

Nothing could more effectually serve their purpose than the pretended loyalty of the officers remaining attached to the Navy Yard who effectively cajoled the Commandant, who was old and feeble, and actually distracted by reason of the turmoil. At the final moment he was left alone, without one officer, and with but 40 marines attached to the Yard to support his authority.

The attack on Fort Sumter and its surrender affected the people of the North and of the South quite differently; while those who captured the fort boasted that they had "finished the war," the people of the North awoke to a painful realization of the fact that a war existed that must be fought to the end, and they girded up their loins as best they could; but

---

[1] After the 4th of March, 259 officers of the navy resigned their commissions or have been dismissed the service (Report Secretary Navy, July 4, 1861). Many others, belonging to States that had already seceded, had previously resigned.

the North was long in attaining that intensity of purpose that is so potent when untrained bodies of troops meet in conflict. Fort Sumter was regarded in the public mind, North and South, as the citadel of the fortress, the incarnation of rebellion, and as such it was attacked and defended.

Failing in the fleet attack, with grim satisfaction, after a time the men of the North saw its walls crumble and fall from the fire of guns four thousand yards away, until from their point of view, it had no longer shape nor semblance of a fort, nor was a single piece of ordnance permitted to stand upon what had once been its walls ; but the satisfaction of the North was not complete until, in the most formal manner, the flag that had been hauled down, four years to the day and hour from that event, again floated over the mass of ruins known as Fort Sumter.

In the confusion at the North, growing out of numerous resignations hastily sent in, abandonment of duty on the part of others, and in some cases of treachery, it is not to be wondered that the Norfolk Navy Yard fell into the hands of the Confederates, with its three thousand cannon, its fine dry dock, numerous well-appointed workshops, material, and small arms. It is not too much to say now, that it should have been held at any cost of life, long enough at least to have destroyed the cannon, workshops, and ships.

There is an extenuating fact that may be stated as a partial justification of officers who were recreant. For half a century perhaps, there had existed a kind of culture of fealty to a State, instead of to the Government which they served ; it was paraded as a dogma, and was in a degree acknowledged by some officers from the South in the military service of the Government, more than half of whom, prior to the Civil War, either came from the slave States or had married within them. Able and educated men, acknowledging this " doc-

trine," thought they had only to resign to hopelessly embarrass the Government. There was certainly for a time
great confusion, and in the case of the Norfolk Yard, great
loss. The difficulties are very properly stated in the Report
of the Secretary of the Navy, before referred to. " With so
few vessels in commission on our coast, and our crews in
distant seas, the Department was very indifferently prepared to meet the exigency that was rising. Every moment
was closely watched by the disaffected, and threatened to
precipitate measures that the country seemed anxious to
avoid. Demoralization prevailed among the officers, many
of whom, occupying the most responsible positions, betrayed
symptoms of that infidelity that has dishonored the service."

Turning to the vessels of the navy in commission, we find
that they had been placed as far as possible in positions to
render them least available. On the 4th of March the home
squadron consisted of twelve vessels, and of these only four
were in Northern ports; two of these were small steamers, a
third a sailing store-ship. The fourth had only a month before entered a Northern port; the commander, a South Caro-
linian, had loitered off the coast apparently undecided. After
reaching port he remarked to an officer of the vessel that he
had hesitated whether to obey his orders or go to Charleston,
and was quite thunderstruck when told that his hesitation
had been observed and he would have been put in irons had
he made the attempt. Several of the vessels in Southern
ports or at Vera Cruz were commanded by Southern officers,
who it was supposed would deliver their vessels into the
hands of the Confederates, but principle or policy was sufficient to spare such an attempted national disgrace.

The sailing frigate Sabine, 50 guns, the sailing sloop St.
Louis, 20, and the steamers Brooklyn, 25, and Wyandotte, 5,
were at Pensacola; and the sailing vessels Macedonian, 24,

Cumberland, 24, and the steamers Pocahontas, 5, and Powhatan, 11, were returning from Vera Cruz.

On the coast of Africa were the sailing sloops Constellation and Portsmouth, 22 guns each, the store-ship Relief, 2 guns, and the steamers Mohican, 6, Mystic, 5, Sumter, 5, and San Jacinto, 13. The steam frigate Niagara, 20, was returning from Japan, and arrived at Boston April 20th.

No one versed in naval matters can read the above disposition of force without feeling indignant at the fact that it was so placed solely to favor the conspirators. Those on the coast of Africa were out of the way of the receipt of orders, as is apparent from the fact that they were issued as soon as possible after the 4th of March, and it was not until the 15th of September that the first of these vessels reached the coast of the United States.

To the vessels in the Mediterranean the mails were more accessible ; the last of the three steam vessels there reached home July 3, 1861. The Richmond, 16, Susquehanna, 15, and Iroquois, 6 guns, were then available. The sailing frigate Congress, 50 guns, and the steamer Seminole came from the coast of Brazil, the last-named arriving home August 12th. From the East Indies, on December 30, 1861, the steamers Hartford, 16, Dacotah, 6, and sail sloop John Adams were *en route*. The steamers Pensacola, 19, fitting out at Washington, and Mississippi, 11 guns, at Boston, should be added as available. There were some old sailing vessels that might have been put in commission, but those in service were found of so little use that they were laid aside as steam vessels could be obtained. In rather indifferent condition in the Northern navy yards were the steam frigates Wabash, Minnesota, Colorado, and Roanoke, of 40 guns each. These last-named at as early a date as possible were put in commission and sent as a supporting force to vessels blockading from Cape Hatteras to the Rio Grande, the far-off boundary with Mexico. To maintain even the appearance of a blockade over the harbors, sounds, and numberless inlets required the purchase of every vessel under the flag that had possibilities of usefulness.

At New York and Boston Navy Yards there were dry docks, and at each several ways for building ships, and at Portsmouth, N. H., and Philadelphia more limited facilities for construction. To supply the needs and waste of war required the employment of every shipbuilding yard in the land.

The personnel of the "old navy," as it was called, depleted as above described, was quite insufficient to meet the exigencies of the Civil War; instead of 5,000 men afloat, as before that event, no less than 50,000 were required. To officer these men, intelligent officers and seamen from the merchant service were sought, who, after passing examinations to establish their professional fitness, were given acting appointments in various grades. It is proper to add that as a whole they fairly fulfilled reasonable expectations, and after the war was over and passing other examinations, more than fifty of these volunteer officers, many of whom would do honor to any navy, entered the regular service under provisions of law.

Just previous to the Civil War our naval vessels were as well supplied with smooth-bore shell guns and with boat howitzers as any service afloat; this was effected with considerable difficulty by the late Rear-Admiral Dahlgren when in an inferior grade. The special value of rifled ordnance under certain conditions had not yet been properly established, and there were but few pieces afloat, but they soon formed a part of the battery of every vessel.

In pages that follow, the inferiority for service of vessels "improvised" for war purposes will become painfully appa-

rent. The machinery of steamers built for commercial purposes is far more exposed than of vessels designed to carry
guns ; the question of war is simply one of *relative strength*
and preparation of the combatants ; in that respect the National vessels in commission, as a whole, were immensely
superior to those of the Confederates, or any that could be
built and fitted for service within the limits of the Confederacy. The difference between a very vulnerable naval force
and another still more so, was not only regarded with gratu-
lation, but in sheer ignorance and vanity was magnified and
expressed in the grandiloquent phrase that "the United
States had the strongest navy in the world," when nine-
tenths of the vessels bearing guns under the National flag
would have been quite powerless to meet vessels of war of
the same tonnage of any civilized nation. Toward the
close of the war we had several double-turreted vessels of an
improved Monitor type that were in their day by all odds the
strongest vessels then afloat, yet at the present time they
would be but "paper ships" under the fire of many vessels
of nearly all of the navies of the world.

It is so pleasant to deceive ourselves, that now, when our
flag waves over a wide and broad land, with its fifty-two
millions of inhabitants, some of our legislators insist that
"no nation would dare attack us." Others speak of "appro-
priating liberally for the building up of a navy" and then
gravely propose the munificent sum of $1,300,000 for the
cruising navy and half that sum, more or less, to complete an
improved Monitor. To the naval mind, or to the person
who looks at forces relatively, there is something painfully
ludicrous in such propositions. The men "who fought out
the war" are rapidly passing away ; their rude experiences,
on both sides, now happily capable of serving a common and
National purpose, will soon be wholly of the past. Then, in

1*

wars that we invite, from a lack of preparation in what plight will we be on land or on the seas ? To the old officer, whether of the land service or that of the sea, these are pain- ful reflections ; so far as he is individually concerned, for usefulness he has almost passed away ; his experiences have taught him what a lack of practical experience and a want of preparation costs a nation in a struggle with another whose military and naval establishments are constant and trained to their duties.

Recognizing the necessity of professional education in the extremity of war, in May, 1861, the Secretary of the Navy applied for an assistant, and Gustavus V. Fox was appointed Assistant Secretary. He entered the naval service as mid- shipman in 1838, passed through the professional instruction existent, and the intervening grades, to that of lieutenant, and resigned in 1856 to engage in civil pursuits.

Abroad we had enemies who desired our downfall and aided it as far as could be done without openly declaring their hostility ; so far as a lack of friendship was concerned, it applied quite as much to the South as to the North; nothing but probable complications nearer home, growing out of hostile interference, as well as the shame of attacking us without reasonable pretext, prevented " armed interven- tion," as it would have been called.

At home we had what were known as " sympathizers," spies, and even traitors in the civil services, who obtained the most accurate information of intended movements and gave it to the enemy. Certainly the skies were dark for years, yet through all the difficulties and shortcomings the nation supported its existence with fearful cost of life and treasure.

Beyond the Capes of Virginia and to Cape Florida, in re- lation to which this volume treats, a blockade, first of form and later of fact, was being established, but so far as hostile guns of opposing forces were concerned within this region they opened first at Hatteras Inlet, more than four months after the war had taken definite shape. The capture of Hatteras Inlet seemed at first of little import to the military mind, but it grew in its proportions, and as will be seen by the following chapters, was no mean event, more important, too, from successive developments, for which it was the gateway.

From the time of the fall of Sumter vessels were prepared and despatched to blockade Charleston, and operations of this nature were extended as the means at hand permitted; it may be readily supposed, however, that until the capture of Port Royal, at least, it was rather nominal than real. If vessels were captured, even in entering the principal ports, it was due rather to the stupidity of the persons attempting to run the blockade than to the effectiveness of the force employed to prevent it. Should a vessel of ordinary or light draught be desired to reach Charleston, she could be taken into Stono, or North Edisto Inlets, or into any of the channels of St. Helena, or into Port Royal Harbor, and from thence in a few hours find her way into Charleston; and if desired to reach Savannah, and fearing to approach Tybee Bar, she could enter either Warsaw or Ossabaw Sound, and find her way to her destination without difficulty. To prevent all this, and eventually, effectively as far as possible, and for securing a military base of operations it was essential that a good port on the Southern coast should be seized and held, and for that purpose not one was more desirable in every point of view than Port Royal. As the Confederates had few vessels of war, and none when military operations began, the blockade ot the coast, and effective aid to the army in the capture of forts, was naturally

regarded as the limit of usefulness of the navy, and when, at
Port Royal, the guns of the navy alone secured the fall of
the forts; then the army had to occupy and secure them
against the attacks of the enemy, and naval guns then became subsidiary or auxiliary, within their power of action,
to army operations, as well to strengthen military lines as
to extend them as far as deemed practicable, to embarrass
and hold in check as large a land force of the enemy as possible.

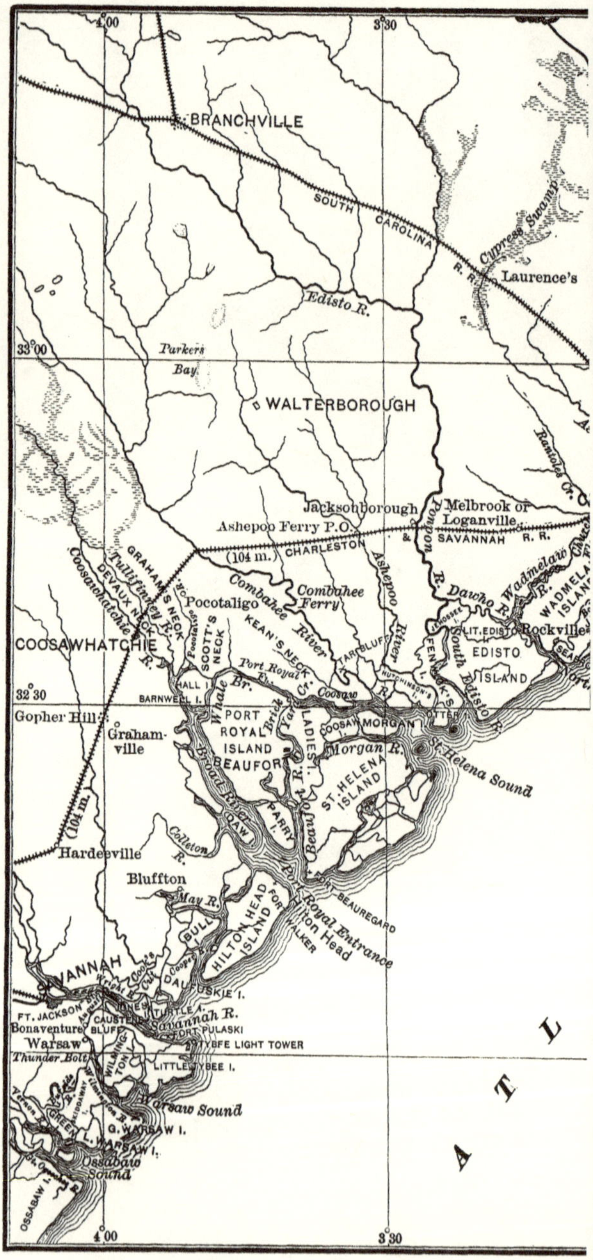

BRANCHVILLE
SOUTH CAROLINA R. R.
Cypress Swamp
Laurence's
Edisto R.
Parkers Bay
WALTERBOROUGH
Jacksonborough
Melbrook or Loganville
Ashepoo Ferry P.O.
CHARLESTON & SAVANNAH R. R.
(104 m.)
Combahee Ferry
Pocotaligo
COOSAWHATCHIE
Gopher Hill
Grahamville
Hardeeville
Bluffton
PORT ROYAL ISLAND
BEAUFORT
ST. HELENA ISLAND
St. Helena Sound
EDISTO ISLAND
Rockville
Port Royal Entrance
Hilton Head
HILTON HEAD ISLAND
FORT BEAUREGARD
FORT WALKER
SAVANNAH
Savannah R.
FT. JACKSON
Bonaventure
Warsaw
Thunder Bolt
FORT PULASKI
TYBEE LIGHT TOWER
LITTLE TYBEE I.
Warsaw Sound
G. WARSAW I.
Ossabaw Sound
OSSABAW I.
DAUFUSKIE I.
A T L

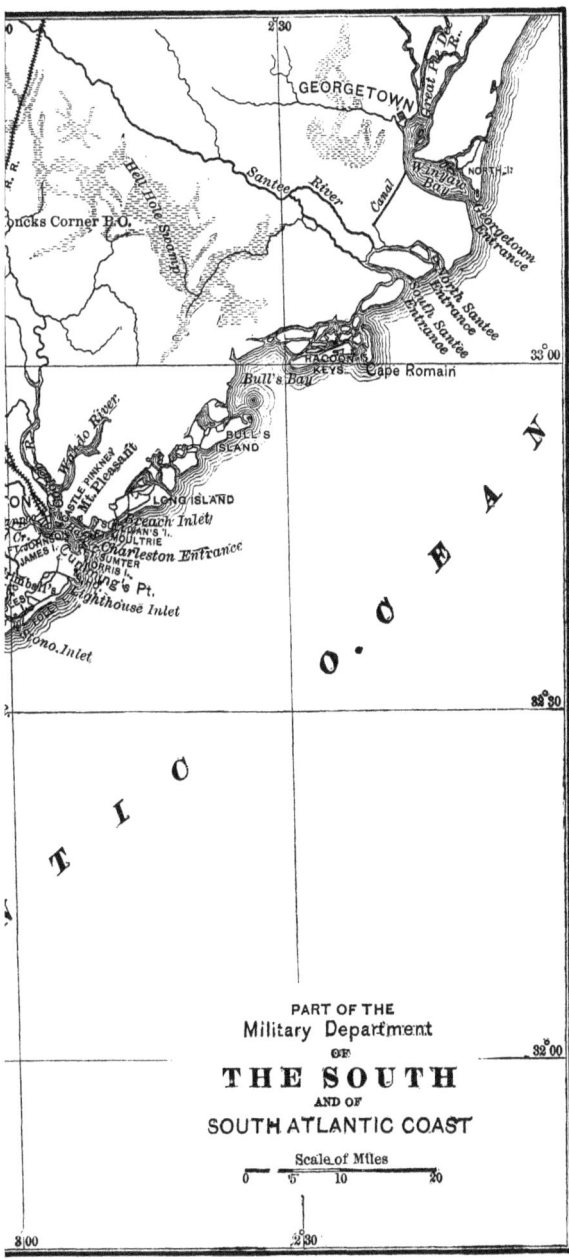

PART OF THE
Military Department
OF
THE SOUTH
AND OF
SOUTH ATLANTIC COAST

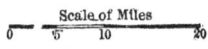

Scale of Miles

0   5   10   20

CHAPTER II.

THE PORT ROYAL EXPEDITION.

In the early part of October, 1861, the steam frigate Wabash was sent from blockading duty to the harbor of New York, to fit for service as the flag-ship of a force destined to our Southern coast, for the purpose of capturing and holding some convenient Southern port to serve as a depot for coal and other supplies, for the use of the vessels maintaining the blockade of the many inlets, harbors, and sounds that lie along the coast from the northern limits of South Carolina to the southern cape of Florida, over which district, what was known as the South Atlantic blockading squadron held its watch. The possession of a harbor was essential to maintaining a proper blockade, as coaling in rough water, if not impossible, is at least a slow and difficult operation. To go around Cape Hatteras to Hampton Roads in order to coal, as had been the case, hundreds of miles from the blockaded ports, lessened the effectiveness of the blockade by the absence of a large number of vessels going and coming, and when they arrived out, much of the coal taken in was already exhausted.

On the 10th of October Flag-Officer Samuel Francis Dupont hoisted his flag on board of the Wabash, commanded by Commander C. R. P. Rodgers. Every effort was made on the part of the flag-officer and his staff to make necessary requisitions and get on board the necessary stores and fitments required for the vessels of war, and for other vessels purchased for war purposes, few of which were adapted to carrying heavy batteries and to withstand the buffetings of rough seas, but they were the best to be had, and as a whole served the required purpose. This heterogeneous fleet of purchased vessels, ferry-boats, and freight steamers of small size, were despatched to Hampton Roads as soon as fitted, and the flag-ship, accompanied by the vessels of war proper, including four gunboats built on contract for completion in ninety days, left for the same destination on the afternoon of the 17th and arrived the day following, exercising at target practice during the passage. The XI-inch pivot guns on board of the gunboats were found handy and effective within their range.

Hampton Roads at that time was crowded with vessels of war, transports, and coaling schooners. Those destined for the command of Flag-Officer Dupont were supplied with stores and coal as soon as possible, as were also the numerous steam transports carrying some 12,000 men, under the command of General T. W. Sherman, with provisions and army outfits of all kinds. A steamer called the Governor, suitable for inland waters rather than to the sea, having on board a battalion of marines numbering 600, under the command of Major John G. Reynolds, was also attached to the expedition.

After receiving sealed orders as to destination—to be opened only in the event of separation—this motley force, numbering fifty vessels, steamed out of Hampton Roads on the morning of the 29th of October. There was considerable delay in forming a double echelon line outside of Cape Henry, and then the fleet proceeded slowly toward Cape Hatteras. The day previous to this force leaving, the flag-officer had despatched twenty-five coal-laden schooners relieved in part of their cargoes, under convoy of the sail sloop

of war Vandalia, with orders to rendezvous off Tybee Bar in
the event of parting company. This with the view of con-
cealing the destination of the fleet.

At 1 A.M. of the 31st the breeze was fresh from the eastward, and the sea rough. Owing to the set of the current and
by getting too far to leeward, two of the transports struck
lightly on Hatteras shoals, when, with a view to their safety,
they all steamed out to the eastward, causing some confusion. After passing Hatteras the course was shaped along
the coast. At noon on the 1st, a dull heavy sky and south-
easterly wind, constantly increasing, gradually settled into
a heavy gale. In the afternoon, the flag-officer made signal
that the vessels would take care of themselves. As darkness
settled over a stormy sea they were seen here and there
under such storm sail as their commanding officers directed.

It was an anxious night; a furious gale swept the waters,
and as many of the vessels were certainly indifferent sea
boats, grave apprehensions arose as to their safety. The gunboats behaved well, which had been doubted from their
motions in rough water when in Hampton Roads.

Throughout the night, which was very dark, the driven
drops of rain struck the face roughly as pellets when keeping a look-out to windward, and phosphorescent animalculæ
lit up the sheet of foam that covered the rough sea. At
3 A.M. the wind, without abating in violence, hauled suddenly
to the westward and the vessels felt more than ever the force
of the sea. When broad daylight came, only one gunboat
was in sight from the masthead of the flag-ship. As the day
advanced several others came in view and followed in her
wake. The Wabash, and such other of the vessels as were
properly fitted, were under sail and using steam as necessary
to maintain position. The wind was from the west and the
vessels were "by the wind on the port tack," that is to say,

the course was toward Bull's Bay, one of the ports supposed desirable to occupy as a coaling and supply station. At 9 P.M. the Wabash tacked ship and headed southwest, the wind having changed some two points. It was apparent, then, to the commanders of such vessels as had not opened their instructions, that Bull's Bay was not the objective point, but that it was probably Port Royal, having a more central position, and was well known to be the best harbor for vessels of heavy draught along the whole coast.

On the forenoon of the 3d, the flag-ship made signal for the commanding officer of the Seneca to come on board. A letter for Captain J. L. Lardner, commanding the steam frigate Susquehanna, off Charleston, was given him, as also verbal instructions that the vessels designated would not leave the blockade of the harbor until nightfall; they were then to proceed to the entrance of Port Royal, where the vessels of the fleet were concentrating, and where Flag-Officer Dupont would be found.

The Seneca proceeded on her way to Charleston Bar, some thirty miles distant. No sooner had she been sighted from Fort Sumter, than a signal gun was fired, and repeated farther in, probably to announce the arrival of the fleet of which this vessel was the *avant courier*. Immediately after the capture of Port Royal it was well known that the Confederates had been correctly informed as to the destination, although it was only determined a few days before, and was supposed to be a profound secret.[1]

---

[1] RICHMOND, November 1, 1861.
Governor Pickens, Columbia, S. C.: I have just received information which I consider entirely reliable, that the enemy's expedition is intended for Port Royal.
J. P. BENJAMIN,
Acting Secretary of War.
[Same telegram sent to Generals Drayton and Ripley.]—Vol. VI., p. 306, Official Records of the War of the Rebellion.

Flag-Officer Dupont, in writing to the Secretary of the Navy, on the 6th of November, the day preceding the battle, says: "Upon taking into consideration the magnitude to which the joint naval and military expedition had been extended, to which you (the Secretary of the Navy) have called my attention, I came to the conclusion that the original intention of the Department, if first carried out, would fall short of the expectations of the country and of the capabilities of the expedition, while Port Royal I thought would meet both in a high degree." [1]

Notwithstanding the violence of the gale, it was ascertained that only one vessel attached to the naval force, the steam transport Governor, had been lost, and that all save seven of the persons on board had been rescued, through the exertions of the officers and crew of the sail frigate Sabine, Captain Cadwalader Ringgold, aided specially and greatly by the Isaac Smith, Lieutenant-Commander Nicholson. In the heavy gale the last-named vessel would have foundered, had not the broadside guns been thrown overboard. The hog braces of the Governor had first given way, then she lost her smokestack, and finally the use of the enginery. It was a lucky chance that of her human cargo, numbering 650 or more, so few were lost.

---

[1] This plainly indicates that the Department had left to Dupont the selection of the point of attack, to be agreed upon, however, with General T. W. Sherman, whose orders, dated August 2, 1861, are as follows: "You will proceed to New York immediately, and organize, in connection with Captain Dupont, of the navy, an expedition of 12,000 men. Its destination you and the naval commander will determine after you have sailed." . . .

The "confidential" order of October 12th, to the flag-officer, says: "In examining the various points upon the coast, it has been ascertained that Bull's Bay, St. Helena, Port Royal, and Fernandina are each and all accessible and desirable points for the purposes indicated, and the Government has decided to take possession of at least two of them. Which of the two shall thus be occupied will be committed to your discretion after obtaining the best information you can in regard to them." . . .

The Peerless, an army transport laden with stores, was discovered in a sinking condition by the steam sloop Mohican, Commander S. W. Godon, and the crew rescued. In effecting this, Lieutenant H. W. Miller of the Mohican was very highly mentioned by the captain.

It is sufficient to say that certain naval vessels that came down in the fleet were detailed to relieve the war vessels proper blockading off Charleston, and that during the forenoon of the 5th all the vessels that were expected had assembled at the rendezvous with the exception of the Pocahontas, mentioned hereafter, and that all of the army transports arrived before the attack on the 7th, with the exception of the Peerless, already reported as lost, and the Belvidere, Union, and Osceola, none of them having troops on board, but army equipment and supplies, whose failure to arrive seriously affected army movements and also the means of transportation.

The bar of Port Royal lies ten miles from the nearest low sandy shores which form the land-locked harbor; only the tops of the taller trees are visible, except in certain states of the atmosphere when the mirage brings up to view continuous forests on Hilton Head to the west, and Bay Point on the east side of the harbor. Several of the vessels of war, among them the gunboats and the surveying steamer Vixen, were directed to feel their way in with the lead, and buoy out the bar, and secure the safe entrance of the heavier vessels. This was effected by 3 P.M., and all vessels of the fleet having a draught not exceeding eighteen feet, entered forthwith, and anchored some five miles outside of the headlands, in good holding ground, and fairly sheltered by shoals to seaward. Flag-Officer Dupont says: "To the skill of Commander Davis, the fleet captain, and Mr. Boutelle, the able assistant of the coast survey, in charge of the steamer

Vixen, the channel was immediately found, sounded out and buoyed."

Seamen will appreciate this celerity of movement, and the fact that on the first high tide thereafter all of the vessels were taken within the bar.

The gunboats Ottawa, Seneca, Pembina, and Penguin had anchored, after aiding in sounding out the channel, only some three miles outside of the headlands upon which the earthworks were plainly visible without the aid of a glass. Near sunset three steamers came out from between the headlands, and at long range opened fire on these vessels. They were soon under way, stood toward the enemy's vessels, commanded by Commodore Josiah Tatnall, formerly of the U. S. Navy, and opening fire, soon caused them to retreat.

Shortly after sunrise the following day (the 5th), the same manœuvre was repeated by the enemy. Just at this time Commander John Rodgers, accompanied by Brigadier-General H. G. Wright, had gone on board of the Ottawa for the purpose of making a reconnoissance of the batteries of the enemy. The Ottawa made signal to the Seneca, the Curlew, and the Isaac Smith to follow, and standing in, opened fire on Tatnall's steamers, and drove them within the headlands, coming themselves within a distant cross-fire from Fort Walker on Hilton Head, and Fort Beauregard on Bay Point. Flag-Officer Dupont says : " These vessels made a reconnoissance in force, and drew the fire of the batteries on Hilton Head and Bay Point sufficiently to show that the fortifications were works of strength, and scientifically constructed." In this affair the rigging of the gunboats was considerably cut by the shells from the earthworks, but no other damage was sustained. They had the satisfaction of noting an explosion at Bay Point, which General Drayton stated in his report to have been caused by a rifle-shell striking a caisson.

About noon a single steamer of the enemy came out, and at long range opened fire on the nearest vessel, but soon left on receiving a ricochet XI-inch shell from the Seneca, which lodged in the hog braces, as was known later. The failure of the fuze, doubtless, prevented serious results.

At 11 A.M. the flag-ship crossed the bar and anchored some five miles from the forts; she was followed by the Susquehanna and the heavy army transports, which anchored somewhat farther out. Signal was made for the commanding officers of vessels to come on board the flag-ship. On entering the cabin of the flag-officer they were made acquainted with the plan of battle, and instructions were given them as to their position in line.

The vessels designated for the attack were of course quite ready, but the day was well advanced when the special instructions had been given and the necessary buoys planted, particularly on Fishing-rip Shoal. The flag-officer says: "This rendered the hour late before it was possible to move with the attacking squadron. In our anxiety to get the outline of the forts before dark, we stood in too near this shoal, and the ship grounded. By the time she was gotten off it was too late, in my judgment, to proceed, and I made signal for the squadron to anchor out of gunshot of the enemy."

The day following a heavy westerly wind prevailed; although the water was not rough, an attack would have been made at great disadvantage. The morning of the day following was calm and beautiful. In his report of the battle and abandonment of Port Royal, General Drayton, who commanded the Confederate forces, says: "On the 6th instant, the fleet and transports, which had increased to about forty-five sail, would probably have attacked us had not the weather been very boisterous. . . . At last the memorable 7th dawned upon us, bright and serene; not a ripple upon the broad expanse of water to disturb the accuracy of fire from the broad decks of that magnificent armada about advancing, in battle array, to vomit forth its iron hail, with all the spiteful energy of long-suppressed rage and conscious strength."

At early dawn of the 7th signal was made from the flagship "go to breakfast," and after the usual time given, the signals "get under way," "form line of battle," and "prepare for action," followed in due time. The vessels of war were then lying more than four miles outside of a straight line connecting the earthworks, situated, as General Drayton states, two and five-eighths miles apart and soon to be the objects of attack. The commanding officers of vessels, previously instructed, on weighing anchor took position in lines as follows : Main column, flag-ship Wabash leading, Commander C. R. P. Rodgers; side-wheel steam frigate Susquehanna, Captain J. S. Lardner ; sloop Mohican, Commander S. W. Godon ; sloop Seminole, Commander J. P. Gillis ; sloop Pawnee, Lieutenant-Commanding R. H. Wyman ; gunboat Unadilla, Lieutenant-Commanding Napoleon Collins; gunboat Ottawa, Lieutenant-Commanding Thomas H. Stevens ; gunboat Pembina, Lieutenant-Commanding John P. Bankhead, and sail-sloop Vandalia, Commander Francis S. Haggerty, towed by the Isaac Smith, Lieutenant-Commanding J. W. A. Nicholson. It will be remembered that the last-named vessel, to prevent foundering, had thrown her broadside guns overboard in the gale of the 1st.

The flanking column consisted of the Bienville, Commander Charles Steedman, leading ; the gunboat Seneca, Lieutenant-Commanding Daniel Ammen ; gunboat Penguin, Lieutenant-Commanding P. A. Budd, and the Augusta, Commander E. G. Parrott.

At half-past eight the vessels were as fairly in position as

attainable when not under good steerage way, and as they
steamed ahead at nine, signal was made for close order, and
the line of battle was fairly developed, at distances intended,
of a little more than a ship's length apart, the flanking column appearing through the intervals, as it were, and at a distance from the other line of a ship's length. The reader will
bear in mind the ample sheet of water between the earthworks.
The order given was, that the main column, in passing in,
should deliver its fire on Fort Walker (Hilton Head) and the
flanking column on Fort Beauregard ; when the vessels had
passed within where the guns could no longer be trained
on the works of the enemy, the main column would turn
toward Hilton Head, pass again toward the sea and against
the flood tide, steam quite slowly, delivering their fire, and
when again reaching a point where their guns could no longer
be brought to bear on the batteries of the enemy, the vessels
would be turned toward mid-channel, and pass as in going
in first, following the flag-ship in line. This made the vessels describe an ellipse, the curves of which, in relation to
the distance from Fort Walker, were chosen by the flag-ship.
In passing in, the shortest distance from Fort Walker was
probably about eight hundred yards, and heading outward
is given as six hundred yards. This evolution was to be
continuous until the reduction of the fort, or until further
orders.

The flanking column was to deliver its fire in passing in
on the Bay Point batteries, then turn its attention to the
force of the enemy afloat, and after sinking or driving it
away, take up a position to the north of Fort Walker, the
best attainable to enfilade that work. In giving these instructions the flag-officer stated that he knew Tatnall well;
he was an officer of courage and plan, and that it was not at
all unlikely in the heat of action and smoke of battle he

would endeavor to pass out and destroy the transports, and the vital duty of the flanking column was to take care of Tatnall, and destroy his vessels if he attempted that movement.

With these explanations the reader is prepared to consider the vessels with a speed of six miles per hour, fairly formed in two columns and at 9.26 coming within long range of the earthworks, when the enemy opened. The force of Commodore Tatnall lay just within an imaginary line connecting the two forts. The vessels composing it were poorly adapted for successfully opposing those advancing and now within fair range of the earthworks. Tatnall's were what are known as "river steamers," extremely vulnerable, boilers and machinery fully exposed, and the guns carried, although rifled, were of inferior calibre.

The vessels entering were not long in replying to the guns of the enemy; with carefully studied elevations and well-directed aim, the heavy shells fell fast within the earthworks, burying themselves and exploding, throwing sand into the guns, covering platforms and gun-traverses with sand, and disturbing much the accuracy of aim and rapidity of fire of the enemy.

As the columns advanced, Tatnall's steamers withdrew, but when the main column turned they again put their bows toward the fleet, perhaps under the impression that the vessels found the fire from the earthworks too heavy to be borne, and were withdrawing. However that may be, seeing the vessels again returning, the Seneca was again headed toward them from a position just reached north of Fort Walker, and on her opening fire, they entered Scull Creek, the entrance to which has no great depth and is intricate; it is situated four miles northwest of Fort Walker.

The Wabash, followed closely by the Susquehanna, swept

again slowly and majestically in face of the earthworks at a distance not exceeding six hundred yards, delivering with accuracy and great dexterity their heavy broadsides. Having passed beyond the point which would admit of training the guns, again they turned, and heading into the harbor continued their broadsides. This was too much for troops not habituated to the use of heavy guns nor trained to war. Before the vessels entered, they saw in the cannon which they served what they fancied and believed a sufficient means to sink or destroy a fleet, and yet, with painful slowness and automaton-like regularity it swept around, delivering broadsides of shells with surprising rapidity, exploding them on the parapets and within their works, covering them up alive, as it were, in what they called their "sacred soil." Their guns were struck and broken or dismounted, guns' crews killed or wounded, and the mighty engines of yesterday seemed to have no potency to-day, wielded as they supposed deftly, but in reality clumsily. They saw the vessels were not impeded and did their will.

There is a force in the logic of war. Indisputably rude it is, yet more powerful than that of the bar, or even that of the pulpit; in undisciplined troops it addresses itself specially to what is equivocally called the "meanest comprehension."

To the battering force in front, that passed along in grim procession, was added the enfilading fire, described by General Drayton as follows : "Besides this moving battery, the fort was enfiladed by the gunboats anchored to the north off the mouth of Fish Hall Creek, and another on an edge of the shoal to the south. This enfilading fire on so still a sea annoyed and damaged us excessively, particularly as we had no gun on either flank of the bastion to reply with, for the 32-pounder on the right flank was shattered by a round shot, and on the north flank, for want of a car-

riage, no gun was mounted. After the fourth fire, the X-
inch columbiad bounded over the hurter, and became useless.
The 24-pounder rifled was choked while ramming down a
shell, and lay idle during nearly the whole engagement."

"The vigorous attack of the enemy continued unabated,
with still no decided damage to any of their ships. At half-
past twelve I again went out of the fort with my Assistant-
Adjutant-General, Captain Young, for the purpose of muster-
ing together the infantry and reserves, and have them in
readiness for any eventuality. Before leaving, however, I
turned over the command to Colonel Heyward, with direc-
tions to hold out as long as any effective fire could be
maintained."

"Having mounted our horses, we rejoined the troops near
Hospital Number 2. I received information through one of
the videttes that a steamer and small boats were sounding
near the beach. I detached Captain Berry with three
companies of his battalion under the guidance of Captain
Ephraim Barnard, volunteer aid, by a road marked R, to
watch the enemy, beat them back if they attempted to land,
and give notice if he wanted support. I then, with some of
my staff, rode to collect together the other troops, who,
through ignorance of our inland roads, had lost their way,
and had not yet come up."

General Drayton was misinformed as to a steamer and boats
sounding north of Fort Walker. The Seneca was returning
from the direction of Scull Creek, as near to the shore as the
depth of water would allow, and as usual, men were sounding on each side of the vessel. Some of the enemy stupidly
fired at the vessel, and although they were unseen the smoke
marked the spot ; 20-pounder rifle shells were returned, with
loss of life to the enemy, as the reports show.

The reader will perceive the painful perplexity of General

Drayton at this moment; he doubtless had the apprehension, if not an entire conviction, that the earthworks would soon be abandoned. His report says : "Two o'clock had now arrived, when I noticed our men coming out of the fort, which they had bravely defended for four and a half hours against fearful odds, and then only retiring when all but three of the guns on the water front had been disabled, and only five hundred pounds of powder in the magazine; commencing the action with 220 men inside the fort, afterward increased to 255, by the accession of Read's battery. These heroic men retired slowly and sadly from their well-fought guns, which to have defended longer would have exhibited the energy of despair rather than the manly pluck of the soldier."

At the time of the occurrences first quoted, several of the vessels of the main line took up positions to the northeast of Fort Walker at a distance of twelve hundred yards or more; the Vandalia, in tow of the Isaac Smith by a long hawser, swept in long, graceful, but inconvenient curves, past and among these vessels. The Unadilla, whose enginery was disabled, pursued her eccentric orbit, her commanding officer hailing and requesting other vessels to get out of the way as "he could not stop." As he swept by again and again the droll song of the man with the cork-leg that would not let him tarry was brought to mind.

Before the close of the bombardment, the Pocahontas, Commander Percival Drayton, entered the harbor, and taking position opened fire on Fort Walker. The vessel had received injuries in the gale of the 1st which delayed her reaching Port Royal at an earlier hour. Her commander was the brother of General Drayton, from whose report quotations have been made.

The report of Flag-Officer Dupont states that at 1.15 P.M. the Ottawa made signal that the works at Hilton Head had been abandoned, and that the same signal was soon after made by the Pembina. At that time, the enfilading vessels north of Fort Walker, drifting with the ebb tide, were within five hundred or six hundred yards of the works, and in addition to the XI-inch guns were using the 20-pounder rifles and 24-pounder howitzers.

In his report the flag-officer says : "After the Wabash and the Susquehanna had passed to the northward, and given the fort the fire of their port battery the third time, the enemy had entirely ceased to reply and the battle was ended. . . . As soon as the starboard guns of this ship and the Susquehanna had been brought to bear a third time upon Fort Walker, I sent Commander John Rodgers on shore with a flag of truce. The hasty flight of the enemy was visible, and was reported from the tops. At 2.20 Captain Rodgers hoisted the flag of the Union over the deserted post."

At 2.45 the flag-ship anchored, and Commander C. R. P. Rodgers was ordered on shore with a detachment of seamen and marines, who threw out pickets and guarded Fort Walker until the arrival of General H. G. Wright. The transports came in from their anchorage, and by nightfall a brigade had landed and the fort was formally turned over to General Wright by order of the flag-officer.

Soon after the fate of Fort Walker was decided the flag-officer " despatched a small squadron to Fort Beauregard to reconnoitre, and ascertain its condition, and to prevent the rebel steamers returning to carry away either persons or property."

Captain Elliott, in command of Fort Beauregard, reports to Colonel Donavant, commandant of the post on Bay Point, as follows : " The last gun from my battery was fired at 3:35 P.M., being the eighth to which the enemy had not replied. A few moments afterward Colonel Donavant entered the fort and said to me, 'Captain Elliott, what is the condition of things over the river?' I replied, 'Fort Walker has been silenced, sir.' 'By what do you judge?' 'By the facts that the fort has been subjected to a heavy enfilade and direct fire, to which it has ceased to reply, that the vessels having terminated their fire, the flag-ship has steamed up and delivered a single shot, which was unanswered, and that thereupon cheering was heard from the fleet.' 'Then, sir, it having been proved that these works could not accomplish the end for which they were designed—that of protecting the harbor —you will prepare to retire from a position from which our retreat may readily be cut off, and which our small force will not enable us to hold against a land attack.' I then prepared my command for a retreat, destroyed the greater part of the powder, spiked the guns, and an hour later took up the line of march for Eddings's Island." So the troops on Bay Point also stole away, without giving themselves the trouble to fold their tents.

About 4 P.M. an officer who had landed near Fort Walker met the body-servant of General Drayton and took him on board the flag-ship for personal examination. It was then ascertained, if not known before, that the Confederate troops could escape from Hilton Head Island by means of the steamboats that had entered Scull Creek, there being a wharf about one mile from the entrance. It was supposed, naturally enough, with a march which General Drayton gives as six miles from the fort to the wharf, that before a force could get through the intricate channel of Scull Creek, the embarkation would have been completed, which was not the case, however, as we learn from General Drayton's report that it was not fully effected until 1.30 A.M. of the 8th.

Not seeing the Seminole, that had been sent over to guard the approach from Bay Point—that vessel having by mistake gone up Broad River—as darkness set in the flag-officer ordered the Seneca to proceed to the vicinity of Bay Point, communicate with the Seminole and inform her commander that at daylight he would make a careful reconnoissance of the Bay Point batteries, and if found abandoned, would land and hoist the flag over the works.

At daylight the Seminole was not found in the vicinity of Bay Point. After a sufficient inspection the commanding officer of the Seneca landed with thirty armed men and hoisted the flag of the Union on the flag-staff over a small frame house near the earthworks, which had been the headquarters of the enemy. He went into the house without a suspicion of possible injury, and found everything had been removed. The earthworks and magazines were hastily examined, and the encampment under the pine trees half a mile distant was then visited; the tents were standing undisturbed and within them many personal effects, wearing apparel, private arms, and some small arms were also found, which showed that when the enemy left they had not stood much on the order of their going. A single wounded soldier was found in a tent. The only animate life visible was a flock of turkeys that had the good taste to remain; they strutted around in stately pride and in the belief that they were superior birds—as indeed they were.

Returning to the vicinity of the earthworks, where our flag had been hoisted an hour before, a dull explosion was heard, a cloud of smoke went up, and when it passed away there was no vestige of the small frame house upon which our flag had been hoisted. A sailor walking near had fallen into the snare by his foot striking a wire fastened to a peg, through which a "spur tube" had exploded a quantity of powder placed under the floor of the house. The sailor was knocked down and stunned for a few minutes, after which he was able to get up and walk off. So much for so mean a mode of warfare.

It was curious to observe the inherent love of plunder that takes possession of the victor. Articles absolutely useless, as a feather-bed and quilts, were brought down to the beach from the tents on Bay Point; had there been a bedstead in camp some fool would have brought that also. If it had been permitted, the vessels would have been filled with trash, for no other reason than that " to the victors belong the spoils."

The vicinity of the magazine was avoided, and the facts reported to General I. I. Stevens, to whom the works were turned over on his arrival with his troops at noon.

The armament and character of the earthworks of the enemy which the navy had captured are described in Lieutenant Barnes's official report as follows :

FORT WALKER.—Upon the sea front of said fort there are mounted, upon the best improved modern barbette carriages, circular railways, the following guns : One VI-inch rifled gun (right angle sea face) in good order; six 32-pounders, of 62 hundred weight each; one has the cascabel knocked off, three are dismounted, and carriages ruined—all loaded and generally in good order; one X-inch columbiad, 13,220 pounds weight, in good order; one VIII-inch columbiad, 9,018 pounds weight; three sea-coast howitzers, VII-inch, 1,600 pounds weight, in good order, loaded; one rifled VI-inch, in good order, loaded (in left angle of sea front)—at or surrounding each gun ammunition is placed in great profusion; five large chests filled with powder for the various guns in front of them; shot, shell, and rifled projectiles are scattered about without limit ; in the centre of the fort are two furnaces for hot shot, and one pump with water. In the left wing are : one 32-pounder, one sea-coast howitzer, not mounted, in good order. Outer work, in rear, commanding land approach, are mounted two 32-pounders in good order ; one VIII-inch heavy howitzer, mounted on navy carriage, loaded with canister, just put up, commanding approach to angle of outer work, the only gun in embrasure ; ammunition-chest full; one English siege gun, 12-pounder, behind embankment at right of right

wing ; one ditto, mounted to the right of the magazine to command
the ditch of the main work. In the right wing are mounted three 32-
pounders, making a total of twenty-three guns. There are also, in the
covered way leading to the shell-room and magazine, about two hundred
and fifty X-inch, one hundred VIII-inch shells, some loaded and fixed
with sabots and straps ; fifty 42-pounder shot, fifty boxes (four shell in
each) rifled VI-inch shell of three patterns ; three hundred VIII-inch
and VI-inch canister, rammers, sponges, primers, and tools of all de-
scriptions. The magazine door, being locked, was not entered.

FORT BEAUREGARD, on Bay Point, has four faces, upon which guns
are mounted, each face looking on the water, and each gun so mounted
as to command the water approach to Broad and Beaufort Rivers. The
guns are thirteen in number, of the following sizes : five 32-pounders ;
one rifled VI-inch, new (gun burst and carriage entirely destroyed) ;
five sea-coast guns, 42-pounders, long and very heavy, all in good order ;
one X-inch columbiad, weight 13,226 pounds (spiked and loaded) ; one
VIII-inch columbiad, in good order. There is also, upon each flank of
the main work, at a distance of about one hundred and fifty yards from
it, a small work, built to command the land approach along the beach,
as well as the channel abreast. Upon the outer works on the left flank
are mounted two 24-pounders. Upon the outer works on the right
flank are mounted three 32-pounders. Within the fort are also two
field-pieces, VI-pounders, old Spanish pattern, making, in all, twenty
pieces of ordnance. Within the fort was found a great amount of ammunition scattered about in disorder. In the shell-room were several
hundred shells, filled and fused for the various sizes of guns. The
magazine is filled with powder, put in cylinders ready for use ; the
powder appears to be of most excellent quality. There are two furnaces for heating shot, both filled with shot, some of them partly
melted. The ammunition-chests are nearly full of powder. In a pool
of water in the rear large quantities of ammunition are lying, where it
was thrown by the enemy before retreating.

At Braddock's Point, at the far end of Hilton Head Island,
the enemy abandoned one X-inch columbiad and two 5½-inch
rifled guns, and near the wharf, in retreat, left two fine 12-
pounder bronze howitzers.

In the attempted defence of these works General Drayton

reported casualties as follows : Killed in Fort Walker, 10 ;
wounded, 20 ; killed in Colonel De Saussure's regiment, 1 ;
wounded severely, 15 ; missing, 4 ; wounded in Fort Beauregard, 13.

The total of casualties on board of all of the vessels is
given by the flag-officer as follows : Total killed, 8 ; wounded
seriously, 6 ; wounded slightly, 17.

The earthworks had not traverses of the height that the
enemy learned to make thereafter, which served him so well
at Fort Fisher and elsewhere. Looking from the direction
of the enfilading fire from the north at Fort Walker, the
wonder was that the ammunition at the guns had not been
exploded, and that many more of the men who served the
guns were not killed. It seemed almost a miracle that explosions did not occur in the passage-way from which powder
and shells were supplied.

It will be remembered that Fort Beauregard was not the
direct object of attack. In entering the harbor, the flanking
column alone delivered its fire in that direction, and afterward in passing to the northward the Wabash and Susquehanna gave it some shells.

General T. W. Sherman, commanding our troops of the
Port Royal expedition, in his report of November 8th, says :
" The beautifully constructed work on Hilton Head was severely crippled and many of the guns dismounted. Much
slaughter had evidently been made there, many bodies having been buried in the fort, and some twenty or thirty were
found some half mile distant. . . . On clearing out the
fort the body of Doctor Buist, surgeon of the fort, was found ;
he was killed by a shell and buried by the falling in of
a parapet. The number of pieces of ordnance that have
fallen into our hands is fifty-two, the bulk of which is of the
largest calibre, all with fine carriages, etc., except eight or

nine, that were ruined by our fire, which dismounted their pieces."

In speaking of the transports he says : " The transport steamers Union, Belvidere, Osceola, and Peerless have not arrived (on the 8th). Two of them are known to be lost, and it is probable they all are. It is gratifying, however, to say that none of the troop transports connected with the land forces were lost, though the Winfield Scott had to sacrifice her whole cargo, and the Roanoke a portion of her cargo to save the lives of the regiments on board. The former will be unable to again put to sea."

The loss of these army transports, all of them of light draught, interfered seriously with the intended movements of our troops immediately after the battle of Port Royal, and the lack of shells for the large guns of the smaller navy vessels imposed quiet upon them for a time.

On the afternoon of the 8th General T. W. Sherman made a reconnoissance several miles up the Beaufort River on board of the Seneca. Lumps and bluffs and ruined houses had the semblance of concealed batteries, but there were none; the preparations for defence by the enemy were confined to the works captured, so far as the waters of Port Royal Harbor and the creeks and rivers were concerned. The same day all of the troops yet on board of the transports were debarked, mostly on Hilton Head, and the construction of a large entrenched camp was immediately begun.

The navy vessels for the most part that had been engaged in the attack on Port Royal were sent at once to blockade duty, leaving the smaller gunboats to an examination of the internal waters, and soon after, the harbors in the vicinity. The Unadilla was sent up Broad River, and the Seneca, Pembina, and Penguin went to Beaufort, under the supposition still that guns would be found in position, in

2*

which case the orders were to get out of the range of them and acquaint the flag-officer, that a proper force might be sent for their reduction. On reaching a marshy island half a mile below Beaufort there was a great commotion; a crowd of persons and several men on horseback left hastily; crowds of negroes were in the streets, others plundering the houses, and loading every scow and boat that they could lay their hands on. They were wild with joy, and had, in their belief, wealth that should satiate desire. Only one white man was found, a Mr. Allen, who was brought on board. He appeared to be suffering from some strong excitement or the effects of liquor. After giving to him assurances of protection to life and property, which the flag-officer had directed to be given to peaceable inhabitants, he was sent on shore.

On the return of the vessels to Port Royal they were boarded by boat crews of negroes, who stated that many of the slaves had been shot by their masters in endeavoring to escape being driven off the island. They were informed that they were free to go to Beaufort or to Hilton Head; they said they would first go to Beaufort and afterward would come to Hilton Head, as would all of the blacks, to escape being murdered by their masters. The mail taken from the post office was delivered to the fleet captain, who found curiously vindictive letters; earnest hopes that the fleet had gone down in the heavy gale that had swept the coasts, or if any survived and entered the port that none were to be left afloat, and thus they would wipe out the disgrace of Hatteras Inlet!

At the headquarters of General Drayton a chart of the coast was found on which were marked in red, points in different harbors which were conjectured, rightly, to indicate the positions of batteries; this information proved of great value to the flag-officer in directing operations along the coast.

No white persons were in Beaufort, nor indeed upon the
island, and the negroes were enjoying, in the stereotyped
language of the Irish orator, "the proudest and the happiest
day of their existence." The South Carolinians had agreed
among themselves, or rather the more violent and dictatorial
had proclaimed, that any communication with the National
forces should be considered an act of treason; that every in-
habitant must remove himself and family beyond the limits
of our occupation. This entailed widespread misery on all
concerned, but fortunately it fell principally upon those who
had been active in bringing about the rebellion. The
wretchedness resulting was not the less distressing because
it was self-imposed, inasmuch as, if non-combatants had
remained, they would not have been molested or interfered
with in any manner. The object, probably, of this insane
action was to prevent any weakening of the feeling of intense
bitterness which was apparent from everything written or
uttered at that time.

Commander John Rodgers in the Flag, with the Seneca
and Pocahontas, was directed to proceed to the Savannah
River and "push his reconnoissance so as to form an approxi-
mate estimate of the force on Tybee Island, and of the possibility of gaining an entrance." A day or so before he had
made a partial examination from beyond the bar, and arrived
at the supposition that the earthworks guarding the entrance
had been abandoned. Arriving at noon of November 24th,
he found the bar quite rough and the ranges for crossing
it destroyed. He therefore went on board of the vessel having the least draught, crossed the bar, and shelled the earthworks without receiving a reply. A closer examination
showed that they had been abandoned and dismantled, as
was found to be the case at all of the points along the coast

within ready and an unembarrassed attack by the gunboats, with the exception of the little inlet of Stono, close to Charleston, and of course the defences of that city and of Savannah.

While Commander Rodgers was making his reconnoissance in one direction, other officers with proper vessels were sent elsewhere, with the same objects and like results. Commander Drayton in the Pawnee, to which he had been transferred, accompanied by the Pembina and the coast survey steamer Vixen, entered St. Helena Sound on the morning of the 26th. On the point of Otter Island was found an abandoned bastioned work, triangular in shape, with two faces looking upon the water, and surrounded by a ditch. The magazine had been blown up and the armament removed.

Continuing his reconnoissance up the Coosaw, at the mouth of Barnwell's Creek was found another deserted redoubt, which had an armament of three guns; one had been removed and the others destroyed. The carriages, a sling cart, and intrenching tools that were found were taken on board of the vessels.

Commander Drayton, with the Pembina and Vixen, some four miles up the Ashepoo found another deserted earthwork; its armament, save three small guns, had been removed; two of these had already been destroyed and the third was put in like condition.

Commander Drayton recommended that the fort on Otter Island be occupied, as it commanded the inland route to Charleston. No single point commanded all of the entrances to St. Helena Sound, as it is five miles across. The Otter Island fort would command the best entrance, and its vicinity would give excellent anchorage for vessels blockading the other channels. He expressed great indebtedness to Captain Boutelle of the Coast Survey, whose services had

been important. Under further orders, on the 5th of December Commander Drayton again revisited those waters in
the Pawnee, accompanied by the Unadilla, Isaac Smith, and
Coast Survey steamer Vixen. He extended his observations
up the Ashepoo River to the entrance of Mosquito Creek,
where the inland route to Charleston commenced. A day or
so thereafter he continued up the river and landed on
Hutchinson's Island; two days earlier the negro houses,
overseer's house, and outbuildings had been burned by the
enemy. An attempt had been made at the same time to
drive off the negroes, many of whom had escaped into the
woods, and he was told that many of their number had been
shot in attempting to escape. " The scene was one of complete desolation; the smoking ruins and cowering figures
which surrounded them, who still instinctively clung to their
hearthstones, although there was no longer shelter for them,
presented a most melancholy sight, the impression of which
was made even stronger by the piteous wailing of the poor
creatures, a large portion of whom consisted of the old and
decrepit." The vessels left soon after dark, when a bright
signal light was burned on the place to announce to the
enemy the departure of the vessels.

The following morning Commander Drayton went up the
Coosaw River with his command. Soon after leaving, the
Unadilla was disabled by the breaking of a cross-head; the
two other vessels proceeded. Off Fort Heyward, before described but not named, the Isaac Smith was left, her size
not permitting her to go farther with safety. Commander
Drayton proceeded in the Vixen to the entrance of Beaufort
Creek, known as the " Brick-yards," where a fort was said to
be. The plantation of Mr. Blythewood was visited, where a
great number of negroes was seen. Here the cotton-house
with its contents had just been burned, and all of the slaves

that could be caught had been driven away. Many of them that remained begged to be taken away, as they had neither shelter nor food. They were permitted to go on board of the vessel. Leaving the blockading force, the Pawnee then returned to Port Royal, and Flag-Officer Dupont informed the Navy Department that he would hold Otter Island and Tybee Roads by a naval force until it was convenient for the army to occupy the islands, when several of the vessels could be sent to other points for blockading purposes.

At the same time, Commander C. R. P. Rodgers was making a reconnoissance of Warsaw Sound with the gunboats Ottawa, Seneca, and Pembina. This force left Tybee Roads on December 5th, and approaching the fort on Warsaw Island found it abandoned. It was octagonal in form, with platforms for eight guns on the water faces; the land faces were protected by an abatis. The guns had been removed, the magazine blown up, and the platforms destroyed. Adjoining the work, huts and sheds for a large garrison had not yet been removed.

From the mouth of Wilmington River, another work on the river was sighted, bearing north 60° west, distant about three miles; this was surrounded by a large encampment. Five guns, apparently of large calibre, were mounted on the face of the battery toward the river; only one gun was visible on the other face.

The Henry Andrew was added to the force, and Commander Rodgers crossed Ossabaw Bar and examined the Great Ogeechee and Vernon Rivers. An earthwork of eight guns, not yet completed, was seen on the eastern end of Green Island; seventy-five tents were counted and a derrick was seen for the work in progress. This fort commanded Vernon River, the Little Ogeechee, Hell Gate, and the passage from Vernon River into the Great Ogeechee. From a distance of two nautical miles a rifle shell was thrown at the Seneca, which fell astern ; another, a heavy smooth-bore, fired at the Pembina fell far short.

On the 15th of December Commander Drayton crossed the North Edisto Bar. An earthwork was seen on the west side facing the bar, and shells were thrown into it without a reply. The works proved to be two abandoned redoubts for five guns each, connected by a long curtain, and protected in the rear by a double fence of thick plank, with earth between, and loopholed. The guns and platforms had been removed. The Seneca proceeded several miles up the river, when on all sides cotton-houses and outbuildings were set on fire. Many of these fires were miles in the interior, and were known only by the dense volumes of white smoke rising above the pine forests that outlined the horizon. Their property was far beyond the reach of molestation, even had a design existed. Such conduct indicated the actual insanity that reigned among the inhabitants in the region, and the terror inspired by the bombardment of the forts at Port Royal.

Escaped slaves reported a Confederate force of 500 men at Rockville, a handsome-looking village on a bluff about three miles distant. Captain Drayton determined to pay them a visit at daylight and went on board of the Vixen for that purpose, taking with him marines and armed boat crews from the Pawnee and the Seneca. The Vixen got aground in the creek, which prevented her reaching the town until 8 A.M. of the 18th. Fifty men were landed, there being no sign of life on the wharf. On reaching the town large numbers of the blacks were found pillaging commissary stores.

A deserted encampment was found one mile from the water, the troops having left when they saw the vessels entering the creek. The blacks were found "as busy as bees," and had already possessed themselves of what they found in camp. Forty-four Sibley tents were taken on board the Vixen.

In relation to this, Colonel John L. Branch, whose encampment was visited, reported as follows : "On Tuesday the 17th, at 4.30 P.M., it was reported to me that four of the enemy's vessels had crossed the bar or were in sight and firing shells. I at once prepared to make observations for myself and saw the vessels, one considerably in advance of the others, coming up the Edisto River. I ordered the regimental line to be formed without knapsacks and marched out of camp, supposing that a fire of shells would at once be opened upon it. This was not done, however, and the advanced steamer continued up the river, while others stopped near the entrance to Bohicket Creek."

"On this river, and the several bold creeks connected therewith, are many places where troops could be landed, and by a forced march to our rear gain possession of the only two bridges connecting Wadmelaw with John's Island, and thereby cut off my entire command, two hundred and ninety-two rifles. . . . It is needless to say that had no demonstration been made to cut us off from John's Island, no retreat, save beyond the reach of the enemy's shells, would have been ordered, unless a very heavy force had been landed at Rockville." He further states that the "activity and energy of the quartermaster deserve the highest commendation," and that the losses sustained were due to insufficient means of transportation.

Several hundreds of slaves who had collected on board of the vessels were sent on shore and located themselves in the wood near the earthworks on the southeast end of Edisto Island, and for their protection and the maintenance of a more effective blockade, the Penguin, Lieutenant-Commanding Budd, was brought into the harbor.

This colony maintained itself for months, eventually reaching more than one thousand in number, although those that desired were taken to Port Royal by the gunboats when going. Corn that had been housed and sweet potatoes that had been buried, and an occasional supply of beef from cattle that they would look up on the island, were quite sufficient to supply their simple wants throughout the winter, and the branches of trees and palmetto leaves placed over poles served them for shelter in true Arcadian simplicity.

Returning to Port Royal, the Pawnee visited the southwest end of the island, where an abandoned earthwork of two redoubts was found. These had been armed with eight guns.

A great deal was said by the enemy and by his putative friends in Great Britain of the sinking of a "stone fleet" on December 20, 1861, in what was termed the main ship channel to Charleston Harbor, and, a month later, in Sullivan Island Channel. It was assumed that these vessels would "destroy the harbor." The official reports of the enemy, obstructing channels by sinking vessels before that time wherever it suited his purposes, made the complaint ridiculous.

It was at most a temporary embarrassment to blockade-runners that had a sufficient draught to require an actual channel ; nearly all of them could pass over any part of the bar near high water, except "Drunken Dick" shoal, which lies within a half mile of Sullivan's Island. As the sea here breaks at all times, it might be regarded rather as a guide than a danger. The range lights, one on Sumter and the other on St. Michael's Church, gave a fair guide into the harbor, even when not running on the range.

In the immediate vicinity where the "stone fleet" was sunk, a better channel than had existed at any recent period was at once formed a little south of east of Lighthouse Inlet. So, too, in the narrow inlets where vessels had been sunk by either of the combatants, a wash soon opened a deeper channel than existed before the obstruction had been placed. Finally, it may be said, every one acquainted with those waters knew that a few months at least would be sufficient for the *teredo navalis* (marine worm) to dispose of any timber that might be placed as an obstruction.

While the navy had been busy as above described, and in maintaining a blockade at the many entrances required, the army had completed a very large and strongly intrenched camp on Hilton Head, which surrounded Fort Walker. It had also occupied Beaufort, and picketed the whole of Port Royal Island, upon which the town is situated, as also the whole of Hilton Head Island, and had established a post on Tybee and other islands.

The enemy had somewhat recovered from the heavy blow of the battle of Port Royal, and the forced abandonment of so many earthworks that had been constructed with so much labor. But he was by no means idle, and had formed the design of swooping down suddenly and capturing a regiment or more of National troops occupying Beaufort and the island of Port Royal. For this purpose he supposed a necessary preliminary was to place obstructions at Seabrook's Point, on Whale Branch, two and a half miles from the ferry, on the one side, and at Boyd's Neck, on the Coosaw, five miles below the ferry, to prevent the ascent of gunboats ; then by constructing a heavy battery at Port Royal Ferry and another on the shore opposite Seabrook's Point, he could cross a sufficient force rapidly and sweep over Port Royal Island. Many of

the slaves that had been driven off had returned, and among
them were spies sent by their masters to keep the enemy informed as to the number and disposition of the National
troops, and there were yet others who visited the main
stealthily, and watched the movements of the enemy with
anxiety and were informed, too, by slaves who were probably
in the Confederate camps.

Apprised of this intended movement on the part of the
enemy, General Sherman sent to Flag-Officer Dupont a confidential letter, stating that the time had come for action, and
requested a naval quota to second the army movement.

A conference was had and Commander C. R. P. Rodgers
detailed to command the naval forces, consisting of the
Ottawa and Pembina gunboats, the armed tug Hale and four
boats of the Wabash armed with howitzers, under charge
of Lieutenants Upshur, Luce, Irwin, and Acting Master
Kempff, which force was to enter the Coosaw by the Beaufort River, and the Seneca and other gunboats to move as a
co-operative force up Broad River, and entering Whale
Branch attack a battery supposed to be placed opposite
Seabrook's Point, and from thence go on to attack, as an
auxiliary force, the enemy's batteries at Port Royal Ferry.
The part assigned to the force first named was to protect the
troops landing first at Heyward's plantation, to cover the
march of the advancing column to the second point of debarkation of troops, and then to attack the batteries.

The attack was fixed for the 1st of January ; the vessels
first named, under the immediate command of Commander
Rodgers, remained at Beaufort until dark and then ascended
the river until within two miles of the Coosaw, where they
anchored until daylight. At 4 A.M. Commander Rodgers
moved on with the launches, and at daylight joined General
Stevens, commanding the army forces, in Mulligan's Creek,

where the general had secured a number of flats ; the gunboats followed at early daylight. The troops having embarked in the creek and passed into the Coosaw, through the
Brick-yard Creek to the first landing, at 8 A.M., the first detachment landed on Chisholm's Island with two light navy
howitzers and their crews, under cover of the gunboats that
had in the meantime come up. The landing was made on
the north bank of the Coosaw, four miles below the ferry.
The embarked troops and the naval force then proceeded to
the second point of debarkation, higher up at Adams's plantation, where they arrived at 10 A.M. At that point the gunboats anchored, and they and the launches covered the debarkation, during which time Commander Rodgers went on
board of the Hale, and to within range of the battery of the
enemy at Port Royal Ferry, on Chisholm's Island, into which
shells were thrown. This fire dislodged troops lying in an
adjoining field, but no response came from the battery.

At 1.30 P.M. the troops moved toward Port Royal Ferry,
the gunboats and launches shelling the woods in advance of
the skirmish line, and then advancing rapidly shelled the
batteries and anchored in front of it at 2.30 P.M. On visiting
the work Commander Rodgers found the enemy had carried off all of the guns save one. He was followed almost
immediately by the troops that had marched along the banks
of the Coosaw. A quantity of VIII-inch and 30-pounder
rifled shells were found in the magazine.

The Seneca and the Ellen had in the meantime entered
Whale Branch, and after ascending two miles, Captain Elliott,
of the Seventy-ninth Highlanders, came on board the Seneca
from Port Royal Island, and one mile higher up pointed out
an earthwork at Long Point, on Barnwell's Island, at a ten-
second fuse range. The channel being quite narrow the vessels anchored and shelled the work, without receiving a reply.

Captain Elliott embarked a force of 300 men in scows from a creek one mile below Seabrook, and landed on the site of the earthwork. Signals from him indicated the position of the enemy, and as requested the vessels opened fire until signal was made to discontinue. A platform for one heavy gun was in place ; the incomplete earthwork was designed for a number of guns. Captain Elliott destroyed the magazine and wood-work by fire, as well as some wood that had served as a concealment.

At 2.30 Commander Rodgers, from the Ottawa at Port Royal Ferry, signalled the Seneca and Ellen to join him ; this was effected at once by the last-named vessel, but owing to intervening shoal ground the Seneca could not get over until the following morning, when at 10 A.M. she, in common with the other vessels having heavy pivot guns, shelled the enemy at long range, as requested by army signals.

General Stevens wrote to the flag-officer in relation to the co-operation of Commander Rodgers as follows : "Whether regard be had to the beautiful working of the gunboats in the narrow channel of Port Royal, the thorough concert of action established through the signal-officers, or the masterly handling of the guns against the enemy, nothing remained to be desired."

The official report of the enemy gives a total of 8 killed and 24 wounded, the greater number attributed to shells from the gunboats. The result of the action was an abandonment of any future attempt on the part of the enemy to plant batteries near those waters, or to make preparations with the view of landing troops on Port Royal Island.

CHAPTER III.

On January 26, 1862, Fleet-Captain Charles H. Davis and Commander C. R. P. Rodgers, with the Ottawa, Seneca, Smith, Potomska, Ellen, and Western World, and the armed launches of the Wabash, accompanied by the army transports Cosmopolitan, Delaware, and Boston, having on board the Sixth Connecticut, Fourth New Hampshire, and Ninety-seventh Pennsylvania regiments, a total of 2,400 men, commanded by Brigadier-General H. G. Wright, entered Warsaw Sound. The following morning General Wright and Major Speidel went on board of the Ottawa, upon which vessel Captain Davis was. Two companies of the Sixth Connecticut having been sent on board of the Ottawa and Seneca, the vessels got under way, and proceeded into Tybee River. Owing to shoal water on the bar it was 8.30 A.M. before the vessels got in, and 1.30 P.M. before they reached the point nearest to Pulaski on its land side. It was amusing to note the bustle. No shots were fired at the vessels, because no rifled or heavy guns were mounted on the side which was supposed unapproachable by vessels of war. Great preparations were made in shifting guns for use when the vessels returned, but as it was simply a matter of choice with the vessels as to when they would return, they preferred doing so under the cover of the night.

The gunboats passed on, and reaching the part of the river

nearest to the highest land on Wilmington Island, their farther progress was at least temporarily prevented by a double
row of heavy piles driven across the channel. They anchored
and despatched boats from the different vessels to examine
numerous creeks and the upper part of the river. At 5 P.M.
five Confederate steamers, one bearing the flag of Commodore Tatnall, came to anchor at the upper end of St. Augustine's Creek. The telegraph wire was seen on the marsh
between Savannah and Fort Pulaski, and was cut. General
Wright and others made careful examination as to the advantage of a military occupation of Wilmington Island, to which
General Sherman had directed his attention.

At 11.15 A.M. of the following day (28th), five Confederate
vessels attempted to pass down the Savannah River to Fort
Pulaski, with scows in tow. A force of gunboats under
Commander John Rodgers, then in Wright River, on the
opposite side of the Savannah, and the force under Captain
Davis opened fire on the enemy, which was returned with
spirit. The flag-ship and another steamer of the enemy
were sufficiently affected by the fire to put about ; the other
steamers reached Pulaski. The object, without doubt, was
to carry necessary stores to the fort should the vessels intercept further communication.

The distance apart of the two forces between which the
Confederate steamers passed measures, on a good chart,
three statute miles. On their return from Pulaski they chose
low tide, and were thus protected from a ricochet fire, as the
gunboats lying in the narrow creeks found the marshy banks
quite near and high above them. On the morning of the 29th,
at 4 A.M., the Union vessels passed down and out, having
accomplished fully the intended object, which was to frighten
the enemy as to an impending attack on the city of Savannah by a sufficient force, this being merely a reconnoissance,

and perhaps a blind. Captain Davis reported : " As a demonstration, the appearance of the naval and military force in Wilmington and Warsaw Sounds has had complete success. Savannah was thrown into a state of great alarm, and all the energies of the place have been exerted to the utmost to increase its military defences, for which purpose troops have been withdrawn from other places."

On February 18th, Captain John Rodgers had carried out the objects for which he had been sent into Mud and Wright Rivers, and after mooring the small steamer Hale to protect an army battery planted at Venus Point, on the Savannah River, he returned to Port Royal with the force under his command. In relation to this the flag-officer informed the Department that Captain John Rodgers had a force of four gunboats and two purchased steamers, and had rendered the most efficient support and protection to the military parties in the planting of this battery.[1]

For some time the flag-officer had been making arrangements for an attack on Fernandina, by collecting or getting ready the vessels doing duty on blockade that would best serve the purpose. At length, on the last day of February, he left Port Royal in the Wabash. On the 2d of March the Wabash and other large vessels anchored off St. Andrew's Inlet, twenty miles north of the sea entrance to Fernandina. The flag was temporarily hoisted on board of the Mohican, Captain S. W. Godon, and the force intended for that inlet formed by signal and entered in the following order : Ottawa,

---

[1] These two demonstrations were known at the time, in the fleet, to be intended to weaken the defences at Fernandina, particularly by withdrawing the guns for the defence of Savannah. Whether they only drew the attention of General Lee to the impossibility of defending Fernandina with the rear approach unguarded, is of little import. The guns at St. Simon's and at Jekyl Island had been previously sent to Savannah, and those at Fernandina were in process of removal when the expedition reached that point. The troops on board the transports remained in Warsaw Sound until they left for Fernandina.

Mohican, Ellen, Seminole, Pawnee, Pocahontas, Flag, Pembina, Isaac Smith, Penguin, Potomska, armed cutter Henrietta, and armed transport McClellan, the latter having on board the battalion of marines under the command of Major Reynolds.

The army transports followed, the Empire City, Marion, Star of the South, Belvidere, Boston, and George's Creek, carrying a brigade under the command of Brigadier-General H. G. Wright. A black man who had been picked up in a small boat informed the flag-officer that the Confederates had hastily abandoned all of the defences of Fernandina, and were at that moment retreating from Amelia Island, carrying with them such munitions as their precipitate flight would allow.

The enemy had seen this formidable force enter St. Andrew's and, aware that it would proceed by way of Cumberland Sound, knew he had not a moment to lose. He had spent four weary days and nights in the effort to get his heavy rifles out of the strong and isolated sand batteries that guarded the sea approach to Fernandina, endeavoring to save as much of his heavy ordnance as possible. He had been aware, too, for some time, that in failing to guard the approach to St. Andrew's he might as well have left St. Simon's and Jekyl Islands unfortified, and had even then begun the removal of the heavy guns from them, but the attacking force had no further knowledge than the black man gave as to the situation. To the enemy it seemed, doubtless, a mean proceeding to enter by a back door when so much careful preparation had been made to receive a force at the sea entrance of the port, but at the last moment he had abandoned everything, and practically it made no difference to him where the vessels entered.

The flag-officer at once detached a force of light-draught

vessels, under Commander Drayton in the Pawnee, from those that entered the Sound in line the previous day "to push through the Sound with the utmost speed to save public and private property from destruction." This force despatched, at daylight the flag-officer crossed the bar in the Mohican and proceeded to the sea entrance of Fernandina, but rough weather prevented the vessel from entering the harbor until the 4th. In the meantime Commander C. R. P. Rodgers with three armed launches of the Wabash had gone on board of the Pawnee, which vessel was diligently threading her way through the narrow and tortuous channels in the marshes of Cumberland Sound, followed by the Ottawa, Seneca, Huron, Pembina, Isaac Smith, Penguin, Potomska, Ellen, and armed cutter Henrietta. The Pawnee, Ottawa, and Huron were the only vessels that succeeded in crossing "the flats" at the dividing point of the tides. The vessels left behind had no pilots, but at high water they got over and groped their way as they best could, as also the transports Boston and McClellan, the first with the Ninety-seventh Pennsylvania regiment, Colonel Guss, the second with the marine battalion, Major Reynolds.

Commander Drayton proceeded with the vessels that had succeeded in crossing "the flats," until 3 P.M., and when only three miles from Fort Clinch, the Pawnee and Huron grounded with a falling tide. He therefore went on board the Ottawa, to which vessel Commander C. R. P. Rodgers also proceeded with his three armed launches.

On arriving near Fort Clinch it was found deserted, and an officer with an armed boat's crew was despatched to hoist the American flag over it, in order to apprise the flag-officer off the harbor of the condition of affairs. The Ottawa continued on. At Old Fernandina a white flag was hoisted. Passing on, at New Fernandina rifle-shots were fired at the vessel from the bushes. A railroad train with two locomotives was on the point of starting. The track passed for some distance along the water, offering an opportunity for shell practice, but it was without further result than the killing of two soldiers on the train.

A small steamer, known afterward as the Darlington, was seen endeavoring to escape up the river through a drawbridge; the armed launches captured her. Besides women and children on board, the steamer was loaded with mules and army wagons; a Confederate surgeon was also found on board.

It was now 8 P.M.; an armed launch was left to guard the drawbridge, and Captain Drayton returned to the Pawnee, which had been left aground. Commander Rodgers with two armed launches went on board of the Ottawa, and left for the town of St. Mary's, ten miles up the river, for the purpose of securing the guns that had been hastily removed from Fort Clinch, and were supposed to be at that place.

At daylight of the 4th the Pawnee and Huron were anchored off the town of Fernandina. Confederate soldiers in the early morning fired on the crew of the launch guarding the drawbridge, and set fire to the end of the trestle-work leading to the bridge. The Huron was sent up; the Confederate soldiers vanished, and the fire was put out. Captain Drayton reported: "The batteries on and near Fort Clinch on the southern part of Cumberland Island and at New Fernandina, although many guns had been removed, might have offered very serious obstacles to our approach."

As stated before, the enemy had been busy for several days in removing heavy guns, for the purpose of transporting them beyond the reach of gunboats. At 8 P.M. of the 2d a telegram to Fernandina from Brunswick stated that twenty-four armed vessels were in Cumberland Sound. This produced a panic, and by noon of the 3d the garrison, which consisted of 1,500 men, and most of the inhabitants had left.

The long line of vessels entering St. Andrew's was really a beautiful and impressive sight; to the naval eye, however, there was not much that was really formidable in it. A punster might be pardoned in calling it an imposing force.

Fernandina was garrisoned on the morning of the 4th by the marines of the Pawnee and a company from the Wabash. At 9 A.M. the Isaac Smith arrived, and later in the day the other gunboats that had passed through the Sound. In the afternoon the Mohican came in by the sea entrance with the flag-officer on board.

We will now note the earlier movements of the enemy. General Trapier reports that on February 23d he received General R. E. Lee's order to withdraw from the islands, securing the artillery, etc. This order was sent by special messenger to the officer commanding the post at Amelia and Talbot Islands, and to Colonel McBlair, commanding the batteries, " to dismantle the batteries with all possible expedition and caution, and then to withdraw the troops and abandon the post."

" The fourth day after the receipt of this order the enemy made his appearance simultaneously in Cumberland Sound, having entered by St. Andrew's, and off the town of Fernandina. At that time the greater number of the guns had been dismounted and removed, and all of the guns that protected the direct entrance to Fernandina. A defence was therefore deemed impracticable, and the order was given to retire from the island. Thirty-three pieces of heavy ordnance were upon these islands, of which eighteen were carried off, as also all of the ammunition. When it is remembered that this was accomplished in four days, no other conclusion can be formed than that the utmost energy, industry, and vigor were exhibited by both officers and men."

"Five of the guns were subsequently lost, having been put on St. John's Bluff, for the defence of St. John's River. The enemy's prompt movements in that direction rendered it impossible to remove them, as was directed by an order of March 1st."

The Ottawa, previously mentioned as leaving for the town of St. Mary's at midnight, soon reached that place and landed a force without delay. A cavalry force of the enemy left without their horses and equipments. The greater number of the inhabitants had already deserted the town. The Ottawa and an armed launch remained, and Commander Rogers returned to Fernandina in the other launch.

In the defences surrounding Fernandina only thirteen guns were found, one 120-pounder and one 80-pounder, both rifled.

The flag-officer reported that "it is impossible to look at the earthworks on the sea face and the other defences without being surprised that they should have been abandoned. The batteries on the north and northeast shores are as complete as art could make them. Six are well concealed and protected by ranges of sand hills in front, perfect shelter provided for the men, thoroughly covered by the natural growth and by land contours, that striking them from a vessel would be the merest chance. A battery of six guns is equally well sheltered and masked. These batteries and the heavy guns on Fort Clinch commanded the sea entrance completely; another battery of four guns on the south end of Cumberland Island commands the channel after crossing the bar. Within the harbor was found another well-constructed battery." Our "forces had captured Port Royal, but the enemy had given us Fernandina."

Brigadier-General H. G. Wright came into the harbor on the 5th with his brigade, and the forts and public property were at once turned over to him. The flag-officer reports: "I desire to speak here of the harmonious councils and cordial co-operation which have marked throughout my intercourse with this able officer. Our plans of action have been matured by mutual consultation and have been carried into execution by mutual help."

Of the many National defences that had fallen into the hands of the Confederates upon the secession of the Southern States, the National flag was first hoisted over Fort Clinch; it was soon flying over all the others, save Jackson at Savannah, Moultrie and Sumter at Charleston, Caswell below Wilmington, and Gaines and Morgan at Mobile.

The Ottawa, Lieutenant-commanding Stevens, made a reconnoissance up the St. Mary's, as far as navigable for vessels of ten feet draught, fifty miles to Woodstock, and placed notices at various points that all peaceable citizens would be protected in their persons and property. While returning, at a narrow stretch known as the Brick-yards, he was fired on with field artillery and small arms. Of this intended attack he had been given warning, and replied with grape, canister, and small arms, with supposed effect.

Nothing more was seen of the enemy until just above the plantation of a Mrs. Campbell, when a large body of cavalry appeared near the river bank, some twelve hundred yards distant. A few XI-inch shells thrown among them caused great haste and confusion. Three miles below, where the river leaves the high land and enters the marshes, the enemy was discovered in ambush, but before he had an opportunity of firing, the Ottawa opened with XI-canister and from three howitzers, it was supposed with great effect. Captain Stevens acknowledged the good conduct of those under his

command, and the efficient services of Midshipman Pearson
of the Wabash. One master's mate was seriously wounded,
and three of the crew less so.

The army was now in occupancy of Fernandina, and vessels despatched in the performance of duties as above shown,
when the Wabash, now the flag-ship, left her anchorage off
Fernandina, accompanied by a bevy of gunboats, and anchored off St. Augustine on the evening of March 8th. The
fact was ascertained that no armed resistance was practicable or intended at that point, and the gunboats were ordered
to the mouth of St. John's River, some forty miles north,
to buoy out the entrance and to cross when the tides and
state of the sea permitted. The Wabash remained off St.
Augustine, and sent a boat on shore as soon as the state of
the sea permitted. Commander C. R. P. Rodgers went in
with a flag of truce. As the boat approached a white flag
was hoisted on Fort Marion. The boat landed at the wharf,
and Commander Rodgers was there received by the Mayor,
who conducted him to the town-hall, where the municipal
authorities were assembled. He stated that a vessel of war
had arrived off the bar for the purpose of restoring the authority of the United States; it was deemed more kind to
send an unarmed boat to inform them of the fact than to
occupy the town by force of arms. He wished to calm any
apprehensions of harsh treatment, and would carefully respect the persons and property of all citizens who submitted
to the lawful authority of the United States; so long as they
respected this authority and acted in good faith, municipal
affairs would be left in the hands of the citizens.

The Mayor informed Commander Rodgers that the place
had been garrisoned by two companies of Florida troops
who had left the previous night; that the Mayor and council
gladly received the assurances given, and placed the town

in the hands of Captain Rodgers, who then recommended
them to hoist the National flag over Fort Marion, which was
at once done by order of the Mayor.

Of a population of two thousand, about one-fifth had left.
"The men acquiesce in the condition of affairs we are now
establishing. There is much violent and pestilent feeling
among the women. They seem to mistake treason for courage, and have a desire to figure as heroines." [1] Three heavy
32-pounders and two VIII-inch howitzers, with some shot
and powder, were found in the fort.

Commander Godon, in the Mohican, with the Pocahontas
and Potomska, had been sent to St. Simon's Inlet, which
they entered on the 8th, and anchored within two miles of
the forts. The following morning they proceeded in, and
finding the forts apparently abandoned, three armed boats
were sent to St. Simon's, and a suitable force to Jekyl
Islands. Two strong earthworks of twelve embrasures and
several well-constructed magazines were found on St. Simon's, which commanded the entrance and the Sound ; the
guns had been removed ; a few X-inch shot remained, which
showed the calibre of the former batteries. The two batteries on Jekyl Island were of greater strength. The outer
one commanding the main channel had a bomb-proof constructed of palmetto logs, sand-bags, and railroad iron, well
supported and braced within. Three casemated guns, carriages, and ammunition had been removed. The other battery, five hundred yards landward, consisted of two casemates, and arrangements for four barbette guns, magazine,
and hot-shot furnace.

On February 16th, General Mercer, in command at Brunswick, Ga., informed General R. E. Lee that all of the guns

---

[1] Commander Rodgers's report.

STRATEGIC RECONNOISSANCES.   57

had been removed from St. Simon's and Jekyl Islands, and
solicited instructions as follows : " Before finally evacuating
this position, I beg to bring to the consideration of the General the question of burning the town of Brunswick, for
the moral effect it would produce upon the enemy."   . . .

No orders appear. The General may not have appreciated
the "moral effect" of burning the property of their own
people, which, if left undisturbed, could have been of little
advantage to their enemy, even though he had thought fit to
occupy the place.

The abandonment of the St. Simon's and Jekyl Islands
batteries had awakened the fears of General Trapier, who informed General Lee that the defence of Fernandina de-
pended upon them, to which General Lee on February 24th
replied as follows : " The withdrawal of the troops from St.
Simon's and Jekyl Islands can only affect the inland communication between Brunswick and Cumberland Sound, ren-
dering it less secure and certain.   The batteries commanding
the principal entrance into Cumberland Sound can be as easily
turned through St. Andrew's Sound as St. Simon's, which is
nearer and as accessible as the latter.   I had hoped that guns
could be obtained in time to defend those rear approaches,
but as I now see no possibility of doing so, and as the means
are incompetent in your opinion for its defence, you are authorized to retire both from Cumberland and Amelia Islands
to the main land."

The question here presents itself with singular force :
Had the National troops held Norfolk Navy Yard only long
enough to destroy the three thousand cannon stored there,
what would have been the ability of the Confederacy to establish defences against a respectable naval force ?

On February 10th General Lee wrote from Savannah to
Governor Brown of Georgia as follows : " I have the honor
   3*

to receive your letter of the 8th in reference to the withdrawal of the batteries from St. Simon's and Jekyl Islands. . . . I find it impossible to obtain guns to secure it as I desire, and now everything is requisite to fortify this city."

After an examination of the St. Simon's and Jekyl Islands earthworks, Commander Godon went in the Potomska to the town of Brunswick and found the railroad depot and wharf had been set on fire and a train of cars on the point of leaving. The Mohican and Pocahontas were then brought up and anchored off the town and a large party of armed men were sent on shore; the town was entirely deserted and house furniture generally removed. Proclamations were posted, "urging the inhabitants to return to their homes and promising protection to the property of all good citizens." The landing parties returned to their vessels; no houses that were not open were entered, and no property of any kind was taken.

The Pocahontas and Potomska were then sent up Turtle River as far as navigable for vessels of their draught. On their return the Pocahontas on the 11th sent a boat on shore in the vicinity of Brunswick to procure fresh beef for the crew. Returning, the boat had scarcely left the beach when she was fired into by a party of 40 Confederate soldiers; two in the boat were killed, two seriously and four others slightly wounded. Assistant-Surgeon Rhoades, in charge of the boat, was then called upon to surrender, which he refused to do, and aided by Paymaster Kitchen and the uninjured portion of the crew, pulled as well as they could for the vessel. The Mohican and the Potomska, observing the attack, opened fire with shells on the enemy, who had been joined by a considerable force. The brave conduct of Surgeon Rhoades received high commendation.

Leaving the Mohican in these waters, Commander Godon

proceeded on the 13th in the Potomska, accompanied by the Pocahontas, to open the inland route to the Altamaha; in doing this he had to remove two double rows of piles several miles apart. They had been sawed off at low water mark to make them more difficult to remove. Their removal took so much time that he did not arrive near Darien until late; he there found two steamers leaving under a heavy head of steam. The brass sleeves of the propeller shaft of the Potomska had given out, which induced him to return to Doboy Island. Darien, as well as Brunswick, had been deserted.

The operations against Fernandina led to the abandonment of the entire coast line defence by batteries, and to points sufficiently high up on the rivers to embarrass an attack by gunboats, except the defences of Charleston, and of Pulaski, the outer defence of Savannah, which was soon to fall. Skiddaway and Green Island batteries were reported abandoned, and the guns taken for the defence of the immediate vicinity of Savannah.

After establishing the lawful authority of the National flag at St. Augustine, the Wabash proceeded to the entrance of the St. John's River, where the admiral had the day before sent several gunboats. The bar had been sounded and buoyed, but in the rough state of the sea only the Ellen, having a lighter draught, could enter, which she did, with two armed launches of the flag-ship. The earthworks in face were found deserted, and the American ensign was hoisted on the lighthouse as a sign of quiet possession.

At high water on the afternoon of the 10th, the gunboats Ottawa, Seneca, and Pembina crossed the bar and at sunset anchored near Mayport Mills, three miles up the river. Every vessel had on board a company of troops of the Fourth New Hampshire.

The Wabash then left the anchorage for Mosquito Inlet,

fifty-one miles south of St. Augustine. It had been used to some extent by small vessels transporting arms from Nassau. The Penguin and the Henry Andrew had been sent some days before, the first-named to remain off the inlet and the second to pass within and protect from destruction a large amount of Government live-oak ready for shipment.

The commanding officers of those vessels, with 43 armed men, had gone some fifteen or eighteen miles up the river, and having returned within sight of the Henry Andrew, the line of order was no longer observed. The two commanding officers, quite in advance of the other boats, landed at an abandoned earthwork, near a dense growth of live-oak with underbrush, and were fired upon from the thicket. Lieutenant-Commander Budd and Acting Master Mather with three of the boat's crew were killed, and the two other men in the boat were wounded and taken prisoners. As the other boats came up they were fired into and retreated up the stream. Under cover of the night they passed out to the vessels with one man killed. The flag-officer was then lying off the inlet. In his report he says: "The loss of gallant lives has expiated the error of judgment which enthusiastic zeal had induced."

The officers and crews of the gunboats that the flag-officer had seen safely cross the difficult bar of St. John's River before leaving for Mosquito Inlet, saw the western sky illuminated throughout the night, and conjectured rightly that the Confederates were burning saw-mills and other buildings at Jacksonville. At daylight they were under way and at noon at anchor off Jacksonville. The troops were landed without delay and the outskirts of the town picketed. Two pieces of heavy ordnance, that the enemy had in transit, were found on the wharf, but time had failed him to carry them farther.

The Ottawa proceeded eighty miles up the St. John's to

Orange Mills, as far as the draught of the former would permit, and the Ellen passed some miles beyond; they then returned to Jacksonville. In a few days the Darlington, the small steamer captured at Fernandina, was repaired, put in service, and on the 17th was off Jacksonville. Lieutenant-Commander Stevens employed her in the recovery of the famous yacht America, that had been used in blockade-running and on the arrival of the National forces had been sunk in a creek.

The gunboats thereafter patrolled the navigable waters of the St. John's, to the entire subversion of the Confederates getting arms through the small inlets of Florida, to which they had been compelled to resort through a vigorous blockade of all of the harbors for vessels of even ten feet draught. The Confederates were not content, however, with having the gunboats in the upper waters of that river, and again endeavored to exclude them, but the effort proved wholly fruitless, and cost them nine more rifled guns in the earthwork on St. John's Bluff, the September following.

After the operations on the coast of Florida were fully completed, the flag-officer returned to Port Royal. During his absence the army had planted batteries of rifled guns and heavy columbiads on the sand-hills of Tybee Island, for the purpose of reducing Fort Pulaski, which the flag-officer described as a "purely military operation, the result of laborious and scientific preparation, and of consummate skill and bravery in execution. . . . General Hunter, with a generous spirit long to be remembered, permitted the navy to be represented on this interesting occasion by allowing a detachment of seamen and officers from this ship to serve one of the breaching batteries."

Commander C. R. P. Rodgers with a detachment of men reached Tybee on the morning of the 10th of April, just be-

fore the firing commenced, and too late to participate that
day. As many of the artillerists were quite untrained, until
ranges were obtained the practice was inaccurate. On the
following day, although there was a high wind, the firing
from both the rifled guns and columbiads was excellent,
"the former boring like augurs into the brick face of the wall,
the latter striking like trip-hammers and breaking off great
masses of masonry that had been cut loose by the rifles."

The four nearest batteries were more than sixteen hundred
yards from the fort; four rifled guns in battery Sigel, one of
those nearest the fort, had been assigned to the men from
the Wabash. The batteries were occupied at daylight, and
" kept up a steady and well-directed fire until the flag of the
fort was hauled down at 2 P.M." Commander Rodgers commended the conduct of Lieutenant Irwin, Master Robertson,
and Midshipmen M. L. Johnson and F. H. Pearson, and also
of petty officers Lewis Boun and George H. Wood.

" Before the fort surrendered the barbette guns had been
silenced and many of them dismounted. The breach was
practicable for storming in two places, and the projectiles
were passing through and knocking down the opposite wall,
which protected the magazine, so that the garrison was convinced that in an hour or so the magazine must be blown
up." [1]

The heavy XIII-inch mortars inflicted little injury; the
shells falling upon the casemates did not seem to shake
them at all, and those that fell within the fort rolled into
the deep furrows that had been made to receive them, where
they burst without doing injury. Less than one year had
passed since the seizure by the Confederates of all of the
forts within their power, and again the National ensign

---

[1] Commander Rodgers's report.

floated over three of them. The blockading duties did not prevent the officers commanding vessels from more pronounced action when circumstances appeared to favor it. Lieutenant-Commanding A. C. Rhind, in the Crusader, at North Edisto, had sent a boat's crew to assist a Government agent. In performing this duty Master Urann was severely wounded by the enemy. Colonel Fellows, Fifty-fifth regiment of Pennsylvania, kindly detailed a force under Lieutenant Bedell to accompany Captain Rhind. A force of 60 men with a light field howitzer reached the vicinity of the enemy at 3 A.M. of the 19th of April, but not without discovery and the precipitate flight of the enemy. Shortly after daylight a considerable force of mounted riflemen were seen advancing rapidly. They opened fire, but after a skirmish of half an hour retired as hastily as they had advanced. In this affair three of the sailors were wounded, and the force returned unmolested at leisure to the vessel.

On the 29th, the same officer on board of the Hale, Lieutenant-Commanding Gillis, with Assistant-Surgeon Brintnall, Mate Henry Parsons, 22 men, and a boat armed with a howitzer, proceeded to destroy a battery of the enemy near the junction of the Dawho, Paw Paw, and South Edisto Rivers. When the Hale was within eighteen hundred yards, the battery opened fire and continued as the bends of the river favored. One long reach had to be made under a raking fire, but the shells from the Hale had been so effective that when the vessel was making a direct course for the battery the enemy abandoned it in haste. The wood in the rear was shelled; 20 men were landed and reached the work by passing over some three hundred yards of marshy ground. Two fine 24-pounder field pieces were found, one of them loaded and primed. This piece was discharged against the other one to destroy it, and the second was destroyed by other means. All of the woodwork was piled under the carriages and set on fire. This was accomplished by 11 A.M., and the Hale then attempted to ascend the Paw Paw to a rice-mill for the purpose of destroying a vessel lying there, but owing to the ignorance of the pilot, when a mile within the river, the Hale grounded and remained fast until 5 P.M. It was too late to accomplish the object, and the ignorance of the pilot made it necessary to return by the Dawho and run the gauntlet of an ambuscade that they well knew would be prepared at a favorable point near Slamm's Bluff. That locality was reached at 8 P.M., and of course proper disposition made to receive the close fire of the enemy. As anticipated, the enemy opened a heavy fire upon the Hale with field pieces and small arms. The men then jumped to their guns and replied with grape, canister, and shells. No one was injured on the vessel. A 32-pounder was rendered useless by a shot knocking out a piece of the muzzle.

The blockaders in Doboy Sound enlivened the dull routine by ascending the Riceborough River with the object of destroying a brig supposed to have entered through Sapelo Sound. Lieutenant-Commanding A. A. Semmes in the Wamsutta, accompanied by the Potomska, on the 26th of April started up this narrow and tortuous stream. The following morning they had reached within a mile of Dorchester, and were informed that the smoke seen the previous day was from the burning brig. The object of their visit having been accomplished, the vessels began a difficult return. At Woodville Island they received the fire of the enemy from small arms at close range. Two men were killed on the first fire. In transit the vessels were of mutual assistance, the one with grape and canister enfilading, as it were, the sharpshooters that attacked the other. The vessels got out of their difficult position without further loss of life, and it was supposed had inflicted much greater loss on the assailants. The records of our former enemy, so far as published, give no details of these minor affairs.

A very interesting episode of the war was that of Robert Small, a slave and the pilot of the Planter, carrying that vessel to the blockading force off Charleston. The account given is substantially the report of the flag-officer to the Department. The vessel was engaged in the transportation of ordnance and army stores. On the morning of the 13th of May, the Planter was lying at the wharf close to army headquarters, with steam up and the captain on shore. Small had the fasts cast off, and with a Confederate flag flying passed the forts, saluting them as usual by blowing the whistle, and passing beyond their line of fire, hauled down his flag and hoisted a white one just in time to avoid the fire from a blockading vessel. The Planter was armed with a 32-pounder pivot gun, a 24-pounder howitzer, and had on board four heavy guns, one of which was a VII-inch rifle, intended for a new fort on the middle ground in Charleston Harbor. Eight men, five women, and three children were on board of the vessel. The flag-officer remarked: "Robert Small is superior to any who have come within our lines, intelligent as many of them have been. His information has been most interesting, and portions of it of the utmost importance." Small afterward served most usefully and with great intelligence on the Southern coast as pilot throughout the civil war, and later, for several sessions as a member of Congress from South Carolina.

Acting under definite but not compulsory instructions, the officers commanding blockading vessels were vigilant in following up by reconnoissance the changed lines of defence which had been established in such manner as not to allow an attack by any considerable number of gunboats.

Commander G. A. Prentiss in the Albatross passed into Winyaw Bay, the entrance to Georgetown, S. C., on May 21st, accompanied by the Norwich. A redoubt near the lighthouse was found deserted. Within, on South Island, an extensive work was seen, with apparently several large barbette guns. On a nearer approach, they were found to be what are known as "Quakers." From this view Cat Island was visible, and on it a well-built fort, with cavalry in the skirts of the woodland, who were scattered by shells. The vessels found these works deserted also and in like manner armed with "Quaker" guns. The work was quadrangular, fitted with platforms for mounting ten guns, with bomb-proofs, magazines, and furnace for hot shot. The woodwork was collected and set on fire, as also a large quantity of timber intended for obstructing the channel.

The following day the vessels passed up the river to Georgetown and steamed slowly along the wharves, the muzzles of the guns within thirty yards of the houses. A brig loaded with turpentine was set on fire to prevent the approach of the vessels, but they continued on, passed the vessel on fire and turned with some difficulty in the narrow channel to retrace their route, "tarrying to see if the town authorities were disposed to communicate." Commander Prentiss had judiciously "sent word to the Union men to make no demonstration whatever, as he was not prepared to hold the place permanently. A few, however, appeared on the wharves, and indicated by gestures or words their joy at seeing us, while the masses of citizens kept aloof. . . . While passing up, a woman appeared in the belfry of a church or city hall, and spread a rebel flag over the bell. I was greatly tempted to send on shore and seize it, but refrained, from the consideration that a contest in the streets would have compelled me to destroy the city, involving the ruin of the innocent with the guilty." [1]

From information derived from Robert Small, a reconnoissance of Stono Inlet was made, and on the next day the gunboats Unadilla, Pembina, and Ottawa crossed the bar under Commander Marchand, and proceeded up the river to the old fort opposite Legaréville. The enemy fired the barracks on the approach of the vessels. A picket guard of six at the magazine of the fort were taken prisoners. On the 29th of May the Pawnee crossed the bar, the Huron having entered the day before; the inlet was entered at extreme high water, nevertheless the Pawnee struck heavily twenty times. Nothing was more trying on officers commanding vessels than thumping them over bars, often with great risk of leaving them there.

The Pawnee ascended to Legaréville; from thence Captain Drayton in the Ottawa, a smaller vessel than his own command, accompanied by the Huron and Pembina, reached the last bend of the river below Wappoo Cut, when the enemy opened fire from a very heavy rifled gun, some of the shot falling only a little short of the vessels. The Pembina and Huron were left for the night a little above Newtown Creek. The removal of a few piles from an obstruction enabled Captain Drayton to bring the Pawnee up the river, which he did, with the Ellen accompanying, as far as Newtown Creek. From that point Captain Drayton continued on in the Ellen, and rounding a point they were in sight of the fortification from which they had been fired upon the previous day. From Parrott rifled guns, shells fired on board of the Ellen, with 16° elevation and 20″ fuzes, just reached the enemy. He replied with accuracy from the heavy rifle before mentioned.

---

[1] Prentiss's report.

After a dozen shots on each side, the Ellen returned with such information as was thus obtainable. Contrabands informed Captain Drayton that torpedoes had been laid in the river above. He adds in his report, that " even were this not the case, I do not think the gunboats could go beyond where I had been, and not stick in the mud. To sum up, we are in as complete possession of the river as of Port Royal, and can land and protect the army whenever it wishes. Beyond the reach of our guns I cannot, of course, be responsible, for it must, to a certain extent, then look out for itself." With a good map, the military student will note an opening here for successful operations through information which the admiral justly styled of " the utmost importance."

The battery of the enemy was near Wappoo Cut, and consisted of a heavy rifled gun and seven heavy columbiads. The vessels above mentioned remained for some time in the river.

The Upper St. John's River, running nearly north and south, important for the transportation of small arms, that for some time had been obtained through some of the many insignificant inlets of the peninsula, was patrolled by several gunboats. There were many men in that region who had been actually driven into the Confederate ranks, and who had escaped into the wilds of Florida. To hound them, a set of men known as " Regulators " were permitted to remain at home. One of these, known as George Huston, commanded a squad and resided near Black Creek. He boasted of having hung the negro pilot when Captain Budd was shot near New Smyrna. It was supposed that " his capture would secure the general tranquillity of persons along the river, most of whom would gladly acknowledge the authority of the Government of the United States were they not in fear of violence from men of this character." To capture him 40

men were detailed from the Seneca, and a reserve of 30 men
from the Patroon, under the command of Lieutenant John
G. Sproston of the Seneca. The party landed at early daylight and proceeded rapidly to Huston's house. A negro
woman saw the party and gave the alarm. Huston appeared
at the door armed with a double-barrelled gun, two pistols
and a bowie knife ; to a demand to surrender he fired a pistol at Sproston within a few feet, killing him instantly. He
fired the other pistol and the gun, wounding a sailor slightly,
and was shot and bayonetted at the same time ; he was
brought on board and died within a day or two, his wounds
being necessarily fatal. The party not having been thrown
around the house, several persons escaped who had fired
from it without effect. The death of this officer was a loss
to the navy, and was deeply regretted by his many friends in
and out of the service. He was a gallant officer of great
professional merit, and had with others, on the 13th of September, 1861, distinguished himself in the destruction of
the privateer Judah at the Pensacola Navy Yard ; and afterward as executive officer of the Seneca in the battle of Port
Royal, and on other occasions.

While in those waters the Seneca recovered two field-
pieces and carriages at a creek below Yellow Bluffs. It was
known that a certain Neils Johnson had been present in
throwing them into the water, and he was sent for. He
acted the simpleton, but he was informed that his feigned
stupidity would not answer, and that he would be held as a
prisoner until he aided in the recovery of the guns. He no
longer feigned, but wept earnestly and said he could not do
so, as the " Regulators " would kill him. A compromise was
effected, resulting in the recovery of the guns, upon his being given a paper stating that he aided under penalty of
otherwise being shot. At Yellow Bluffs, before this occur-

rence, the Seneca was fired on at a distance of sixty to one hundred yards by a company of "Regulators," and two of the crew dangerously wounded. Although the attack was wholly unexpected, and the commanding officer, pilot, and others were grouped, and the mass of fire was directed at them, none of the group were struck, although many bullets hit the hammock netting and the bulwark opposite.

As stated before, the enemy were most desirous of closing the upper part of the St. John's, to permit the transportation of small arms through the inlets of the peninsula, and for that purpose had erected a battery of seven VIII-inch and two IV$\frac{1}{2}$-inch rifled guns on St. John's Bluff, some seven miles from the mouth of the river.

Commander Steedman in the Port Royal suggested that a co-operating land force should be sent to secure the guns when silenced by the vessels under his command. General Mitchell, then in command at Port Royal, promptly sent a force under General Brannan, which was landed at a favorable point. The gunboats attacked the battery on the 5th of October, which led to the hasty abandonment of the works and the seizure of them by our troops. The armed steamer Darlington, captured, as the reader will remember, by Commander Rodgers at Fernandina, Lieutenant-Commander Williams, with Company E Forty-seventh Pennsylvania regiment on board, and the Hale, Lieutenant-Commander Snell, ascended the river to Lake Beresford, two hundred and thirty miles, and captured the steamer Morton, one of the best on the river and engaged in the transportation of arms and munitions. General Brannan wrote to the flag-officer : "Commander Steedman exhibited a zeal and perseverance in every instance, whether in aiding my forces to effect a landing, the ascent of St. John's river two hundred and thirty miles, or the assistance to one of my transports, unfortunately injured in crossing the bar, that is deserving of all praise."

An expedition designed to destroy the Pocotaligo bridge was less fortunate in its results from a series of miscarriages. The naval force, as before, was under Commander Steedman in the Port Royal, and the troops again under the command of General Brannan. Officers commanding naval vessels were assembled on board the Vermont and received instructions as to order of sailing, etc. In aid of the transports, every naval vessel carried an assigned quota of troops. At sunset the vessels proceeded some miles and anchored in the mouth of Broad River. Four armed launches in tow of a small tug carrying one hundred troops were sent in advance to a point some two miles below Mackey's Point, from whence half the force was to proceed to Mackey's, and the other part to Cuthbert's Landing to capture the pickets. The guide to Mackey's was incompetent and the picket was not captured; the other force was successful in that object.

Soon after midnight the signal was made for the vessels to get under way; the Paul Jones with transport De Ford proceeded up the river, apparently without observing the fact that they were unaccompanied. These vessels anchored above Mackey's at 4.30 A.M. The failure of the naval vessels was due to the fact that the Conemaugh, the third vessel in line, did not see the signal to get under way, and when she moved, passed on the wrong side of the lights placed to carry them over shoal ground. She then grounded and disarranged the line, and the Marblehead and Water Witch collided. As a result of these mishaps the vessels did not leave Broad River until daylight; however, they reached Mackey's and landed the troops on board by 10 A.M., those on board of the De Ford and the Paul Jones having landed on arrival.

At the request of General Brannan the Uncas proceeded

up the Pocotaligo River and the Patroon and the Vixen up the Coosawhatchie, the last-named to cover the landing of Colonel Barton's forces from the Planter. The services of these vessels are officially commended. Also at the request of the general, the three howitzers of the Wabash, in charge of Lieutenant Phenix and Ensigns Wallace, Pearson, and Adams, were landed and sent to the front; the conduct of these officers and the men under their command was highly commended by the general commanding the troops. A message from the general that he was falling back was received at 5 P.M. The next day (23d) the troops re-embarked and the whole force returned to Port Royal. The escape of the picket was in itself sufficient to make the move abortive, and the failure of the vessels to arrive for five hours after those leading, was also enough, as the troops of the enemy in half that time could be sent to the line of railroad from Savannah and from Charleston.

While the intended results of the expedition, to make a lodgment on the Charleston and Savannah Railroad, were not attained, the services of the naval co-operating force were duly acknowledged by the military commander in his official report.

On the afternoon of January 30, 1863, the gunboats Commodore McDonough, Lieutenant-Commander George Bacon, and the Isaac Smith, Acting Lieutenant F. S. Conover, were lying in Stono Inlet. At 4.40 P.M. the Isaac Smith got under way and proceeded up the river above Legaréville, for the purpose of making a reconnoissance, and being fired upon from concealed and unsuspected heavy field batteries, hotly engaged them. The McDonough proceeded to her relief, but before getting within supporting distance a white flag was seen flying over the Isaac Smith. A nearer approach showed that the vessel was apparently aground [1] and two of her

---

[1] Confederate reports say "she dropped anchor and unconditionally surrendered." No surrender of a vessel has come to the knowledge of the writer that

boats were taking the officers and men on shore. Three field batteries then opened on the McDonough, one of six guns, on John's Island; the fire from the enemy was at once returned, the engines reversed and the vessel dropped down the stream.

The report of the officer commanding the Smith states that he anchored opposite Grimball's plantation, four and a half miles from the inlet; an excellent lookout was at the mast-head and nothing suspicious was seen. A few minutes later a battery of three rifled guns on James Island six hundred yards distant, and concealed by trees, opened fire; the vessel at once was got under way and engaged the battery. At the same time two other batteries lower down, on John's Island, also opened fire on the vessel. An endeavor was made to pass down, but for a mile or more the vessel was exposed to a raking fire and unable to reply, except occasionally from a pivot gun. Passing by the two batteries, at an estimated distance of from two to four hundred yards, a broadside of shell and grape was delivered, but the vessel received a shot in her steam-chimney which at once disabled her, and there was nothing left to do but surrender. Eight men had been killed and 17 wounded, some of them mortally. The batteries were properly supposed to be composed of siege and field guns, and their fire was supplemented by a number of riflemen on or near the banks of the river.[1]

The Isaac Smith was a vessel of four hundred and fifty-three tons, purchased in 1861, and was armed with one 30-pounder Parrott and eight VIII-inch columbiads.

---

was not *unconditional.* January 31st the McDonough reports the Isaac Smith " still on shore at the same place. She must have been injured below the water-line or else they would certainly have gotten her off at high tide this morning."

[1] " Their artillery force was composed entirely of field and siege guns brought down and concealed in the bushes " (report of Lieutenant Conover).

CHAPTER IV.

RAID OF THE CONFEDERATE IRONCLADS OFF CHARLES-
TON.—ATTACK ON FORT M'ALLISTER.

EARLY in the morning of January 31, 1863, two ironclad vessels, known afterward as the Palmetto State and the Chicora,
built and lying in Charleston, came out of the main channel.
A thick haze and an entire calm favored the movement.
The Powhatan and the Canandaigua, the two most powerful
vessels on the blockade, were temporarily absent, coaling at
Port Royal, leaving only one vessel of size built for war purposes, the Housatonic, with nine other vessels blockading.
The others, except the gunboats Ottawa and Unadilla, were
purchased vessels whose steam-pipes, chimneys, and machinery were much exposed when under fire. Such vessels,
built of iron, if penetrated by a shot or shell would receive
little injury from the ingress, but if it were not arrested
by some solid body within, on its egress a whole sheet would
be carried away, perhaps at the water-line, and the vessel
might sink at once, as did the Hatteras, after an engagement
with the Alabama off Galveston, Texas. The Mercedita,
Captain F. S. Stellwagen, just such an iron vessel as described, was the first approached by a ram. In the early part
of the evening she had overhauled a transport passing with
troops and afterward returned to her position and anchored.
About 4 A.M., one of the armor-plated vessels (the Palmetto

State) suddenly appeared through the mist. She was hailed
and an order given to fire, but it was found the ram was so
close that the guns of the Mercedita could not be sufficiently
depressed to strike her. A heavy shell from a rifled gun on
the ram entered the starboard side of the Mercedita, passed
through the Normandy condenser and the steam-drum of
her port boiler, exploding against the port side of the vessel
and tearing a hole four or five feet square. The shell killed
the gunner in his room, and the escape of steam three firemen and coal-heavers, and badly scalded three others. The
enginery was disabled, and as demanded, an officer was sent on
board of the attacking vessel and gave a parole for the officers
and men "not to take up arms against the Confederate States
during the war, unless legally and regularly exchanged as
prisoners of war." Repairs of a temporary character enabled
the Mercedita to reach Port Royal during the day without
being towed.

The rams then approached the Keystone State. An extract of the log-book of that vessel, over the signature of her
commanding officer, is more circumstantial than his official
report given also in the appendix to the Report of the Secretary of the Navy, and therefore forms the basis of what
appears below.

Between 4 and 5 A.M. a gun, supposed from the Mercedita,
was heard, lights were seen, and soon a dark object a little
ahead of her, and a column of black smoke rising as was
supposed from a tug; another column of black smoke was
seen more to the north and east. The suspicions of the captain were aroused, and he ordered the forward rifle trained
upon the vessel approaching from the Mercedita. The battery was made ready, engineer directed to have steam, the
cable was slipped and the vessel was under steerage way.
The vessel was hailed, a reply of "Halloo" with unintelligi-

ble words following, and a gun was fired which was at once
responded to by the ram. The order was given to fire the
starboard battery as the guns would bear, the helm was put
aport for a northeast course, when a ram was seen on each
quarter. The shell from the enemy had entered forward and
there was fire in the fore-hold ; in ten minutes it was found
the water was shoaling and the course was changed to southeast for about ten minutes longer, to extinguish the fire,
which was supposed to have been effected, but it broke out
again. After it was extinguished, full steam was ordered, a
black smoke was seen and steered for, with the intention of
running the vessel down, and approaching exchanged shots
rapidly with the ram, striking her repeatedly but making
no impression, while every shot from her was striking.
About 6.17 a shell entering on the port side forward of the
forward guard destroyed the steam-chimneys, filling all of
the forward part of the ship with steam. The port boiler
emptied, the ship heeled to starboard nearly to the guard,
and the water from the boilers and two shot-holes under
water led to the impression that the vessel was sinking;
eighteen inches of water was reported in the well. The
steam forward cut off the supply of ammunition for the time.
Boats were got ready for lowering, the signal-books thrown
overboard, and also some small arms. "The ram being so
near, and the ship helpless, and the men slaughtered by almost every discharge of the enemy, I ordered the colors to
be hauled down, but finding the enemy were still firing upon
us directed the colors to be rehoisted and resumed our fire
from the after battery. Now the enemy, either injured or
to avoid the squadron approaching, sheered off toward the
harbor, exchanging shots with the Housatonic, which vessel
was in chase. Fore and aft sail was put on the ship, sent
yards aloft and bent sails ; the Memphis took the vessel in

tow for Port Royal. The port battery was run in to heel the ship, to prevent inflow from shot-holes at the water-line."[1] Surgeon Gotwold and 19 men were killed and 20 wounded, the greater number of the casualties being caused by the steam.

The Housatonic, Captain William Rogers Taylor, senior officer present on the blockade, was at anchor farthest to the north and east, near Rattlesnake Shoal. The firing had been heard, but as it was a very usual occurrence, no apprehension of attack was entertained; the cause of the firing was conjectured to be due to an attempt to run the blockade. At early dawn the Housatonic got under way and shaped her course for three vessels, one of which was known as the Augusta, next in station on the line of blockade. Some time previous this vessel had made a night signal which was not understood. As the Housatonic proceeded, a black smoke was seen ahead, and as the light increased, "an ironclad ram bearing the Confederate flag" was made out, steering toward the entrance of the harbor, and the Augusta was firing; later, another ram was seen to the southward and westward, also making for the harbor. The Housatonic was sheered in as near as the soundings would permit, and opened fire on the nearest ram, which deviated twice from her course in order to return the fire. The Housatonic was not struck, however, and it was supposed she had injured the pilot-house of the ram and shot away her flag-staff.

The rams entered Charleston Harbor, and were not seen until late in the afternoon, when the mist partially lifted and showed them at anchor in the Maffitt Channel, near Fort Moultrie, visible from the assigned anchorage of the Housatonic.

---

[1] See Le Roy's Report.

The following proclamation was issued :

HEADQUARTERS NAVAL AND LAND FORCES,
CHARLESTON, S. C., January 31, 1863.

At the hour of five o'clock this morning the Confederate States
naval forces on this station attacked the United States blockading
fleet off the harbor of the city of Charleston, and sunk, dispersed, or
drove off and out of sight, for the time, the entire hostile fleet. Therefore, we, the undersigned commanders, respectively, of the Confederate
States naval and land forces in this quarter, hereby formally declare
the blockade by the United States of the said city of Charleston, S. C.,
to be raised by a superior force of the Confederate States, from and
after this 31st day of January, A.D. 1863.

G. T. BEAUREGARD,
General Commanding.

D. N. INGRAHAM,
Commanding Naval Forces in South Carolina.

Official : THOMAS JORDAN, Chief-of-Staff.

The results of the engagement are: two vessels sunk, four set on
fire, and the remainder driven away.

Yesterday afternoon General Beauregard placed a steamer at the disposal of the foreign consuls to see for themselves that no blockade existed. The French and Spanish Consuls accepted the invitation. The
British Consul, with the commander of the British war-steamer Petrel,
had previously gone five miles beyond the usual anchorage of the blockaders, and could see nothing of them with their glasses.

Late in the evening four blockaders reappeared, keeping far out.
This evening a large number of blockaders are in sight, but keep steam
up ready to run. The foreign consuls here held a meeting last night.
They are unanimously of the opinion that the blockade of this port is
legally raised. [This information appended is not attested.]

In relation to this extraordinary proclamation, Colonel
Leckler and others wrote Admiral Dupont as follows :

HEADQUARTERS 176TH REGIMENT PENNSYLVANIA MILITIA,
ST. HELENA SOUND, S. C., February 21, 1863.

SIR: Having seen a proclamation issued by General Beauregard and
Commodore Ingraham to the effect that upon the morning of the 31st
ult. they had, by force of arms, succeeded in dispersing the blockading
fleet which was lying off Charleston Harbor, and also a statement pur-
porting to have come from the English Consul for that port, and the
commanding officer of the English man-of-war Petrel, that they had
gone out to a point five miles beyond the usual anchorage of the blockading fleet, and that not a single vessel could be seen, even with the aid
of powerful glasses, and that, consequently, the blockade had been
most effectually raised, and knowing, as we do, the above statement to
be utterly false in every particular, we feel constrained to tender our
evidence as corroboratory of that already furnished.

On the evening of January 29th, the One Hundred and Seventy-
sixth Regiment Pennsylvania Militia (with which we are connected)
left Morehead City, N. C., on board steamer Cossack, destined for Port
Royal. Upon the morning of the 31st, when near Charleston, could
hear firing distinctly. Upon our arrival off the harbor, which was at
about 8.30 A.M., found lying there the blockading squadron, some of
which were at anchor, and also the prize steamer Princess Royal. The
distance from land at which they were was estimated to be from four
to five miles; and although the morning was somewhat hazy, yet the
land could be plainly seen on each side of the harbor. Vessels could be
seen in the inlets, and by the aid of a glass a fort, said to have been
Sumter, was visible. We were right in the midst of the fleet, so near as
to be able to carry on a conversation with the Housatonic—were boarded
by officers from it and the Quaker City. We remained there until about
nine o'clock. Shortly after we departed, the Princess Royal followed.

Being thus near the site of the engagement, and so soon after it came
off, we do not hesitate in the least to pronounce the statement that the
blockade was raised not only absurd, but utterly and wilfully false in
every particular. And the statement of the English Consul and the
commander of the Petrel, that the squadron could not be seen even
with the aid of powerful glasses, is one equally false, and one that im-
pels us to conclude that it would require a powerful glass, truly, to be
able to discover one particle of truth or honesty in the composition of
these gentlemen.

The entire regiment can substantiate the above facts, and burn with indignation that gentlemen occupying high stations, as they do, should resort to such base fabrications to prop up a failing cause.

We have the honor, sir, to be your most obedient servants,

A. A. LECKLER, Colonel Commanding 176th Regiment.

W. F. FUNDENBURG, Surgeon 176th.

TAYLOR C. NEWBURY, Commanding Steamship Cossack.

Rear-Admiral S. F. DUPONT,

Commanding South Atlantic Blockading Squadron.

At an earlier date the commanding officers of vessels blockading that were sufficiently near to be cognizant of the facts wrote the following letter:

U. S. STEAMER NEW IRONSIDES,

OFF CHARLESTON, February 10, 1863.

We, the undersigned officers, commanding various vessels of the blockading squadron off Charleston, have seen the proclamation of General Beauregard and Commodore Ingraham, herewith appended, as also the results of the so-called engagements, viz.: two vessels sunk, four set on fire, and the remainder driven away; and also the statement that the British Consul and the commander of the British war-steamer Petrel had previously gone five miles beyond the usual anchorage of the blockaders, and could see nothing of them with their glasses.

We deem it our duty to state that the so-called results are *false in every particular*. No vessels were sunk, none were set on fire seriously. Two vessels alone were injured of consequence: the Mercedita had her boiler exploded by a shell from the only gun fired at her, when surprised by an attack by night. A thick haze was prevailing; and the Keystone State also had her steam-chest injured at the moment of attempting to run down one of the rams. The Keystone State was at once assisted by the Memphis, which vessel exchanged shots with the iron ram as she was withdrawing toward the bar, after having fired at the Keystone State, as did also the Quaker City. So hasty was the retreat of the rams, that, although they might have perceived that the Keystone State had received serious damage, no attempt was ever made to approach her. The Stettin and Ottawa, at the extreme end of the line, did not get under way from their position till after the firing had ceased, and the Stettin merely saw the *black smoke* as the rams disappeared over the bar. The Flag was alongside the Mercedita after, it seems, she had yielded to the ram, supposing herself sinking. The rams withdrew hastily toward the harbor, and on their way were fired at by the Housatonic and Augusta, until both had got beyond reach of their guns. They anchored under the protection of their forts, and remained there.

No vessel, *ironclad or other*, passed out over the bar after the return of the rams in shore. The Unadilla was not aware of the attack until the Housatonic commenced firing, when she moved out toward that vessel from her anchorage.

The Housatonic was never *beyond the usual line of blockade.* The Quaker City, in the forenoon, picked up her anchor which she had slipped to repair to the point of firing. The Flag communicated with the senior officer on board the Housatonic that forenoon, soon after the firing ended, and the blockade continued as before. No vessel ran in or out of the port that day, *nor was any attempt made to run the blockade.* The Keystone State necessarily was ordered to Port Royal for repairs. The Unadilla returned to her usual anchorage, after communicating with the senior officer, where she remained during the day. *Throughout the day two small tug-boats* remained apparently in attendance on the rams, under cover of Forts Moultrie and Beauregard. The prize steamer Princess Royal, which had been lying alongside of the Housatonic, was despatched to Port Royal, by order of the senior officer, *one hour and a half after the ram had returned to the cover of the batteries* and the firing had ceased, or about 9.30 A.M.

These are facts, and we do not hesitate to state that no vessel did come out beyond the bar after the return of the rams, at between 7 and 8 A.M., to the cover of the forts. We believe the statement that any vessel came anywhere near the usual anchorage of the blockaders, *or up to the bar*, after the withdrawal of the rams, to be deliberately and knowingly false.

If the statement from the papers, as now before us, has the sanction of the captain of the Petrel and the foreign consuls, we can only deplore that foreign officers can lend their official positions to the spreading before the world, for unworthy objects, *untruths*, patent to every officer of this squadron.

WM. RODGERS TAYLOR, Captain U.S.S. Housatonic.

J. H. STRONG, Commander U.S.S. Flag.

JAMES MADISON FRAILEY, Commander U.S.S. Quaker City.

PEND. G. WATMOUGH, Commanding U.S.S. Memphis.

C. J. VAN ALSTINE, Commanding U.S.S. Stettin.

4*

The reader may well wonder at the several preceding pages; the proclamation and the refutation at such length. The first-named shows that however able and brave the officers were who signed it, they did not limit their devotion to *fighting* for the Confederacy; they were willing to go far beyond that.

The refutation is inserted somewhat maliciously, to embarrass such persons as either believe what they choose, or assert a belief in what is absurd in itself. In the face of the character of the blockading force off the bar at that time, with three exceptions so entirely destructible by such vessels as the rams, it seems unaccountable that they did not remain outside of the bar during the day at least.

These Confederate rams never ventured out again, although Flag-Officer Ingraham states in his report that they were not struck by a projectile during the raid.

The construction of such vessels at Charleston must have been imperfect from a lack of plant of suitable materials, and of skilled workmen.[1] The wonder is, that under so many disadvantages, they should have ventured to construct any vessels. In every case the labor was without compensating result, if we except the structure on the hull of the frigate Merrimac, known as the Virginia to the Confederates, which, after the destruction of the sailing frigates Congress and Cumberland at Newport News, was soon after consigned to the flames as a result of the fall of Norfolk.

---

[1] Since writing the above, one of their former lieutenants, whose opinion and statements may be relied on, states: "They were well-constructed vessels, covered with four inches of iron, and would steam about seven knots. They drew twelve to thirteen feet, and were each armed with two Brooke rifled 80-pounders, and two 64-pounder shell-guns." He has no recollection as to where the enginery was made. From the experience in the capture of the Atlanta, it may be regarded certain that their casemates would not have resisted XV-inch shells.

Soon after this raid, the New Ironsides, then at anchor in Port Royal, a vessel built under far more favorable auspices than could obtain within the limits of the Confederacy, was added to the blockading force off Charleston. We may suppose, without derogation to the enemy, that she exercised a powerful restraining influence on the Confederate rams within that port.

The enemy, as we have seen, having felt the power of guns afloat where many of them could be brought to bear, no longer contested inferior points of defence, and fully aware of an intended attack on Charleston and under an apprehension of attack on Savannah, turned his attention to strengthening the defences of those cities by every means within his power. He looked with apprehension, as the people of the North looked with hope and expectation, upon the arrival of the monitor class of vessels that were completed and of others under construction, intended particularly for the attack on Charleston. In the early part of January several of them were already south of Cape Hatteras, where the Monitor, the original vessel of that type, foundered at sea, and at the same time the Montauk and the Passaic were in great peril.

Several of these vessels which arrived out in advance of others of their class intended for the attack on Charleston were sent by Rear-Admiral Dupont [1] to the Great Ogeechee River.

The Rear-Admiral informed the Department on the 28th of January that he considered it desirable in every way to test the ironclads of the Monitor type, and to avail himself of their usefulness until the intended number might arrive, he had sent the Montauk, Commander John L. Worden, to Os-

---

[1] The title of flag-officer had been changed by law to that of Rear-Admiral since the operations of the preceding year.

sabaw, to operate up the Great Ogeechee, and capture, if he could, the fort at Genesis Point (known afterward as Fort McAllister), under cover of which was lying the Nashville, a large side-wheel steamer, a blockade-runner fitted for a cruiser under the Confederate flag, and there for the purpose of escaping to foreign waters. If Commander Worden should be successful against the fort, it was thought that the Nashville might be destroyed, and afterward a railroad bridge lying two miles above the fort.

Commander Worden reported his arrival off Ossabaw Bar on the 24th of January, in tow of the James Adger. He crossed the bar at 5 P.M. but had to anchor on account of fog, which also held him fast the following day. The commanding officers of the Seneca, Wissahickon, Dawn, and Williams were called together and instructions given as to the plan of attack on the fort. On the 26th the Montauk anchored just out of range, followed by the other vessels. After dark, Lieutenant-Commander John L. Davis, with two armed boats, went up the river to reconnoitre, and to destroy range marks placed by the enemy. He examined the line of piles driven across the river diagonally below the fort, and found indications that the piles supported torpedoes. At 7 A.M. the Montauk moved to a position about one hundred and fifty yards below this line of piles, and opened fire, and at the same time the other vessels moved into effective range for shells and opened also. The fort at first returned the fire briskly, with fair aim, striking the Montauk thirteen times without inflicting serious damage. Before noon the shells of the Montauk were expended and the vessel withdrew and by signal directed the withdrawal of the other vessels. No casualties occurred on board of any of the attacking force. The fort was found to mount nine guns and was provided with ample bomb-proofs.

On February 1st the Montauk again took position, supposed to be within six hundred yards of McAllister, supported by the same vessels as before. The falling of the tide
made it necessary to drop down to a distance of fourteen
hundred yards, and the firing of shells and the return fire
from the fort continued until near noon, when, Commander
Worden says, "finding it useless to shell any longer, I
withdrew out of range with the supporting gunboats."

The Montauk had been struck forty-six times without sustaining any serious damage, and although her fire had been
delivered with accuracy, no further harm was done than to
tear up the parapet and traverses of the fort.[1]

On March 2d the Rear-Admiral had the satisfaction of reporting the destruction of the Nashville, which vessel had
been successfully blockaded for eight months. He says:
"Through the extreme vigilance and spirit of Lieutenant-
Commander Davis of the Wissahickon, Lieutenant Barnes of
the Dawn, and later, Lieutenant-Commander Gibson, I have
been able to keep her so long confined to the waters of the
Ogeechee.

"For some months the Nashville had been loaded with
cotton, constantly watchful, yet never ventured an effort to
escape. Then she withdrew up the river, and reappeared
after a length of time fitted as a privateer. To defend her
and the railroad bridge above, Fort McAllister was strengthened, and a diagonal row of piles driven, having a line of
torpedoes below them. The vessel had appeared from time
to time ready to make a dash should an opportunity offer.
The vessel was armed with a heavy rifle mounted on a circle,

---

[1] One officer was killed, seven men wounded, and one gun disabled.

Colonel R. H. Anderson, commanding Fort McAllister, in his report of this action states : " The enemy fired steadily and with remarkable precision. At times
their fire was terrible. Their mortar firing was unusually fine, a large number of
shells bursting directly over the battery."

and was 'proverbially fast.' Through the ability and zeal of the officers before mentioned she had been held, and through the quick perception and rapid execution of Commander Worden she has been destroyed."

On the evening of February 27th Commander Worden observed the Nashville in movement above McAllister. In a reconnoissance it was discovered that she had grounded in a bend known as the seven-mile reach, and supposed to be within reach of the guns of the Montauk in her former position when attacking the fort. At daylight she went up with her consorts, into their former positions. The Nashville was seen aground at a distance of twelve hundred yards across the marsh, and a few shells thrown determined the range. In less than twenty minutes she was on fire forward, amidships, and aft. Soon after, the large pivot gun, mounted abaft the fore-mast, exploded from the heat. Twenty minutes later the smoke-stack went by the board, and soon after "the magazine exploding shattered the smoking ruins."

During this time McAllister was busily engaged firing at the Montauk, but in the attendant excitement only struck her five times, without damage to the vessel, and at the same time the firing from the fort on the gunboats was wild and without injury to them. The fire upon the fort destroyed one gun-carriage.[1]

The destruction of the Nashville completed, the Montauk withdrew with her assisting force beyond the reach of guns; in doing so, she ran over a torpedo placed by the enemy, inflicting an injury so serious that, had she not been run aground soon after, she would have sunk. Once on the bottom, a piece of boiler iron was secured over the hole, and stanchioned temporarily, and then secured with tap-bolts,

---

[1] Confederate report.

which enabled her to perform such other service as was required during her continuance on the Southern coast.[1]

The Rear-Admiral thought it desirable to further test the mechanical appliances of the monitors in an attack on McAllister before entering on more important operations, and as well to give the officers and men the advantage of target practice with their new ordnance; he therefore ordered such vessels as were available to a renewed attack.

They were the Passaic, Captain Percival Drayton; the Patapsco, Commander Daniel Ammen; and the Nahant, Commander John Downes, aided by three mortar schooners throwing XIII-inch shells.

Captain Drayton reported that on March 3d the bombardment had been maintained for eight hours by these vessels, the Passaic squarely in front of the fort, upon which seven guns were mounted, protected from an enfilading fire by high traverses. Owing to the slowness of the fire from the monitors, the men in the fort never exposed themselves, usually discharging their pieces while the vessels were loading, or just before the ports came into line. The row of piles and depth of water did not permit a nearer approach to the fort, which was found by spirit-level and necessary elevations to be twelve hundred yards, and seven-second fuzes were found necessary. Two of the guns of the fort were disabled during the engagement; immense craters were dug into the parapet and traverses, but still no injury was done that could not be readily repaired during the night. The three mortar schooners, at a distance of four thousand yards, kept up an ineffective firing during the attack, and until the

---

[1] The officer commanding on this occasion, now Rear-Admiral Worden, regards the destruction of the Nashville, under the attendant difficulties, with more professional pride than the engagement between the Monitor and the Merrimac, which gave him a world-wide reputation.

next morning, the shells generally falling short. The guns on board the Passaic worked satisfactorily, "except that the box round the XV-inch gun, on examination, was found to be almost detached from the side, owing to the breaking of the bolts which secured it to the turret."[1] A close observation showed that a few more rounds would have broken it. The decks of the Passaic were badly injured, being considerably grooved; a mortar-shell filled with sand fell on the deck, and had it not struck over a beam, it would inevitably have gone through. As it was, it completely crushed the planking at the side of the beam, opening quite a hole. The measurement of a fragment of the shell showed it to be but ten inches. The fort directed nearly all its fire at the Passaic. During the action she was struck thirty-four times; nine of the hits were on the side armor; thirteen on the deck, breaking bolts and causing a leak; five on the turret; two on the pilot-house; one on the roof of the turret, and one on the smoke-stack. The indentations were from one-half to two inches; many bolts were broken. Neither of the other ironclads engaged were struck except with Whitworth bolts of small size, and no injury was sustained.

The report of the Passaic does not give the number of shells expended, but the Confederate reports give ninety. Her battery, and that of the Montauk and the Nahant, was a XV-inch and a XI-inch smooth-bore; and of the Patapsco, one XV-inch smooth-bore, and one 150-pounder rifle. Forty-six shells were fired from this rifle, and fourteen shells from the smooth-bore of the vessel last named, the gun machinery working satisfactorily.

---

[1] The XV-inch guns first put on board of the monitors were too short to fairly clear the port; to avoid the counter-blast of powder in the turret, a "box" was fastened with screws to it; a better substitute was found in a cylindrical casting somewhat larger than the bore, which was fastened by bolts around the muzzle of the gun.

On board of the Nahant, the compresser of the XV-inch gun became disarranged at various times, and at the twentieth discharge, the rivets securing the brass guides on the after-part of the carriage gave way, the guides falling down into the turret-chamber, without, however, disabling the gun. A cast-iron "yoke" put in to allow the use of an XI-inch gun temporarily on a carriage made for a XV-inch gun was broken at the thirty-ninth discharge, thus disabling the gun until a new "yoke" could be put in. The foundries were not able to furnish a sufficient number of XV-inch guns when the vessels were completed, hence the temporary use of a smaller calibre, and the fitment of a "yoke" to hold the trunnions of a smaller gun. It should have been made of bronze, cast-iron not having the tenacity to resist the strain brought upon it. The rifle of the Patapsco had, months before, carried away its "yoke" in like manner, and the Ordnance Bureau, being thus informed, had bronze "yokes" sent down, which were substituted, and cured that defect.

After the bombardment the vessels withdrew, as did the mortar schooners and the gunboats Seneca, Wissahickon, and Dawn, that had laid two miles from the fort to signal the effect of the shells.

On the 6th, early in the day, the Passaic, Patapsco, and Nahant left Ossabaw Sound in tow of suitable vessels, and the same evening entered Port Royal Harbor.

The Passaic was at once put under repairs, which were not fully effected until the 28th. She also had a bronze "yoke" put in to avoid a future mishap, such as the Patapsco and Nahant had undergone. The last-named, and indeed all of the monitor class, had bronze "yokes" placed in the carriages upon which the XI-inch guns were mounted. All of them, too, had one-inch plates of iron placed over the magazines, and the vessels that had not powerful centrifugal pumps already were so fitted.

On the 25th the Weehawken, Nahant, Patapsco, and Catskill left Port Royal under tow for North Edisto Inlet—an excellent harbor within twenty miles of Charleston Bar. The repairs and fitments of the Passaic, Montauk, and Keokuk detained them until the 1st of April, when they also proceeded to North Edisto, where they had been preceded by the Nantucket—another monitor which had arrived from the North on the 13th of March. The vessels were amply supplied with ammunition, and were fully prepared, as far as they could be, to make the intended attack on Fort Sumter.

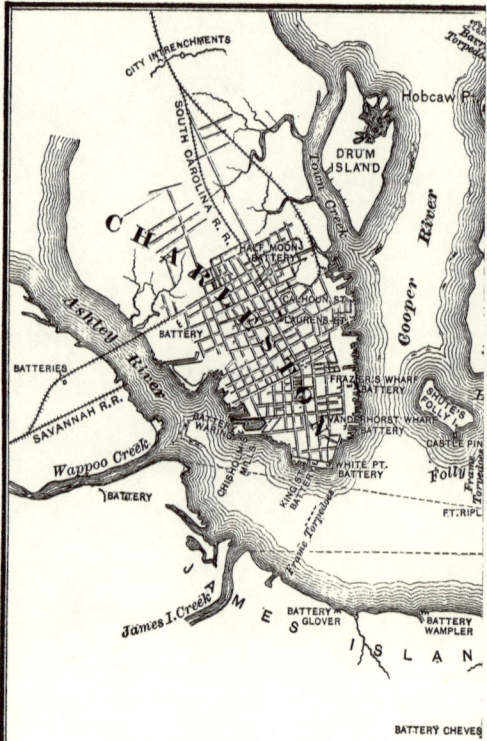

ARMAMENT OF REBEL FORTS.
FEBRUARY 18TH, 1865.

FORTS AND BATTERIES.	DAHLGREN. XI IN.	COLUMBIADS SMOOTH. 8 TO 11 IN.	COLUMBIADS RIFLED. 8 AND 10 IN.	BROOKS. RIFLES. 7, 8, 9, 10 IN.	BLACKELEY'S. RIFLES. 13 IN.	OTHER RIFLES. 5 TO 10 IN.	SMOOTH. 5 TO 10 IN.	10 INCH MORTARS.	FIELD
Sullivan's I.	1	19	2	6		11	19	5	1
Sumter		2		2		1			
James I.		9	3	5		1	2	5	
Mt. Pleasant				2					
Castle Pinckney		3		1					
City Batteries	1	7		3	2				
City Intrenchment									
	2	40	5	19	2	13	21	10	3

GENERAL MAP

OF

CHARLESTON HARBOR,

SOUTH CAROLINA.

Showing Rebel Defences and Obstructions.

—)o(—

Union Batteries.　　*Rebel Batteries.*

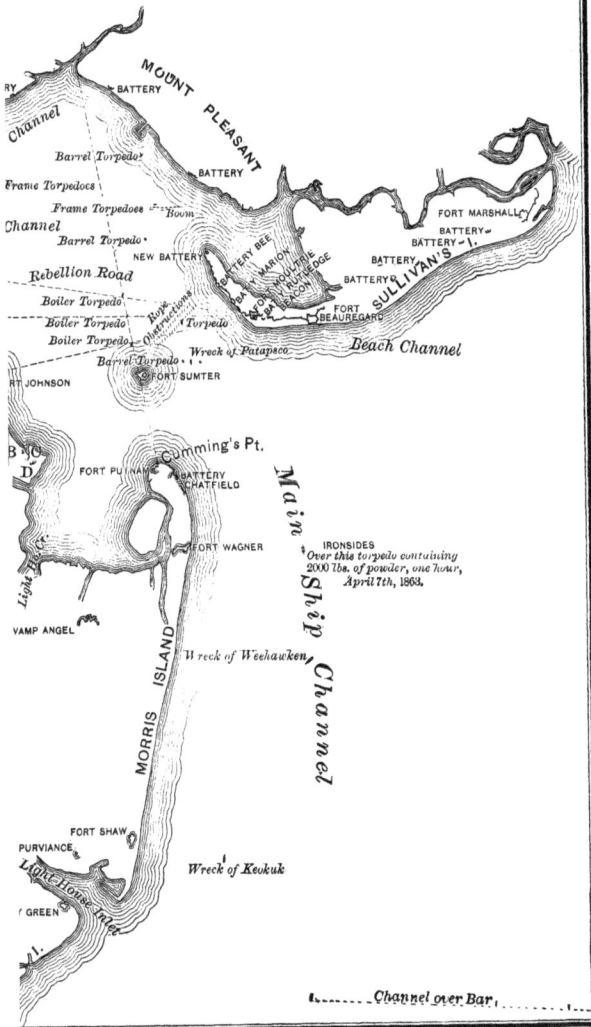

Channel

MOUNT PLEASANT

BATTERY

RY

Barrel Torpedo

BATTERY

Frame Torpedoes

Frame Torpedoes

Boom

Channel

Barrel Torpedo

NEW BATTERY

FORT MARSHALL

BATTERY

BATTERY

Rebellion Road

BATTERY BEE

BATTERY

Fort MARION

SULLIVAN'S

Boiler Torpedo

RUTLEDGE

BEAUCON LODGE

Rope Obstructions

FORT BEAUREGARD

Boiler Torpedo

Torpedo

Boiler Torpedo

Beach Channel

Barrel Torpedo

Wreck of Patapsco

RT JOHNSON

FORT SUMTER

B C

D

Cumming's Pt.

FORT PUTNAM

BATTERY CHATFIELD

Main Ship Channel

FORT WAGNER

IRONSIDES

Over this torpedo containing
2000 lbs. of powder, one hour,
April 7th, 1863.

Light

VAMP ANGEL

Wreck of Weehawken

MORRIS ISLAND

FORT SHAW

PURVIANCE

Light-House Inlet

GREEN

Wreck of Keokuk

Channel over Bar

CHAPTER V.

On April 2, 1863, the Rear-Admiral left Port Royal to join the "ironclads," as the monitors were styled, at North Edisto, and on the morning of the 5th left for Charleston Bar with all of them in tow of suitable vessels. As previously arranged, on arrival, the Keokuk, aided by Captain Boutelle and Master Platt of the Coast Survey, sounded and buoyed the bar of the main ship channel, supported by the monitors Patapsco and Catskill. This was soon accomplished, and before dark these two monitors anchored within. At high tide on the following morning, the Admiral came in on board of the New Ironsides, Commodore Thomas Turner, and was followed by the five monitors yet outside, and by the Keokuk. He intended to proceed the same day to the attack of Fort Sumter, and thence to the city of Charleston, but the weather became so hazy that the ranges could not be seen and the pilots refused to go farther. The state of the atmosphere prevented a satisfactory examination of an earthwork, known afterward as Fort Wagner, on Morris Island, distant about two thousand five hundred yards from Sumter, of the batteries on Cumming's Point, and of the heavy earthworks flanking Moultrie.

The order of battle was "line ahead" as follows: The Weehawken, Captain John Rodgers, with a raft on the bows

to explode torpedoes,[1] led the line; the Passaic, Captain
Percival Drayton; the Montauk, Captain John L. Worden;
the Patapsco, Commander Daniel Ammen; the New Ironsides, Commodore Thomas Turner (as flag-ship), followed
by the Catskill, Commander George W. Rodgers; the Nantucket, Commander D. M. Fairfax; the Nahant, Commander
John Downes, and the Keokuk, Commander A. C. Rhind.

The vessels were ordered to pass without returning the
fire from batteries on Morris Island; when within easy
range of Fort Sumter they were to open upon it, and take
position to the north and west, at a distance of eight hundred yards, firing low, and at the centre embrasure. The
necessity for precision of fire was enjoined. Vessels were to
be prepared to render assistance to each other as far as possible, and a special code of signals was arranged, that could
be operated on board of the ironclads.

Noon on the following day (7th) was the earliest hour that
the pilots were willing to move. Signal was made, and the
vessels got under way. The Weehawken in weighing anchor
fouled the torpedo grapnels attached to the raft before mentioned, on her bows; this delayed movement until 1.15.
The vessels then proceeded up in line ahead at distances
varying a good deal, but intended to be one hundred yards
apart; they steered very badly if obliged to stop the engines,
sheering every way, and the raft on the bow of the Weehawken delayed her, and caused wild steering along the whole
line, so it was about 2.50 P.M. when she was opened on by
Moultrie, followed at once by Sumter, and all of the bat-

---

[1] It was formed of very heavy timbers crossing at right angles, bolted together,
about fifty feet in length, shaped not unlike a boot-jack, the bows of the vessel
propelling within the notch. The after-ends or jaws of the raft were secured by
chains to the bow of the vessel. The wave-motion acting on this cumbrous mass
was quite different from that of the monitor. It proved to be a battering ram,
and loosened the armor plating on the bows of the Weehawken.

teries within effective range. The Weehawken was then somewhat above Fort Wagner. At about 3.05 she opened fire on Fort Sumter, followed by the other monitors, at or before they arrived at the same point, the Patapsco at that time employing a 150-pounder rifle, at the angle of Sumter that was in face. From Wagner up, several buoys of different colors were seen; the vessels passed between them and Morris Island, but nor far from them, perhaps within one hundred and fifty yards. It was observed that the different vessels, in bringing the buoys in range with Moultrie or batteries on that shore, received in turn a heavy fire, and it was supposed probable that they marked torpedoes; they certainly served to indicate distance, and the ranges of the guns had been practically established on them, which greatly increased the accuracy of fire from the forts as the vessels passed. As the narrow part of the channel was approached, the flood tide became strong, setting the vessels in, and made them additionally unmanageable.

Soon after getting within the heavy fire of the batteries, the Weehawken signalled obstructions in her vicinity, and previous to that a torpedo had exploded close to her. Captain Rodgers' report states: "We approached very close to the obstructions extending from Fort Sumter to Fort Moultrie—as near, indeed, as I could get without running upon them. They were marked by rows of casks very near together. To the eye they appeared almost to touch one another, and there was more than one line of them."

"The appearance was so formidable that, upon deliberate judgment, I thought it right not to entangle the vessel in obstructions which I did not think we could have passed through, and in which we should have been caught. Beyond these, piles were seen between Castle Pinckney and the middle ground."

" A torpedo exploded under us or very near to us ; it lifted
the vessel a little, but I am unable to perceive that it has
done us any damage. I have no accident to report."

After approaching the obstructions as above described, the
Weehawken's bow was turned to seaward, in order to prevent
being swept upon the obstructions by a strong flood tide then
running, and steaming a few hundred feet to the southward
enabled the Passaic to turn in her wake, the Montauk following her.

The working of the guns of the Weehawken was entirely
satisfactory. Eleven XV-inch, and fifteen XI-inch shells were
fired ; she was struck fifty-three times in forty minutes ; the
missiles were formidable ; two or three of them struck the
side armor near the same place and so broke the plates that
they remained only in fragments, the wood backing being exposed. The deck was pierced so as to make a hole through
which water ran into the vessel. Thirty-six bolts were broken
in the turret and many in the pilot-house, the number not
ascertained, as they were concealed by an iron lining. At
one time the turret revolved with difficulty, having been
wedged by a fragment of a shell between its top and the
pilot-house.

From the Passaic, next in line, buoys of various descrip-
tions were observed and also the torpedo that burst near the
bow of the Weehawken. When opposite the centre of the
northeast face of Sumter, the vessel was near some obstructions that seemed to extend from Sumter to Moultrie. At the
moment of the fourth discharge from the XI-inch gun the
Passaic was struck by two heavy shot in the lower part of
the turret, which bulged in the plates and beams, and forced
the rails together upon which the gun was worked, disabling it for several hours. Soon after, a portion of the brass
ring surrounding the turret was broken, and temporarily

impeded revolving the turret. A very heavy rifle-shot struck the upper edge of the turret, broke all of the plates forming it, then glancing, struck the pilot-house above, indenting it two and a half inches nearly the whole length of the shot. It disarranged the top of the pilot-house and lifted one side of it three inches. The vessel was struck thirty-five times; several bolt-heads were knocked off and thrown into the pilot-house and turret. The vessel fired four XI-inch and nine XV-inch shells. There was great difficulty in managing the vessel and keeping clear of her consorts, owing to the limited range of vision from the holes in the pilot-house and to the dense smoke.

The Montauk experienced difficulty in maneuvering in the narrow and uncertain channel, with the limited means of vision, under the rapid and concentrated fire of the enemy. The vessel was struck fourteen times without receiving material injury. She fired ten XV-inch cored shot, sixteen solid XI-inch shot, and one shell.

The Patapsco opened fire with 150-pounder rifle when within thirteen hundred yards of Sumter, and when within eleven hundred yards with the XV-inch gun. On the fifth discharge the cap-square bolts of the rifle gave way, disabling that gun for two hours.

The Montauk, next ahead, following the head of the line, turned seaward. At that time several rows of buoys were observed above and near, and further within the harbor, a row of piles. Endeavoring to turn a step's length short of the Montauk's wake, the headway of the Patapsco ceased, and the vessel no longer obeyed the helm. She was backed, and got off, having been stationary long enough to afford the enemy an excellent opportunity, which was availed of, for delivering a heavy concentrated fire. At this time she was supposed to be six hundred yards from Sumter and double that distance from Moultrie. A XV-inch shell fired at Sumter was watched until it struck on the northeast face; the fort was covered with a mass of dust from the bursting shell, and the effect upon the masonry was plainly visible.

The opinion was expressed by her commander that a want of vision from the pilot-house was one of the most serious defects of that class of vessel, making it impossible to fight them advantageously, to avoid dangers, or to make a satisfactory reconnoissance. Owing to the breaking of the cap-square bolts of the rifle, that gun delivered only five shells; the XV-inch fired the same number. The vessel was struck forty-seven times. Forty bolts of the smoke-stack were broken and a chain afterward put around it for security. The vessel was not disabled, but injuries were received which, if multiplied, would have disabled her.

The Catskill reports that at 2.50 the forts and batteries opened on the head of the line. The flag-ship (New Ironsides) becoming unmanageable from shoal water and strong tide, the Catskill passed her, and at 3.35 the first shot struck her. She approached within six hundred yards of Sumter, and one of her XV-inch shells apparently dismounted a barbette gun. The cross fire to which she was subjected was most severe. The same obstructions reported by the four preceding vessels were observed. Surprise was expressed that the vessel suffered so much injury in so short a time. She was struck twenty times; one shot forward broke the deck-plates and deck-planking, and drove down the stanchion sustaining the beam, causing the deck to leak. She fired fifteen XI-inch and eleven XV-inch shells. No complaint as to the working of the turret or the battery.

The commander of the Nantucket, next in line, made the same general observations. The New Ironsides having signalled to "disregard motions of flag ship," he followed the Catskill. When within seven hundred and fifty yards of Sumter he opened fire on it, and for forty-five or fifty minutes was under the fire of three forts, which he describes as "terrific." The effect of the fire of the vessel on the fort was not so observable as that of the enemy on the vessel. After the third discharge the port stopper of the XV-inch gun was jammed, several heavy shot having driven in the plating. The XI-inch gun was fired twelve times. The vessel was struck fifty-one times. During the action the turret was jammed; six or seven nut-heads driven off had fallen inside and rendered it necessary to key up the turret to enable it to revolve.

A number of side-plates were started, so that another shot would probably have broken them off. One rifle-shot was driven through the armor into the wood, and one deck-plate was started from a blow on the side armor. Other serious injuries were named.

The Nahant reports that, following in line of battle, the vessel became hotly engaged. She soon began to suffer from the terrible fire to which she was subjected. At 4.30 the turret, having become jammed from the effects of three shots, refused to turn. One of these shot broke off a piece of iron in the interior weighing seventy-eight pounds, and throwing it violently across the house bent and disarranged the steering gear. Bolt-heads (nuts from the bolts) flying from the inside of the pilot-house struck down the pilot, and fatally injured the helmsman. The commanding officer was the only person in the pilot-house not senseless from injuries. The preventer steering gear was got in working order, and after repeated futile efforts to train the guns on Sumter, the vessel was headed out, the other vessels withdrawing under signal at the same time.

II.—5

The vessel was struck thirty-six times, one man was fatally injured, two others severely, and four others slightly, all by flying bolts or other fragments inside the pilot-house and turret. Several of the plates on the side armor were badly broken, and at one place, where two shots had struck near each other, the plating was partly stripped from the wood, the backing broken in, and the edging of deck-plates started up and rolled back in places. On the port quarter and side the plating was deeply indented and started from the side to the stern. The deck had two very damaging shots, one near the propeller well, quite shattering the plate and starting twenty-five bolts; another starting the plate and twenty bolts. The smoke-stack received three shots; one pierced the armor, making a hole fifteen inches long and nine broad, displacing the grating inside, and breaking seven bolts. The turret received nine shots; fifty-six bolts were perceptibly broken, the nuts stripped from the inside, and the bolts themselves protruded almost their length; some of them, in fact, having actually been forced out, were found lying on the deck; doubtless many others were broken that had not then been detected, as some bolts seemingly sound were afterward found loosened. One shot struck the upper part of the turret, breaking through every plate, parting some of them in two, three, and four places. The pilot-house bore marks of six shots, three of XI-inch diameter, twenty-one bolts were broken and others started, and the plates were much started; in the opinion of the commanding officer, a few more such shot would have demolished it. One of the missiles at the base broke through every plate, and evidently nearly penetrated.

During the action the Nahant fired seven XV-inch and eight XI-inch projectiles. It was not until 5 P.M. of the next day that the turret was sufficiently cleared to be turned, although a corps of skilful workmen under able supervision were engaged at it.

The commanding officer of the Keokuk states that at 3.20, the flag-ship having made signal to disregard her motions, he found it necessary to run ahead of the Nahant to avoid getting foul of her in a narrow channel and strong tide. In consequence, he was forced to take a position slightly in advance of the leading vessel of the line, which brought the Keokuk under a concentrated fire between Sumter and Moultrie, about five hundred and fifty yards from the latter. This position was maintained about thirty minutes, during which time the vessel was struck ninety times. Nineteen shots pierced her at and just below the water-line. The turrets (casemates) were pierced in many places and one of the forward shutters shot away; in short, the vessel was completely riddled.

Finding it impossible to keep her afloat many minutes more under such an extraordinary fire, at 4.40 she was reluctantly withdrawn from action. The gun-carriage of the forward turret was disabled, and so many of the crew of the after gun wounded as to disable that gun. She was anchored out of range of the fire of the enemy and kept afloat during the night, as the water was smooth. At daylight the breeze sprung up, the leakage increased, and it was apparent the vessel must soon go down. Signal was made, assistance arrived, and an endeavor to get the head of the vessel around to tow her into shoaler water, but in that effort she filled rapidly and at 7.20 a.m. of the 8th sunk, her smoke-stack alone remaining partly above water. The wounded had been put on board of a tug a few minutes before the vessel sunk. The casualties were 16 seriously, and as many more slightly wounded.

Commodore Turner, commanding the flag-ship, states that

the pilot-house being insufficient to hold more persons than were required by the Admiral, he had taken personal charge of the battery of the Ironsides. By sounding it was found that the vessel at times was only one foot clear of the bottom. A shot striking the forward facing of a port shutter knocked it off. The damage done to the ship from the fire of the enemy was not material, and the opinion was expressed that at the distance of 1,000 yards the armor plating would prove invulnerable to such shot as were fired at the vessel. He expressed great admiration of the conduct of officers and men, and would fall short of his duty if he omitted to present to especial notice Lieutenant-Commander George E. Belknap, the executive officer. It is proper to note the fact that without exception the commanding officers of all of the vessels engaged spoke in the highest terms of those under their command. The names, which may be seen in the official reports, are omitted for lack of space and fear of taxing the patience of the reader.

Rear-Admiral Dupont, in his several reports to the Department, states that he moved in line of battle as before given, in the New Ironsides, with seven ironclad monitors and the iron-plated vessel Keokuk, and attacked Fort Sumter, intending to pass it and commence action on the northwest face, in accordance with his order of battle. The heavy fire received from Sumter and Moultrie and the nature of the obstructions compelled the attack from outside, which was fierce and obstinate, and the gallantry of the officers and men was conspicuous.

The endeavors of the Admiral in the pilot-house of the New Ironsides to bring the vessel into such close action as he desired were not successful; in a rapid current and narrow channel the vessel became partly unmanageable, and was twice anchored to prevent grounding, and once on account of a collision with two of the monitors. She did not get nearer to Fort Sumter than 1,000 yards.[1]

Owing to the condition of the tide and unavoidable accidents, the vessels were not engaged until late in the day, and toward evening, finding no impression made upon the fort, signal was given for the vessels to withdraw, with the intention of renewing the attack the following morning. The commanders of the monitors came on board during the evening, and stated verbally the injuries the vessels had received, when without hesitation the Admiral determined not to renew the attack, as in his judgment it would have converted a failure into a disaster. He stated that in his opinion Charleston could not be taken by a purely naval attack, and the army could not give co-operation. Had he succeeded in entering the harbor, he would have had 1,200 men, with 32 guns; but five of the seven ironclads were wholly or partially disabled after a brief engagement. He had alluded above only to Forts Sumter and Moultrie, but the vessels were also exposed to the fire of the batteries on Cummings Point, Mount Pleasant, the Redan, and Fort Beauregard.

In a more detailed report to the Department, dated April 15th, Admiral Dupont gives with particularity the fire delivered by the vessels engaged and the injuries sustained by them, and adds, that in his belief any attempt to pass through the obstructions referred to would have entangled the vessels and held them under the most severe fire of heavy ordnance that had ever been delivered, and while it was barely possible that some vessels might have forced their way through, it would only have been to be again impeded

---

[1] Confederate accounts state that no monitor approached nearer than 600 yards to the rope obstructions, which is probably an error, as they turned in line, and at such distance as in a strong tide seemed necessary to clear them. They estimated the nearest approach of the Ironsides at 1,800 yards.

by other and more formidable obstructions and to encounter other powerful batteries with which the whole harbor of Charleston had been lined. He says that the slowness of our fire and our inability to occupy any batteries we might silence are disadvantages of the gravest character, and until the outer forts shall have been taken, the army cannot enter the harbor or afford assistance. A want of success, however, will not prevent him from bringing to the notice of the Department the gallant officers and men who took part in this desperate conflict.

After naming the officers and the vessels they commanded, he says: "They did everything that the utmost gallantry and skill could accomplish in the management of their untried vessels." These commanding officers had long been known to him ; many of them had served in the squadron before, and were present at the capture of the Port Royal forts ; they were men of the highest professional capacity and courage, and fully sustained their reputations, coming up to his requirements. He commended them and their reports, which speak of those under them, to the consideration of the Department.

He then names in the highest terms Commander C. R. P. Rodgers, Lieutenant S. W. Preston, Lieutenant A. S. Mackenzie, and Ensign M. L. Johnson, who were on his staff or serving immediately under his personal observation.

The result of the attack was mortifying to all of the officers and men engaged in it. Had any loss of life been regarded as likely to render another attempt successful, there would have been few indeed who would not have desired it. The opinion before the attack was general, and was fully shared in by the writer, that whatever might be the loss in men and vessels, blown up by torpedoes or otherwise destroyed (and such losses were supposed probable), at all events Fort Sumter would be reduced to a pile of ruins before the sun went down. The damage done to the forts by the very small number of projectiles fired by the vessels, although not known at the time to the assailants, was so considerable as to cause the enemy to fill nearly all of the casemates with sand, and this work was begun and carried on vigorously the very night after the bombardment. (See Appendix A for effect of shells, as given in Confederate records.)

The damage inflicted on the vessels shows that they were incapable of enduring heavy blows sufficiently long to effect the destruction of Sumter, as they were situated, or as it was supposed possible to place them. There was considerable swell even between the forts at the time of the attack, and the flood tide ran strong and irregularly, which added to the embarrassment. Afloat as elsewhere leeks have to be eaten sometimes, whether liked or not, as an old proverb has it.

An examination of the chart of Charleston Harbor, with its batteries and obstructions of various kinds, as shown in 1865, and the experience gained subsequent to the attack (bearing in mind, too, the condition of the batteries of the vessels on the 7th of April), would point rather to the probability of disaster than to success, had an attempt been made to enter.

The reader has been informed of the strength of the attacking force in guns and in material resistance, and the failure of many of the guns to operate when they were most needed. A part of the defences at that time consisted of seventy-six guns of large calibre, which bore over the area occupied for a time by the vessels attacking.

H. R. Ex. Doc. No. 69, Thirty-eighth Congress, First Session, page 85 (Report on Armored Vessels), states : "There was a cylinder torpedo off Fort Wagner under charge of Mr.

Langdon Cheves, who endeavored to explode it for ten minutes. He could not have placed the Ironsides more directly over the torpedo, but the confounded thing, as is usual with them, would not go off when it was wanted." The character of the defences of Charleston and the ability of the attacking force will appear more fully in the closing pages relating to operations on that coast.

The considerations that were operative in the mind of the flag-officer are given in his report of April 15th. He says: "I had hoped that the endurance of the ironclads would have enabled them to have borne any weight of fire to which they might have been exposed ; but when I found that so large a portion of them were wholly or one-half disabled by less than an hour's engagement, before attempting to remove [overcome] the obstructions, or testing the power of the torpedoes, I was convinced that persistence in the attack would result in the loss of the greater portion of the ironclad fleet, and in leaving many of them inside the harbor, to fall into the hands of the enemy."

On the withdrawal of the ironclads at 5 P.M., April 7th, the flag-officer had not even a suspicion that he would not resume operations the following morning. The grave injuries sustained by the vessels in aggressive power restrained him, such as no loss of life, had it occurred, would have done.

On the evening of the attack the flag-officer received a letter, as follows :

CONFIDENTIAL.

NAVY DEPARTMENT, April 2, 1863.

SIR—The exigencies of the public service are so pressing in the Gulf that the Department directs you to send all the ironclads that are in a fit condition to move, after your present attack upon Charleston, directly to New Orleans, reserving to yourself only two.

Very respectfully,

GIDEON WELLES.

Of the same date is the following unofficial letter from the Assistant Secretary of the Navy : " Matters are at a standstill on the Mississippi River, and the President was with difficulty restrained from sending off Hunter and all the ironclads directly to New Orleans, the opening of the Mississippi being the principal object to be obtained. It is, however, arranged, as you will see by to-day's order, that you are to send all the ironclads that survive the attack upon Charleston immediately to New Orleans, reserving for your squadron only two. We must abandon all other operations on the coast where ironclads are necessary to a future time. We cannot clear the Mississippi River without ironclads, and as all the supplies come down the Red River, that stretch of the river must be in our possession. This plan has been agreed upon after mature consideration, and seems to be imperative."

On the night after the attack officers on General Hunter's staff were on board of the Ironsides with the proposition for the flag-officer to co-operate with General Hunter in the reduction of Morris Island, which, for reasons quite obvious, could not then be entertained.

In a reply to a very complimentary letter received from General Hunter at this time, the Admiral says : " I feel very comfortable, General, for the reason that a merciful Providence permitted me to have a *failure* instead of a *disaster*, and if I had ever entertained for a moment any misgiving as to my course, the despatches just handed me would remove it."

The following day, in a note to General Hunter, he says : " I find the ships so much damaged during this short engagement as to force me to the conviction that they could not endure the fire to which they would be exposed long enough to destroy Sumter or reach Charleston. I am now satisfied that

5*

the place cannot be taken by a purely naval attack, and am
admonished by the condition of the ironclads that a persistence in our efforts would end in disaster, and might cause
us to leave some of our ironclads in the hands of the enemy,
which would render it difficult to hold those parts of the
coast that are yet in our possession. I have therefore determined to withdraw my vessels."

The Department and the people of the North counted con-
fidently on the fall of Charleston through the monitors, as
is shown by the orders of April 2d, followed before the receipt of the news of the repulse on April 7th by a letter to
the Admiral from the Secretary of the Navy, dated April 11th,
as follows : "It has been suggested to the Department by
the President, in view of operations elsewhere, and especially
by the Army of the Potomac, that you should retain a strong
force off Charleston, even should you find it impossible to
carry the place. You will continue to menace the rebels,
keeping them in apprehension of a renewed attack, in order
that they may be occupied, and not come North or go West
to the aid of the rebels with whom our forces will soon be
in conflict. Should you be successful, as we trust and believe you will be, it is expected that General Hunter will
continue to keep the rebels employed and in constant apprehension, so that they shall not leave the vicinity of Charleston. *This detention of ironclads, should it be necessary in
consequence of a repulse, can be but for a few days.* I trust
your success will be such that the ironclads can be or will
have been despatched to the Gulf when this reaches you.
There is intense interest in regard to your operations."

The writer has italicised the sentence above, as it would
exert a controlling influence on Admiral Dupont in fitting
for effective service all of the ironclads under him with the
least possible delay.

Immediately following is a despatch from the President :

EXECUTIVE MANSION, April 13, 1863.

Hold your position inside the bar near Charleston ; or, if you have left it, return to it, and hold it until further orders.   Do not allow the enemy to erect new batteries or defences on Morris Island.   If he has begun it, drive him out.   I do not herein order you to renew the general attack.   That is to depend on your discretion or a further order.

A. LINCOLN.

To Admiral DUPONT.

The following day the President issued further instructions :

EXECUTIVE MANSION, April 14, 1863.

This is intended to clear up an apparent inconsistency between the recent order to continue operations before Charleston, and the former one to remove to another point in a certain contingency.   No censure upon you, or either of you, is intended ; we still hope by cordial and judicious co-operation you can take the batteries on Morris Island and Sullivan's Island and Fort Sumter.   But whether you can or not, we wish the demonstration kept up for a time, for a collateral and very important object ; we wish the attempt to be a real one (though not a desperate one) if it affords any considerable chance of success.   But if prosecuted for a *demonstration* only, this must not be made public, or the whole effect will be lost.   Once again before Charleston, do not leave till further orders from here.   Of course this is not intended to force you to leave unduly exposed Hilton Head or other near points in your charge.   Yours truly,

A. LINCOLN.

General HUNTER and Admiral DUPONT.

P.S.—Whoever receives this first, please send a copy to the other immediately.

On April 16th, Rear-Admiral Dupont wrote to the Secretary of the Navy as follows :

I have the honor to acknowledge the receipt this morning, by the Freeborn, of your communication of the 11th inst., directing the maintaining of a large force off Charleston, to menace the rebels and keep them in apprehension of a renewed attack in the event of our repulse.

The Department will probably have known, on the 12th instant, the result of the attack. In my despatch of the 11th instant, dated off Charleston, the Department was made aware of my withdrawal with the ironclads, from the very insecure anchorage inside the bar, and just in time to save the monitors from an easterly gale, in which, in my opinion and that of their commanders, they would have been in great peril of being lost on Morris Island beach. Their ground-tackling has been found to be insufficient, and from time to time they have dragged even in close harbors.

I have since been doing all in my power to push forward their repairs in order to send them to the Gulf, as directed, but I presume that your despatch of the 11th instant, and the telegraphic message from the President, revoke your previous order.

I shall spare no exertions in repairing, as soon as possible, the serious injuries sustained by the monitors in the late attack, and shall get them inside Charleston bar with all despatch in accordance with the order of the President. I think it my duty, however, to state to the Department that this will be attended with great risk to these vessels from the gales which prevail at this season, and from the continuous fire of the enemy's batteries, which they can neither silence, nor prevent the erection of new ones.

.   .   .   .

I have deemed it proper and due to myself to make these statements, but I trust I need not add that I will obey all orders with the utmost fidelity, even when my judgment is entirely at variance with them, such as the order to re-occupy the unsafe anchorage for the ironclads off Morris Island, and an intimation that a renewal of the attack on Charleston may be ordered, which, in my judgment, would be attended with disastrous results, involving the loss of this coast.

.   .   .   .   .   .

I am, however, painfully struck by the tenor and tone of the President's order, which seems to imply a censure, and I have to request that the Department will not hesitate to relieve me by an officer who, in its opinion, is more able to execute that service in which I have had the misfortune to fail—the capture of Charleston. No consideration for an individual officer, whatever his loyalty and length of service, should weigh an instant if the cause of his country can be advanced by his removal.

Chief-Engineer Alban C. Stimers was sent by the Department to look after and correct any deficiencies in the monitors which might be developed in service, and for this purpose
he had under his control a number of skilled workers in iron.
He was either the designer of the raft before described, secured to the bow of the Weehawken, or was closely connected with its construction.   He witnessed the attack of the
7th of April from beyond the bar, and had recommended
the employment of two rafts that he had brought down, one
of which was attached to the bow of the Weehawken.   Each
raft was designed to carry on its forward end a submerged
torpedo to destroy by explosion any obstruction met with ;
the torpedo Captain Rodgers declined to carry, *as he feared
blowing up some of the other monitors against which he might
run by accident.*   Stimers, however, states that his explanation as to the safety of the vessels carrying the torpedo
was not satisfactory, and for that reason they had rejected
" this powerful weapon, for which we have every reason to
suppose the enemy was entirely unprepared, in an attack
which could have few hopes of success without it."

He was agreeably disappointed the following morning,
upon his inspection of the monitors, to find " that there were
no clear passages through the decks, and no penetrations
through the sides of the vessels or the pilot-houses."   He
then institutes a comparison between the vulnerability, as he
supposes, of the plates of 4½ inches in thickness of the New
Ironsides and the five 1-inch plates applied to the sides of
the monitors.   He says : " To the casual observer, therefore,
the solid plates will have the appearance of having withstood the bombardment better than the laminated, but the
unprejudiced engineer will perceive the latter disposition of
the metal is much the more effective in attaining the desired
end."   The falsity of this presented observation of the effect

of shot on laminated plates as compared with their effect on
a solid plate of equal thickness has been established uni-
formly, by very many target experiments, and afterward by
the Ironsides herself.

In his report to the Department he adds : " In consideration of the vast importance to our country that the strong-
hold of rebellion should be reduced, I take the liberty to
express to the Department my firm opinion that the obstructions can be readily passed with the means already provided,
and our entire fleet of ironclads pass up successfully to the
wharves of Charleston, and that the monitor vessels still retain sufficient enduring powers to enable them to pass all the
forts and batteries which may be reasonably expected."

The official history of Chief-Engineer Stimers in relation
to monitors closes as follows : " Chief-Engineer Stimers is
responsible for the detailed drawings of the [21] light-
draught monitors, and for the calculations as to their displacement. It was expected that they would not draw over
six and one-half feet of water, and be out of water amidships
about fifteen inches. The contracts were made generally
in the spring of 1863, and the vessels were to be furnished
in the fall of that year. . . . The Chimo, at Boston, was
the first one finished. She was under the entire direction
of Chief-Engineer Stimers. Instead of being fifteen inches
out of water she was only three inches on an average,
showing a miscalculation of one foot. The Department immediately removed Mr. Stimers from the position of general
superintendent, and placed the question of what should
be done to remedy the difficulties occasioned by his error in the hands of Rear-Admiral Gregory, Chief-Engineer
Wood, and Captain Ericsson " (letter of Assistant Secretary of the Navy, December 15, 1864, to Joint Committee on
the Conduct of the War, vol. 3, 1865).

CHAPTER VI.

THE MONITOR CLASS OF VESSELS.

THE reader is probably already informed that the raising of the hull of the old frigate Merrimac, at Norfolk, and placing an iron casemate upon it, created a very general alarm among the people of the North, and brought into prominence the grave question as to how that vessel could be successfully met or destroyed. The destruction of the sailing vessels Congress and Cumberland intensified the alarm, and at the same time afforded painful instances of the impotency of sailing frigates, armed with small smooth-bore guns, when an adversary plated with iron, though improvised and imperfectly constructed, so readily effected their destruction.

A vessel designed by Captain John Ericsson, named the Monitor, was built in great haste for the purpose of meeting the Merrimac. Her construction gave rise to that of a class known as "monitors," seven of which were sent to Port Royal, as soon as they could be built and equipped, for the purpose of operating against Charleston. At the time they were supposed to be if not invulnerable under the fire of the guns then in use in the forts defending Charleston, at least less liable to destruction. In relation to the effective working of their batteries no doubt existed, or was expressed by any one.

As these vessels have had their day and will pass out of the knowledge of the reader in coming years, it seems worth while to give a particular description of them.

Afloat, in appearance they were not inaptly likened to a cheese-box on a plank. The hull itself, even if freed from the overhang, could not as a model have any pretension to speed. The dimensions of the Passaic, the first vessel built of the improved class, were as follows : Apparent length of vessel, 200 feet ; beam, 45 feet. This was sustained by an iron hull with nearly a flat floor, 16 feet shorter at the bow, and 25 feet shorter at the stern than the deck measurement, and on a cross section at the turret, 37 feet 8 inches wide. The usual draught was something over 11 feet, and displacement 844 tons. The thickness of the mass of wood firmly bolted together that surrounded the hull proper was 5 feet and was plated externally with five 1-inch iron plates.

The turret had a thickness of eleven 1-inch plates, with a height of 9 feet, and an interior diameter of 20 feet. It was designed to revolve at will by suitable machinery ; had iron beams on top to support a light iron cover, and was surmounted by a small cylindrical tower (pilot-house) composed of eight 1-inch plates, some 7 feet in height and 8 feet in diameter. Within this pilot-house was the wheel, and in battle, the commanding officer, the pilot, and the helmsman. It was capped by a circular plate of iron 1½ inch thick. Small circular holes were originally cut through for vision, and afterward, as a necessity, they were chiselled out to give an angle to the view. The plates of the turret and of the pilot-house were held together by numerous bolts, with the heads on the outside and a nut within. The blow of a very heavy projectile would make the nuts fly with great force within the turret, and the rebound of the plates would then at times withdraw the bolts entirely, but more frequently they would stand out like the "quills upon the fretful porcupine."

The hatchway over the windlass-room, another forward of

the turret, and a third over the engine-room, were covered
with iron plates and calked on going to sea, and on going
into action were put on, leaving no egress from below except
through the turret. For ventilation, six holes of 8 inches
diameter were cut through the deck forward and four aft,
and ventilating pipes 4 feet high were fitted with gaskets
to keep out the water; beneath were bull's-eyes that could
be screwed up below to exclude the water when the pipes
were taken off.

Forward of the hull proper, in the "overhang," was what
was known as the "anchor-well," a cylinder into which a
four-armed anchor could be hove up by means of a windlass
in a small apartment called the "windlass-room" in the
bow, the chain passing in through a hawsehole less than
two feet above the ordinary water level. The anchor-well
had a removable ·plate over it, as also had what was known
as a "propeller-well," some fifteen feet from the stern. The
turret was nearly, if not quite, on the centre of the vessel,
and the smoke-stack, made of eight 1-inch plates to a height
of 6 feet above the deck, and then of the usual height with
the ordinary thickness of iron, was 12 feet farther aft. The
deck itself was of heavy wood and covered with two ½-inch
plates of iron. When ready for sea and properly trimmed,
the bow would usually be 2½ feet, and the stern a foot
less above the water level. With a perfectly clean bottom,
a speed somewhat in excess of seven knots was attainable. Lying in the warm salt water of Southern ports soon
caused the bottom to foul in the most extraordinary manner, and reduced the attainable speed to less than four
knots.

The armament intended was two XV-inch guns, but owing
to inability to obtain them in time, one of that calibre was
given and one XI-inch gun, fitted with a "yoke," as before

described. Instead of this gun the Patapsco and Lehigh had 150-pounder Parrott rifles.

It is apparent to the reader that it would require only a foot or so of water in the hold to sink this vessel, and this danger was augmented by the insufficient water-way, which was the trough within the keel, having a chord of 16 inches, and a depth of 3¾ inches, in the form of a lunette. When the vessel was nearly on an even keel this was a very insufficient conduit from the fore body of the vessel to the powerful centrifugal pumps placed in the after body, as we shall presently see in the sinking of the Weehawken.

In a heavy sea the monitors were surprisingly easy in their movements. This was obtained at the cost of great strain on the fastenings of the "overhang." When the engines were stopped the vessel, quite unlike ordinary ones, would sheer one way or the other, and no amount of watching could prevent this. As we have already seen, the gun machinery had not that reliability that it was supposed to possess. When under a fair steam-pressure they steered very well.

In May, 1863, in answer to the requirement of the Navy Department, all of the officers commanding monitors near Charleston (five in number) submitted their opinion in relation to the qualities of that class, which the Department did not think worth while to give to the public in its "Report on Armored Vessels," 1864, made under a Congressional resolution. It might be supposed that this letter had been inadvertently passed over, had it not been that on page 603 Captain Ericsson comments upon one of its paragraphs. Captains Drayton and Worden subsequently saw the letter, and concurred in its contents. It has never been published, and for lack of space is not now given. The closing paragraphs are as follows : " In relation to the qualities of the vessels, we would remark that they have been exaggerated into vessels capable of keeping the seas and making long voyages alone. Some of us have been in heavy gales in them, and, indeed, from the amount of water in them, have had grave apprehensions of their loss. . . .

"Possessing the advantage of a secure harbor and choosing their time of exit, these vessels can, in our opinion, greatly harass a blockading force, making it necessary for wooden vessels to withdraw to such distances from the entrance of the harbors, especially after night, as would make the blockade very ineffective against the entrance of steamers.

"The average time required to load, point, and fire the XV-inch gun does not vary much from seven minutes. It must be remembered that this controls the fire of the lighter piece, or if that be fired oftener, it retards further the slow firing of the heavier gun. We regard a small calibre with a larger proportional charge of powder as desirable, at least when used against brick or stone."

It is necessary to add that the opinion was expressed by the same officers that the monitors could not ride securely to their anchors within the bar off Charleston. This grew out of the fact that several of the vessels had dragged in very moderate weather and not strong tides within Edisto inlet. This opinion, however, was found erroneous; the force of a heavy sea was expended in a great measure on the bar, and the monitors continued within it off Charleston for some twenty months. Heavy moorings, with buoys attached, were put down for them, which ensured their safety so far as dragging was concerned.

Another fitment, however, was necessary to enable monitors to be habitable in that locality. This was the placement of high coamings around the hatchways, so as to allow the battle-plates to be left off, except when going into action, or when a heavy gale set in from seaward. Without this arrangement it would have been absolutely impossible to exist on board of them, as the water was usually swashing over the decks. Admiral Dahlgren did not exaggerate when he said "no one can form an idea of the atmosphere of these vessels" after being closed up and in action for a few hours in a hot climate.

The New Ironsides fairly fulfilled reasonable expectations ; she had all the speed necessary for the purposes of her construction; was not an indifferent sea boat; presented in broadside seven XI-inch shell guns and one 200-pounder rifle. Her battery had rapidity of fire and great precision and usefulness within its range. When in shallow water, like all flat-floored vessels, she steered badly and became unmanageable, if obliged to slow down or to stop the enginery. The armor plating was four and a half inches in thickness, and stood fairly the fire from all the batteries to which she was exposed at all times. Before going into action her deck was covered with sand-bags, and the iron bulkheads of four inches in thickness at her ends were reinforced with sand-bags.

The Keokuk proved to be a hopeless failure under the fire to which she was subjected, and would not have withstood projectiles of ordinary size at any distance at which her battery could have been used effectively. The contract calls for " one iron-clad, shot-proof, steam battery on Whitney's plan, the vessel to be wholly of iron. Length, 159 feet ; beam, 39 feet ; depth of hold, 3¼ feet, and draught, 8 feet. . . . The said vessel shall have capacity and stability safely to carry and work a battery of two XI-inch guns, . . . the vessel and the two turrets and the pilot-house to be shot-proof against ordnance used in the naval service of the United States." The " turrets," as they were called, were two oval casemates. The above comprises all that the contract calls for, so far as invulnerability is concerned, and no mention is made of her in this regard, or of her qualities in the report on "Armored Vessels," 1864. So far as memory serves, the "armor-plating," as it was called, was one and a half or two inches thick, and an inner skin of perhaps three-fourths of an inch. Her rôle was short, and she would not have proved a success anywhere, whether against forts or ships.

By April 13th all of the monitors had been sent to Port Royal for repairs, and as fast as finished were sent to North Edisto, the inland waters of which were contiguous, and actually afforded a better base for menacing or taking Charleston than Morris or Sullivan's Island. Had both of these islands been in possession of the National forces, Charleston would certainly have been a sealed port, but so far as its attack from a land force was concerned, even then an approach from Stono and North Edisto would have been more practicable, considering the support derivable from guns afloat. The admiral had reason to suppose that at any day the monitor force, with the exception of two vessels, would be ordered to the Mississippi, and so it was held in expectancy.

Definite information was obtained of the approaching readiness of the ram Atlanta to leave Savannah, with the intention of sweeping the coast of the weak vessels that for the most part maintained the blockade. The vessel was reputed strong. Timely provision was made to meet her by sending the monitors Weehawken, Captain John Rodgers commanding, and Nahant, Commander John Downes, to Wassaw Sound, from whence she was expected to come out.

The admiral had the satisfaction of reporting to the Department on June 17th the capture of the Atlanta on that day. At early dawn she was discovered coming down Wilmington River, accompanied by a propeller and a side-wheel steamer. The Weehawken and Nahant slipped their cables and steamed outward for the northeast end of Wassaw Island ; the ram and her consorts steamed down rapidly, apparently thinking them in retreat. After preparations were completed and broad daylight had come, at 4.30 the Weehawken and Nahant turned and stood up to meet their adversary. At a distance of a mile and a half the Atlanta fired a rifle shell, which passed over the stern of the Weehawken and struck near the Nahant. She then laid across the channel and awaited an attack. At a distance of about three hundred yards the Weehawken opened fire, and after an engagement of fifteen minutes, at 5.30 A.M., having fired but five shots, the Atlanta hauled down her flag. The Nahant had not the opportunity of delivering a single shot, although close aboard and ready to support her consort.

The Atlanta had gone aground after the action was over. A rising tide soon enabled her to be got afloat and sent with a prize crew to Port Royal. Four shots had struck her. A XV-inch cored shot had struck the casemate at an angle of about fifty degrees with the keel, broken in the armor and wood backing, covered the deck with splinters, and from the concussion and débris prostrated 40 men. Another of the same size struck the top of the pilot-house, knocking it off, wounding the pilots, and stunning the men at the wheel. An XI-inch solid shot struck the edge of the overhang, breaking the plating ; the fourth, supposed to be of the same size, struck a port-stopper in the centre, breaking it in two, and driving many of the fragments into the casemate. The crew was composed of 21 officers and a complement of 121 enlisted men, 16 of whom were wounded. The captured officers estimated her speed at ten knots, and regarded the

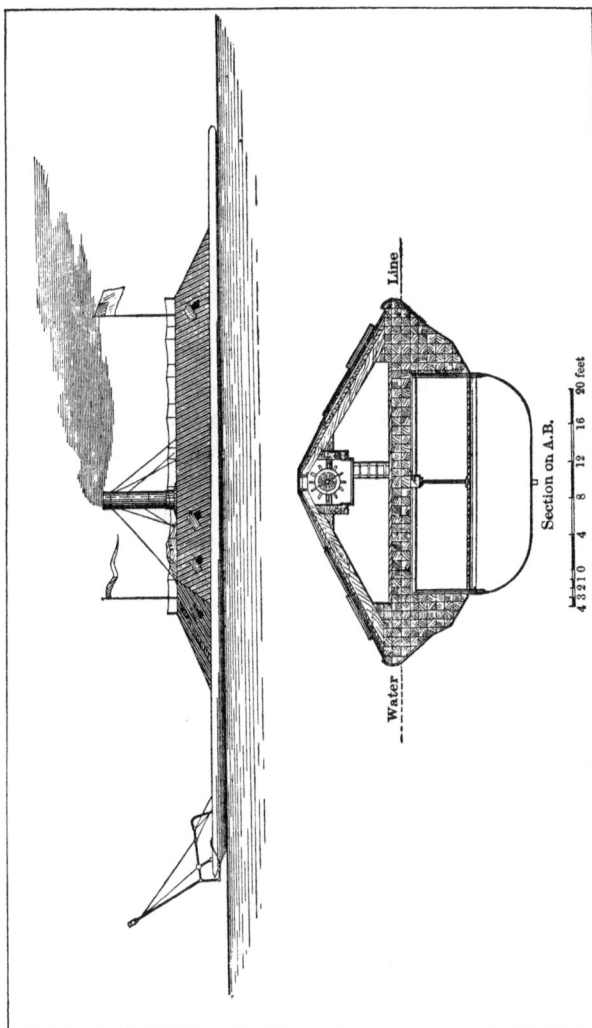

Section on A.B.

4 3 2 1 0   4   8   12   16   20 feet

Water

Line

Confederate ironclad Atlanta, captured in Wassaw Sound, June 17, 1863.

Atlanta as the strongest ironclad of the Confederates, and quite a match for the two monitors.

Confident and enthusiastic friends on board of the two steamers that had come from Savannah to witness the triumph of the Atlanta, saw instead, their pride and their hope in the possession of the enemy. They certainly had not long to wait, and, however painful the suspense, it was of short duration.

The armament of the Atlanta was two VII-inch and two $VI\frac{4}{10}$-inch rifled guns, two of which could be pivoted either on broadside or ahead and astern. Length of vessel, 204 feet; extreme breadth, 41 feet; draught, 16 feet. A more detailed description will be found in the volume of Professor Soley. The superstructure was built on a staunch new steamer known as the Fingal, with excellent enginery. The plating was four inches in thickness, composed of two plates, but of little tenacity, as it shattered almost like cast-iron.

Chronometers and other nautical instruments found on board disclosed the fact that the builders intended the vessel for sea purposes, and the boldness of her commander indicated the belief that she was far superior to any of the rams in Charleston Harbor.

CHAPTER VII.

OPERATIONS AGAINST CHARLESTON.

THE Navy Department, on June 26th, addressed a letter to Rear-Admiral Dupont, from which the following is an extract:

"To your ceaseless vigilance and that of the officers under your command we were indebted, some months since, for the destruction of the notorious steamer Nashville, which the enemy had armed and fruitlessly endeavored to send out to destroy our commerce; and now to your timely measures, and the efficient means provided, do we owe the capture of one of the most powerful ironclads afloat—a vessel prepared after months of toil and great expenditure of money, and sent forth with confidence to disperse our blockading fleet and overcome our monitors.

"You may well regard this, and we may with pleasure look upon it as a brilliant termination of a command gallantly commenced and conducted for nearly two years with industry, energy, and ability."

On the 21st of April the Assistant Secretary of the Navy said to Admiral Dahlgren, in the Navy Department, that it was his wish that he (Dahlgren) should relieve Dupont. Dahlgren says in relation to this:

If I am wanted there now, an order will soon take me there, *as I am an applicant for sea service.* Next day the President came into Fox's room while I was there, and sat some time, talking generally of matters. He said nothing of the Charleston business, in the way of opinion, but remarked that Dupont's last letter showed over-readi-

II.—6

ness to think that his (the President's) letter censured him. Abe was in good humor, and at leaving said, " Well, I will go home ; I had no business here; but as the lawyer said, I had none anywhere else."

May 28th.—Dupont is to be relieved, and three are spoken of in his place—Gregory, Foote, and myself. There is evidently an idea of two commanders, one for the fleet generally, and one for the attack, intended I think, to include Foote and myself (Dahlgren's Memoirs, p. 390).

Admiral Foote was taken suddenly ill, and that gallant officer died in New York on the 26th of June. Admiral Dahlgren was ordered to relieve Admiral Dupont, and left with the least possible delay ; he arrived at Port Royal on the 4th of July. He says:

General Gillmore wished to act, and had called for assistance. Dupont had no specific instructions, but would assist. He preferred to await my arrival. A very loose state of things; no shape or connection. After Rodgers got to the Wabash a note was sent me from Dupont, saying he was 'rejoiced' and would send for me at 10. . . . Dupont was very pleasant. The cabins full of officers.

In the afternoon I went over to Hilton Head to see General Gillmore. He said that his project must now be tiied, or it would be too late in a few days. So I had no alternative but to grant the aid asked (Dahlgren's Memoirs, p. 396).

On the 5th Admiral Dahlgren met General Gillmore on board of the Wabash, and they " put the matter in a definite shape." The admiral " would send in five ironclads to clear the ground on Morris Island, and he would attempt an assault the night before. If it failed, then he would open the batteries. The thing is rather complicated, and, to make it worse, I am new to the squadron and the locality, and my staff likewise. . . . Besides, three of the turrets are being altered, and this work has to be stopped for the occasion " [1] (Dahlgren's Memoirs, p. 397-8).

---

[1] This change in the turret fitments could only be effected by direct orders from the Navy Department, and yet Admiral Dupont was held derelict in not having

On the 6th the command of the squadron was turned over to Rear-Admiral Dahlgren. On the 7th he "received a note from General Gillmore, who asked to postpone one day. Agreed on."

In taking leave of Rear-Admiral Dupont, the writer is impelled to give a sketch of him, perhaps such as is in the memory of every officer who was personally acquainted with him or served near him. Professionally, he was thoroughly able ; he possessed undaunted courage, energy, and zeal ; his education was of a high order, and his character might well serve as a model in every respect. He had the rare ability to make the best use of the personnel and the material under his control, and to maintain over no less than forty harbors, inlets, and channel-ways, as rigorous a blockade as it was in the power of man to accomplish with the vessels which were at his disposal.

In appearance he was distinguished, over six feet in height, admirably proportioned, graceful and urbane, with an intelligent expression and action. It will not be considered adulatory to those who knew him to say that no officer in our navy within the past half century was gifted with a more distinguished appearance or exalted character.

On July 15th the Secretary of the Navy wrote to Rear-Admiral Dupont, after the close of his official duties, as follows : "Elsewhere, and in public official communications, I have expressed my high appreciation of your services and of the ability you have exhibited."

---

the monitors within Charleston bar, and for failing to give co-operation to General Gillmore, *who writes on June 30th :* " *My preparations are nearly completed,* but I can do nothing until Admiral Dupont's successor arrives and gets ready to work. The admiral has no instructions, and does not feel at liberty to put his vessels into action on the eve of relinquishing his command." *General Gillmore, however, was not ready to operate until July 10th,* or four days after Dahlgren was in command.

There was further correspondence between the Navy Department and the admiral of an acrimonious character, which neither the limits nor the objects of this volume could take in. A careful consideration of what is herein presented, will show, however, that certain charges of disobedience of orders were simply technical, namely : the ironclads should have been within Charleston bar, as per order, when they were undergoing repairs from injuries received, and were having base-rings put around their turrets, and pilot-houses increased in thickness, *by order of the Department*, which could not have been done off Charleston; also, a failure to coöperate with General Gillmore as ordered, when Gillmore was not ready to operate until some days after Dahlgren took command.

Admiral Dahlgren, when in an inferior grade, had with great difficulty introduced into the naval service an improved armament of shell guns and boat howitzers, in relation to which Rear-Admiral Dupont, immediately after the battle of Port Royal, wrote him as follows :

But besides this, I am impelled by a feeling of duty to address you. The large ordnance of this squadron has sprung from your inventive genius, and thankful am I, for one, for those long years of study, scientific research, and deductions, which so materially aided in arming the American navy as I believe no other navy is armed. . . . I only now wish you could have seen the practice from this ship during the engagement, not alone for its precision and destructive results, but for the rapidity with which such large guns could be loaded with their heavy shell.

I never get *transporté*, as the French term it, about such things, but I will repeat, to the day of my death, that the second assault of this ship upon the forts, for rapidity, continuity, and precision of fire, has never been surpassed in naval warfare.[1]

---

[1] Although irrelevant, the above is introduced as information valuable in itself, and pertinent to show personal relations and official appreciation.

Admiral Dahlgren, upon assuming command, had shown him by Dupont a letter from Gillmore, to the effect that he was about operating on Morris Island, and asked naval co-operation. This had been declined in order to enable his successor to make all preliminary arrangements.

"General Gillmore had informed him [Dahlgren] that the enemy appeared to be aware of his design, and was working on Morris Island with great activity to defeat it, and would succeed unless speedy action was taken. There being no time to ascertain the views of the Department it only remained for him to furnish the assistance required."

This he proposed to do with the monitors, with what assistance from the wooden vessels was found practicable. He regretted the probability that at the time desired the Ironsides would not be able to cross the bar. He says: "Of course, the most that is expected from the action of these vessels is to relieve the troops as much as possible, and is to be considered of no other consequence."

On the 10th of July General Gillmore opened his batteries, situated on the north end of Folly Island, against those of the enemy occupying the southern sand-hills of Morris Island.

At 4 A.M. the Catskill, Commander George W. Rodgers, the Montauk, Commander D. M. Fairfax, the Nahant, Commander John Downes, and the Weehawken, Commander E. R. Colhoun, passed the bar, the admiral's flag being on board of the leading vessel. General Gillmore opened fire about this time, and as soon as sufficiently near, the monitors opened fire with shell upon the enemy's batteries, which were replying to those of General Gillmore. The fire of the monitors dispersed the enemy wherever seen to assemble. About eight o'clock the land batteries ceased firing and the troops in some force were seen making their way along the beach on Morris Island.

The monitors, with the advance of the troops, now moved parallel to the low, flat ground that extends northward between the sand-hills and Fort Wagner, as near to the island as the depth of water permitted, rolling shells over the surface to clear away any bodies of troops that might be behind a continuous sand-ridge near the beach.

Two or three buildings near Fort Wagner were set on fire by the enemy, for the supposed purpose of unmasking the guns of the fort looking down the beach. The monitors were now laid abreast of Fort Wagner, which is situated about 2¾ miles from the southern end of Morris Island, and 1¼ mile north of the sand-hills situated on that end. The number of guns in Wagner was supposed to be ten or twelve. At 9.30 the monitors opened on the work. The admiral desired to get within grape-shot range, but was not able to get closer than about 1,200 yards, by reason of shoal water. The fire was promptly and vigorously returned till noon, when the monitors dropped down to allow the men to have dinner, after which they re-occupied their position and continued firing until 6 P.M., and then withdrew, the men having been fourteen hours employed. The weather was excessively hot. Five hundred and thirty-four shell and shrapnel were fired during the day, and from the different points of view the practice appeared to be excellent.

The admiral was favorably impressed with the endurance of the monitors. The Catskill was struck sixty times, a large percentage of the hits being very severe. The pilot-house, turret, and side armor, were all more or less damaged. Some of the shots were large; one found on deck after striking the turret proved to be a X-inch; when these heavy shot struck, the concussion was very great. An officer touching the turret at such a time was knocked down senseless and much injured. The iron of the pilot-house was broken through entirely, and a nut from one of the bolts driven against the lining, so as to break it through. The deck-plates were also cut through in many places, so as to make the entrance of water troublesome. The test was most severe, as all admitted who saw the vessel. Yet after firing one hundred and twenty-eight rounds she came out of action in good working order, as was proven by her going into action the next day.[1]

The enemy directed his fire almost exclusively against the Catskill. The Nahant was hit six times, the Montauk twice, and the Weehawken was untouched.

The following morning the admiral received a note from General Gillmore stating that at early daylight he had made an assault on Wagner and had been repulsed. He had learned that the enemy expected reinforcements at 10 A.M., and asked for action to prevent it. In accordance with the request, four monitors were again moved near Wagner, and scoured the ground in that vicinity.

On July 17th the admiral states that since his last report he had been occupied with measures to continue the advance and have the Ironsides with five monitors inside the bar. An attack was made on our forces in the Stono the previous day, which had been repulsed. The Pawnee had been struck forty-two times.

---

[1] The above is a transcript from the official report of the Admiral. It seems entirely admissible, in view of the facts presented, to suppose that he was *not very favorably impressed* with the endurance of the monitors. Captain Rodgers reports "that the deck has been entirely broken through in four places, two of these sufficiently large to admit large quantities of water, requiring shot-plugs. . . . The hull was struck on the port quarter, completely shattering all the plates." Two engineers and several firemen were prostrated by the intense heat in the fire- and engine-room. The distance from the fort, it will be remembered, was given as 1,200 yards. Admiral Dahlgren's Memoirs, seen since writing the above, says, "her armor was very much hurt. The sides of the pilot-house bulged through, and I just escaped the end of a bolt that was dislodged."

On July 19th he states that the previous day a combined attack had been made by the troops under General Gillmore and the vessels under his command. At 11.30 A.M. the admiral led on board of the Montauk, Commander Fairfax, followed by the Ironsides, Captain S. C. Rowan; the Catskill, Commander G. W. Rodgers; the Nantucket, Commander Beaumont; the Weehawken, Commander Colhoun; and the Patapsco, Lieutenant-Commander Badger. At 12.30 the Montauk anchored abreast of Fort Wagner and fired the first gun, the other vessels following. The tide ebbing, the pilot was averse to going nearer. The distance to the fort was about twelve hundred yards. The gunboats Paul Jones, Commander A. C. Rhind; Ottawa, Lieutenant-Commander W. D. Whiting; Seneca, Lieutenant-Commander Wm. Gibson; Chippewa, Lieutenant-Commander T. C. Harris; and Wissahickon, Lieutenant-Commander J. L. Davis, at the same time were using their pivot guns against the fort at long range, and the batteries of General Gillmore, about one thousand yards south, on Morris Island, were firing very deliberately and steadily.

At 4 P.M., with a flood-tide, weighed anchor and closed in to within about three hundred yards of the fort, so that for the day not a shot was fired afterward at the vessels, nor was a man to be seen about it. Near sunset a note was received from General Gillmore stating that he had ordered an assault, and the battalions could be seen advancing along the beach. "Before our troops had reached the works it became too dark to discern them. To this moment an incessant and accurate fire had been maintained by the vessels; but now it was impossible to distinguish whether it took effect on friend or foe, and, of necessity, it was suspended. Very soon afterward the rattle of musketry and the flashes of light artillery announced that our men were mounting to

the attack. This continued without intermission until 9.30
P.M., then gradually decreased and died away altogether.

"The ill-tidings of a repulse were not long coming; the
admiral was of opinion that the number of troops was inade-
quate. The officers and men were zealous, and labored
hard; the general plans were well conceived; but there was
a manifest lack of force."

The following morning the admiral sent a flag of truce on
shore to offer to take charge of our wounded. The offer was
rejected, and the fact observed that dead and wounded were
lying about the ground. The enemy stated that the dead
would be buried and the wounded properly provided for.
Owing to our wounded lying exposed, it was not possible to
do anything that day; the vessels were ordered to withdraw
in order that the men might get fresh air below. The admiral
expresses his satisfaction with those under his command, and
says the vessels were handled with great skill in the narrow
channel.

On July 21st he forwards copies of correspondence between
General Gillmore and himself, and states his belief that an
additional land force is absolutely required to advance operations. "Fort Wagner had been silenced and its garrison
driven to shelter, and that could be repeated; the rest could
only be accomplished by troops."

As a part of the operations against Charleston, the command of General A. H. Terry was sent up the Stono River to
make a diversion. The Pawnee, Commander G. B. Balch;
the McDonough, Lieutenant-Commanding Bacon; and the
Marblehead, Lieutenant-Commanding Scott, were in those
waters to co-operate.

On the afternoon of July 9th the Pawnee, Nantucket
(monitor), the McDonough, and the Williams proceeded up
the Stono, anchored above Strom's Landing, and opened

6*

fire on James Island. The troops followed in transports, landed, and sent a force out on the island. On the 11th a Confederate battery opened fire on the army transport Hunter, and at once received the fire of the McDonough and the Williams. In the afternoon, at the request of General Terry, the Pawnee anchored off Grimball's, near the locality where the Isaac Smith had been captured five months previously, and opened fire in the direction of Secessionville, to assist our troops in making a forward movement, and this was continued, and at ranges designated, until signal was made to cease, when the troops advanced.

On the morning of the 16th the enemy opened a heavy fire on the Pawnee and Marblehead, choosing a time when the position of the vessels would not permit their batteries to bear. The narrow channel, and the steering-wheel of the Pawnee being disabled, made the attempt to drop down perilous, but the movement was effected without grounding, and was most opportune. General Terry signalled that the enemy was advancing in force, and requested the Pawnee to open fire. This was effectively done, and an advance along a causeway was checked. The attack on Terry's troops was very spirited, and, as learned through prisoners taken, the design was to disable the vessels, and by means of a superior force capture the troops.

On the afternoon of that day General Terry stated that he had fulfilled his instructions, and would embark during the night. As proposed, the troops left, and the vessels of war dropped down to the inlet.

Active operations, from causes indicated above, were suspended on Morris Island until the morning of August 17th, at which time General Gillmore opened fire on Fort Sumter from all of his batteries. At the same time Admiral Dahlgren, with his flag on board of the Weehawken,

followed by the Catskill, Nahant, and Montauk, attacked
Wagner, the New Ironsides taking position in face of the
fort. From outside the bar the Canandaigua, Mahaska,
Cimarrone, Ottawa, Wissahickon, Dai Ching, and Lodona
opened also with rifles and pivot guns.

As the tide rose the monitors closed to within a distance of
about four hundred and fifty yards of Wagner, and the Ironsides as near as her draught would permit. After a couple
of hours the fort was silenced, and the fire of the vessels was
less frequent thereafter. During the action Fort Moultrie
made fair practice on the Ironsides.

The batteries of General Gillmore were working effectively
on the gorge of Sumter. Later in the day the admiral
shifted his flag to the Passaic, and, accompanied by the
Patapsco, steamed to within two thousand yards of Sumter,
and opened fire on its southeast face with one rifled 150-
pounder on board of each of these vessels. Sumter scarcely
replied, Wagner was silent, and battery Gregg alone, on
Cummings Point, maintained a deliberate fire at the two
monitors. The vessels were withdrawn at noon, the batteries
of General Gillmore continuing an effective fire at Sumter.
In the afternoon the Passaic and Patapsco again attacked
Wagner to prevent repairs. The fort opened briskly on
them, but in a short time remained silent.

During this day's bombardment a heavy shot striking the
top of the pilot-house of the Catskill, of which vessel Commander George W. Rodgers was in temporary command,
caused the instant death of that gallant officer and of Paymaster Woodbury, who was at his side. The fragments of
iron also wounded Mr. Penton, the pilot, and Master's Mate
Wescott.

Commander Rodgers was the chief-of-staff to the admiral,
but on this occasion had been permitted to take the Catskill

into action. The vessel withdrew temporarily, the bodies were transferred to a tug, and the Catskill resumed her position at 11 A.M. In relation to the death of his chief-of-staff the admiral in his official report says : "It is but natural that I should feel deeply the loss thus sustained, for the close and confidential relation which the duties of the fleet-captain necessarily occasion, impressed me deeply with the loss of Captain Rodgers. Brave, intelligent, and highly capable, devoted to his duty and to the flag under which he passed his life, the country cannot afford to lose such men. Of a kind and generous nature, he was prompt to give relief when he could."

The writer cannot refrain from adding that from the time of separation on leaving the Naval School, he never met his classmate Rodgers without an increased appreciation of his great professional aptitude. He possessed, in a marked degree, all of the high qualities assigned him by the admiral. Eminently useful in all the subordinate grades, had he lived, he would have become a distinguished officer of the highest rank.

After this day's bombardment, by land batteries and vessels, General Ripley, in command of Confederate defences, reports, "Sumter in ruins and all guns on northwest face disabled, besides seven other guns."

On the night of the 21st a "steam torpedo boat" came out of Charleston, and struck the Ironsides. A direct collision was not effected and the electric current failed also. The boat, however, effected her retreat under a heavy fire from the Ironsides and other vessels.

On the 23d of August, before daylight, five monitors were brought within about 800 yards of Sumter and opened fire. Considerable damage was done to the southeast and northeast faces. The fort replied with only six shots, but Moultrie,

with its extended line of earthworks, opened fire with many
large guns and struck the monitors frequently with heavy
shot.   The Weehawken, upon which the admiral was, received two blows on the pilot-house "more forcible than any
he had seen." Notwithstanding the difficulties of manœu-
vring during the night, and in a channel edged with shoals,
only one monitor got aground.   At six it was blowing from
the southeast and the vessels were withdrawn.   The Department was informed that the gorge of Sumter was completely
ruined by the severe fire of the batteries of General Gillmore, aided by four rifled cannon of the navy in battery on
shore under Commander F. A. Parker.   The intention was
expressed of "passing Sumter into the harbor if the obstacles are not of such a nature as to prevent it, as soon as
the weather moderated."

On the 25th of August an exchange of prisoners took place
by agreement.   It was either happily arranged or fortuitous
for the defenders of Fort Wagner.   General Ripley says :
"The enemy opened about daylight both from the fleet and
land batteries.   Wagner was sorely pressed, and the flag of
truce boat was literally a godsend.   The firing continued
until 10 A.M., and for a portion of the time was equal in intensity to the bombardment of the 18th.   One of the more
advanced land batteries of Parrott guns did serious damage ;
the remaining X-inch columbiad on the sea-face was dismounted, and the magazines so much exposed that it became
necessary to remove the ammunition.   The commanding officer, anticipating a renewal of the bombardment upon the
completion of the exchange of prisoners, requested that all
necessary arrangements should be made for the transfer of
the troops from the island in case of necessity.   Four hours
were consumed in effecting the delivery of 105 wounded prisoners and in receiving 39.   The bombardment was not re-

newed, and the time thus allowed was improved to the utmost in repairing the damage that had been done." The casualties in the fort from the 20th to the 31st were 13 killed and 49 wounded.

The admiral states that at his request, on the 21st of September, General Gillmore had knocked down four or five pieces of ordnance that had been seen on the inner fronts of Sumter. Soon after midnight on the 2d he led in the Weehawken and anchored 600 yards from Sumter off the angle between the northeast and southeast fronts. The fire was maintained by all of the monitors, and the Ironsides, within good range, joined in the action. Moultrie opened a rapid and sustained fire from its extended line, which told with effect, notwithstanding the obscurity of the night, which interfered with accuracy of aim. The fire of the monitors was in some degree directed at the floating obstructions that had been reported from day to day. The vessels were engaged for five hours and fired 245 shots and received in all 71 hits. The Ironsides fired 50 shots and received 7 hits.

A round shot which struck the base of the Weehawken's turret drove in a fragment of iron and broke the leg of Fleet-Captain Badger. "He had been with the admiral for eight years, and was one of the best ordnance officers in the navy. The loss of his services was felt greatly."

The enemy evacuated Morris Island on the night preceding the 7th of September. The previous day a steady cannonade had been maintained against Wagner from the land batteries and by the Ironsides, and it was known to the enemy that an assault was intended soon, which in fact was to have been carried out at 9 A.M. At this time General Gillmore's advanced sap was within forty yards of the salient. The army occupied Wagner and Gregg on the morning of the 7th.

From August 17th, the time the land batteries opened on

Fort Sumter from beyond Wagner, having a mean range of four thousand five hundred yards, every day brought ruin, until Sumter had not a single gun mounted. General Ripley's report of August 21st says : "Enemy opened heavily from land batteries on Morris Island on eastern face of Sumter. Four hundred and sixty-five projectiles struck outside, 259 inside, and 219 passed over. The eastern face was heavily battered and 2 barbette guns dismounted." During the night artillery implements, subsistence, and other stores and 9,700 pounds of powder were removed. This removal of stores, etc., was continued steadily, as opportunities favored. The next day all of the barbette guns were disabled except one XI-inch and one X-inch on eastern face. The arches of the northwest face were demolished, of which five and the terre-plein fell in. On the 23d the ironclads came up and engaged Sumter at short distance. Twenty-nine projectiles struck outside, 15 inside, and 17 missed. Considerable damage was done to the parapet and wall. From the land batteries came 282 projectiles outside, 310 inside, and 141 missed. The X-inch gun en barbette was disabled, and three 42-pounder rifles in the northeast salient of second tier. The Confederates were engaged in throwing the dismounted guns off the parapets and transporting them and munitions as they best could. Although the bombardment was almost daily, it is passed over here until the 30th. Four guns were then firing from the land batteries, and disabled three X-inch Columbiads that had been repaired. Three of the casemate arches on the northeast face were demolished, and two breaches made in the scarp wall, exposing the sand with which the arches were filled. September 1st, all of the guns en barbette were disabled, and the entire terreplein of the northeast face, with the exception of two arches, fell in. September 2d, "the Ironsides and monitors came up and

directed their fire principally against Sumter, apparently
with the intention of doing as much damage as possible.
Nearly the whole of the eastern scarp was demolished. The
accumulated débris served to protect the walls." Confederate reports show the steady destruction of Sumter and its
armament, with little loss of life, until the evacuation of
Morris Island, when its appearance from seaward was rather
that of a steep, sandy island than of a fort.

On September 5th, General Ripley wrote a confidential
letter to the officer commanding Fort Wagner, stating that
it was "within the contingencies" that those works would
be evacuated. He alluded to the fact that at different times
they had been supplied with safety-fuse. "This would be
examined and kept in place, and magazines would be prepared for explosion before the evacuation takes place, by
causing safety-fuses, three in number, to be inserted in a
barrel of gunpowder in each magazine and carefully trained,
so that the explosion may not be premature." Elaborate
instructions follow ; but they were carried out so indifferently as to be inoperative when the fort was evacuated. The
commanding officer of the fort reported on the 6th that
"thirty-six hours' severe bombardment, confining the garrison to the bombproofs, had so dispirited the garrison as to
render it unsafe, in the opinion of its officers, to repel an assault. The head of the enemy's sap was within forty yards
of the salient, and he was making rapid progress, unmolested
by a single gun, and with scarcely any annoyance from sharpshooters. In an effort the previous night to repair damages
a loss was sustained of from 60 to 80 men in the working
parties alone. Without having the ability to repair damages
at night, from the effects of the fire of the shore batteries
and the fleet, the work would be rendered untenable in two
days."

The garrison of Fort Wagner was successfully withdrawn without loss, except some 40 prisoners, and later, the failure to blow up the magazines was sharply commented upon by General Beauregard. With so many men in the trenches, close to the work, an explosion would have resulted in great loss of life.

The day following the evacuation of Morris Island Admiral Dahlgren sent a demand for the surrender of Fort Sumter, and was informed that "he could have Sumter when he could take and hold it."

The Weehawken was ordered on the night of the 7th to pass into a narrow, shoal, and tortuous channel between Sumter and Cummings Point, and in the attempt grounded and remained so for two tides. When her condition became known, Moultrie and other batteries on Sullivan's Island opened fire on her, as well as Fort Simkins on James Island. In returning the fire the Weehawken caused an explosion at Moultrie. One of her heavy shells struck and disabled an 8-inch columbiad, and glancing, fired a service magazine, killing 16 and wounding 12 men. Whilst aground she fired 36 shells at Moultrie and Bee and 46 at Sumter. She was struck 24 times, without material damage, and had 3 men wounded. The admiral, on board the Ironsides, and followed by the monitors, had moved up " to feel, and if possible, pass the obstructions north of Sumter." This force received a severe fire from the usual batteries, which was returned until it was thought best to give entire attention to the Weehawken. She was finally got afloat. In this affair Captain Rowan, in the Ironsides, did admirable service ; one of the heaviest guns of the enemy was dismounted, and his fire, if not controlled, was much weakened. When only thirty shells remained, the anchor was weighed, firing kept up from all of the available guns, and she left unmolested, "after one of the severest artillery duels ever sustained by a ship" through a period of nearly three hours. Her armor was battered, but stood the battering fairly, quite disproving Mr. Stimer's assertion, previously noticed, of the superiority of five 1-inch plates over a solid plate of 4½ inches in thickness.

On the night of September 8th an attempt to take Sumter by a boat expedition from the squadron resulted disastrously, not in great loss of life, but in the capture of a considerable number of officers and sailors, as well as the loss of several boats. The demand for the surrender of Sumter had informed the enemy, and boats in tow of tugs from the vessels outside of the bar during the whole of the afternoon left little doubt as to an intended attempt. He did not fail, therefore, to put a considerable force into Sumter for the occasion.

Commander T. H. Stevens was in command, and Lieutenant-Commander E. P. Williams, Lieutenants Remey, Preston, Higginson, and Ensign Craven, commanded the five divisions of boats. A detachment of marines, under Captain McCawley, formed also a part of the force, numbering in all 400. A request for the loan of some army boats brought the information that General Gillmore also intended·making an attack. It was about 10 P.M. before the boats, in tow of a tug, reached the vicinity of Sumter; "a sound of musketry, followed by shells from the adjacent forts, announced the assault." Before the Admiral reached the vicinity the conflict had ceased. Of the 400, 10 officers and 104 men were taken prisoners, and 3 were reported killed.

Commander Stevens reported that on his way up he had communicated with the monitors Lehigh and Montauk and given orders to move up for his support. When within 800 yards of the fort, the boats cast off from the tug, and final instructions and the watch-word were given. Lieutenant Higginson's division was directed to move up to the northwest front for the purpose of making a diversion, and the other divisions were ordered to close up and wait to advance on the southeast front. It was intended to wait until the full benefit of the diversion was attained, "but mistaking his movement, doubtless, as intended for a general one, and in that spirit of gallantry and emulation which characterizes the service, many of the other boats dashed on. Finding it too late to restrain them, the order was given to advance."

The boats, on approaching the fort, were met with a fire of musketry, hand-grenades, lighted shells, and grape and canister, and simultaneously, at a signal from the fort, all of the enemy's batteries, with one of their gunboats and rams, opened fire.

Several of the boats effected a landing, "but the evidences of preparation were so apparent, and the impossibility of effecting a general landing or scaling the walls so certain, that orders were given to withdraw." All who landed were either killed or taken prisoners. They were, in fact, entirely helpless, and when they agreed to surrender were taken around to another face, and helped to get within the fort.

There was a period of comparative quiet until the 5th of October, when a second attempt was made to blow up the Ironsides by a torpedo boat. At 9.15 P.M. a small object was seen by a sentinel and hailed. No answer was received and the sentry fired ; the ship almost immediately thereafter received a very severe blow from an explosion which threw a column of water upon the spar deck and into the engine-room. The object was afterward known to be a torpedo boat, "shaped like a cigar, 50 feet long and 5 feet in diameter, and so submerged that the only portion visible was the coaming of her hatch, two feet above the water surface, and about 10 feet in length.

2

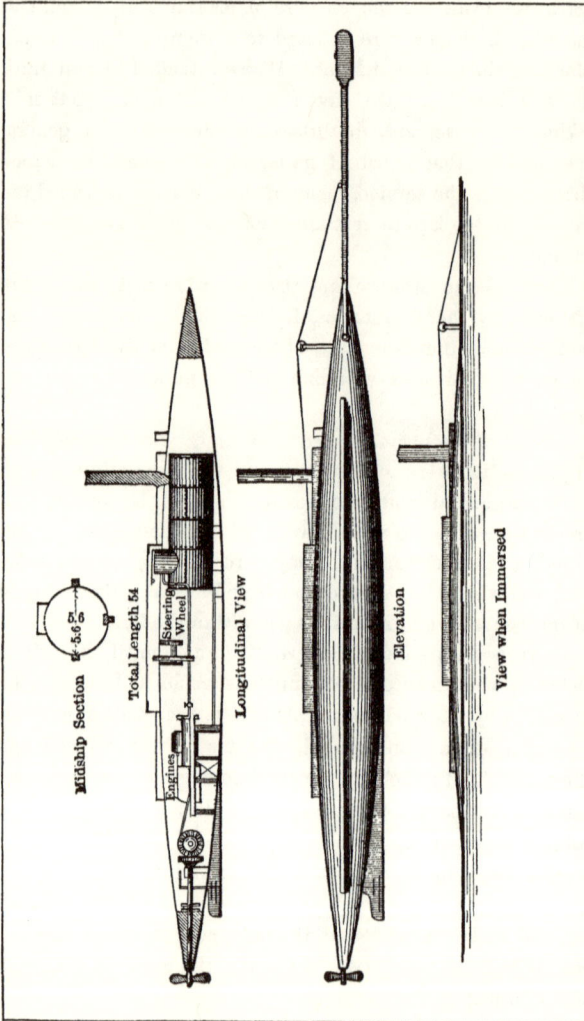

Midship Section

Total Length 54

Steering Wheel

Engines

Longitudinal View

Elevation

View when Immersed

Sketch showing torpedo-boats as constructed at Charleston, S. C.

The boat was commanded by Lieutenant Glassell, formerly of the navy. He was taken prisoner, and stated that the explosion threw a column of water which put out the fires and left the boat without motive power.

The marine guard and musketeers on the spar-deck of the Ironsides saw a small object, at which a very severe fire was kept up until it drifted out of sight, when two of the monitors passed near; then it disappeared. Two boats were sent and made an unsuccessful search. The prisoner stated that he, Engineer Toombs, and a pilot, were compelled to abandon the vessel, and provided with life preservers, swam for their lives. Glassell hailed a coal schooner as he was drifting past, and was taken on board. Confederate reports say the boat and remainder of crew came back to Charleston.

The naval operations before Charleston were now only of blockade, and although the channel was certainly very limited the blockade-runners came and departed, but "the Navy Department was not informed of the fact." [1] The monitors were being patched up where they had been battered, and were beached at high water and the sides were scraped at low water, and when afloat again, the flat floor was cleaned by divers. Their speed even then would not exceed four knots with all the revolutions their enginery could make.

On October 26th the army again opened on Sumter from the nearest attainable points on Morris Island, and were aided by the cross-fire of 150-pounder rifles on board of the Patapsco and Lehigh. This seemed wholly a work of supererogation, as Sumter was in appearance and in reality only a mass of ruins, without a gun mounted upon it.

---

[1] The Secretary of the Navy appeared before the "Joint Committee on the Conduct of the War" and assumed that because "the Department was not informed of the fact" no vessels ran the blockade; actually twenty-one vessels ran in after the ruin of Sumter until the evacuation of Charleston.

On December 6th the monitor Weehawken sunk when made fast to one of the mooring buoys placed for those vessels within the Charleston bar. The previous day Commander Colhoun had been relieved by Commander Jesse Duncan, and a day or so before had taken on board as many heavy shells as the vessel would hold. The capacity of the shell-room of a monitor was found to be entirely insufficient for long continuous operations, hence the fore body was also allotted for their stowage. The hold was little deeper than sufficient to contain a XV-inch shell, below the "flying deck," which means one made of movable sections. The shells were thus conveniently stowed, and easily got up in action, and their weight not only made the monitors lie deep in the water, but also reduced the difference of draught between the bow and stern from a foot and a half to about six or eight inches, and this resulted in a sluggish water flow to the powerful pumps, which, placed aft, were ineffective, since the water could not reach them and hence could not be expelled.

When within Charleston bar, where the swell was often heavy, and usually sufficient to wash over the deck, in order to make the monitors habitable, or existence in them possible in hot weather, high coamings, or "hoppers" as they were called, were fitted around the hatch-openings.

The reader will remember that the "windlass-room" is a small apartment, previously described, in the bow of the monitors into which the anchor-chain is led through the hawse-hole from the "anchor-well." The plate over the latter forms a chamber, and serves as an air-cushion, in a measure preventing the entrance of water through the hawse-hole by slopping. Heavy plaits of strands of rope were made, known as gaskets, which were pliable, and in rough weather, *whether at sea or at anchor*, were, or should have been, carefully mauled in from the windlass-room, around the chain, to fill the entire hawse-hole and thus prevent anything more than a seepage of water through it.

The morning was clear and pleasant; the high coaming at the windlass-room hatch served its purpose until the vessel had considerable water in her; only a little spray flew over it from time to time.

Near noon, a strong ebb-tide kept the broadside of the vessel to the sea; the hawse-pipe was not supplied with a " gasket," and a considerable amount of water slopped in, there being nothing to exclude it. The sea became heavier, the waves washing over the bow, and slopped over the hatchway in small quantities. To prevent water from getting into the cabin, the iron door between it and the windlass-room was closed; the seas increased, and while closing down the battle-plate of the hatch to the windlass-room, several seas went over, almost filling the room. The " limbers" were cleared and the executive officer had no fears that the water would not run aft and be pumped out; a small gutter, six by eight inches in dimensions, permitted a flow with whatever velocity the head would give it. The commanding officer had left the vessel soon after nine o'clock, and was on board the flag-ship near by until signal was made from the Weehawken that she was sinking. At about 1 P.M. Ensign Chadwick, observing that the water partially flooded the captain's cabin, called the assistance of Mr. Allen, the chief engineer, and they put on and secured the cross-bars to the iron door before mentioned. " The water gradually rose in the windlass-room, as indicated by the leak about the door and in about thirty minutes it was on the top of the door" (Reports of Stuyvesant and Chadwick).

A court of inquiry found that the causes of the sinking of the Weehawken were: " The additional weight of ammunition that had been lately put on board of her, leaving her trim so little by the stern as not to afford sufficient inclination for water to get to the pumps freely.

"The neglect to close the hawse-hole, which permitted the rapid accumulation, at the forward extremity of the vessel, of sufficient water to bring her nearly on an even keel.

"The large amount of water that was permitted to come into the vessel under the turret, through the XI-inch port, and down the berth-deck hatch, which assisted to tip the bows of the vessel.

"The amount of water which, owing to the immersion of the forward part of the vessel, came in under the plank sheer.

"The absence of all effort to relieve the forward part of the vessel from its depressed position by rolling shot aft, or moving any weight from the bow."

The reader is doubtless satisfied that the sinking of the vessel was clearly preventable up to within a few minutes of the occurrence. Had an *apprehension* of danger existed at the time the cabin door was securely bolted, it should have been thrown wide open instead; the hawse-hole should then have been filled in around the chain with a gasket, and such weights taken aft as would have been practicable, to increase the "trim by the stern" and the "water flow" to the pumps as much as possible. The fore body of the vessel gradually filled with water, which could not flow aft to the pumps, and it rose to the berth-deck floor.

Five minutes before the vessel went down the signal was made "Assistance required." At this moment no assistance could be rendered, save to rescue the crew from drowning. The vessel heeled over to the right, or, as seamen would say, "to starboard;" the bow settled, the water within rushed forward; for a minute, more or less, she lay on her side, gradually settling, the water pouring in through the turret port, which was open, and through the main hatch, over the "hopper;" a dense steam arose out of the engine-room, the vessel assumed an upright position as she went down, and the top of the smoke-stack alone remained visible when the keel rested on the bottom. Four officers and twenty men were drowned, being below at the time, and unable to reach the deck through the inrush of the water, or, if on deck, unable to keep themselves afloat for the few minutes that intervened until boats were at hand for their rescue.

As the reader will have already observed, the Stono River was frequently a scene of contention between batteries and gunboats; again on Christmas day, at 6 A.M., we find an attack made on the Marblehead, Lieutenant-Commanding Meade. The vessel was at anchor near Legareville, and the batteries were on John's Island. The engagement lasted an hour and a half, with the loss of three killed and four wounded; the hull of the vessel was struck twenty times, and the rigging considerably damaged. Balch, in the Pawnee, lying further down, got under way, and from an enfilading position aided the Marblehead, and the mortar-schooner Williams, Acting-Master Freeman, having a fair wind, came up several miles and opened on the enemy, who abandoned two disabled guns, a dying man, intrenching tools, etc. The carriages were destroyed afterward, and two VIII-inch sea-coast howitzers were brought off by Meade.

Under instructions from the Department on January 28th, the admiral summarized the services of the ironclads under his command. He says : "The vessels thus shared fully with the army in the operation that led to the abandonment of the works on Morris Island, and besides what is already men-

II.—7

tioned, prevented the access of reinforcements, or their accumulation between Wagner and Gregg. A detachment of
seamen and marines, under Captain F. A. Parker, participated
in the practice of the batteries at Fort Sumter, by working
four navy rifle cannon landed for the purpose.

"The Ironsides is a fine powerful ship. Her armor has
stood heavy battering very well, and her broadside of seven
XI-inch guns and one VIII-inch rifle has always told with
signal effect on the enemy.

" On the 19th of July, 1863, an English steamer attempted
to pass into Charleston harbor, having eluded the outside
blockade. The Catskill, Captain G. W. Rodgers, well up
toward Moultrie, ran her on a shoal. Two or three other
blockade-runners within the harbor afterward managed to
escape, and one or two may have gotten in, but that ended
the business of blockade-running at Charleston.

" On the morning of February 4, 1864, Bryson, in the
monitor Lehigh, discovered a blockade-runner ashore on
Sullivan's Island, outside of Moultrie. He opened fire at a
distance of twenty-five hundred yards with an VIII-inch rifle
and struck the vessel nine times in forty-two shots, and the
following day used also a 12-pounder rifled howitzer. The
first day the vessel was set on fire by the shells, but the
flames apparently made little progress; on the second day
she was again set on fire, and destroyed."

Early in February General Gillmore announced to the admiral his readiness to operate on the St. John's River, Florida, and desired a naval co-operation. This was at once
given, the Mahaska, Dai Ching and Water Witch leaving
forthwith. The force off Charleston was left in command of
Commodore Rowan, and the admiral proceeded to Jacksonville. The National troops had landed at that point, and a
considerable force gone into the interior. The admiral re-

turned to Charleston, leaving the Mahaska, Ottawa, and Norwich to second army operations.

The Confederates, notwithstanding repeated failures in the use of torpedo-boats off Charleston, had still sufficient encouragement to continue endeavors, which resulted on the night of February 19th in the destruction of the Housatonic, a fine vessel of war, lying outside the Charleston bar, some four miles from Moultrie.

About 9 P.M. an object was seen moving toward the ship, supposed one hundred yards distant; it had the appearance of a plank on the water; in two minutes it had reached the ship. Within this time the crew had been called to quarters, the chain cable slipped, and engine backed.[1] The torpedo-boat, for such she proved to be, struck the ship on the starboard side, forward of the mizzen-mast, and the Housatonic sunk almost immediately, the hammock nettings being just awash when the keel rested on the bottom. The crew ascended the rigging and were soon taken off by the boats from other vessels blockading. Ensign Hazeltine, and four of the crew were missing; they had been either stunned by the explosion or drowned as the vessel went down.

Pickering, who commanded the Housatonic, was severely bruised by the explosion. The torpedo-boat, which was designed to be wholly submerged if required, went down with the four men in her. She had on former occasions drowned her crews.

Notwithstanding the destruction of this torpedo-boat and her entire crew, another one, at 1 A.M. of March 6th, in North Edisto River, was discovered rapidly approaching the block-

---

[1] Had the vessel gone *ahead* instead of backing, when she slipped her cable, there is a reasonable probability that she would have escaped destruction.

ading steamer Memphis. The chain was slipped and the men called to quarters; the boat was then under the port quarter and no gun could be brought to bear on her; a rapid fire of small arms was delivered into what looked like a hatchway near her centre; she dropped a short distance astern, and came up again immediately under the stern. The propeller then revolving is supposed to have caught and broken the torpedo pole. The boat then appeared disabled and drifted up the river. An armed boat was sent to capture her, but the search was unsuccessful.

On the night of April 18th, the Wabash, lying off Charleston, was made the object of an unsuccessful attack. At 9.45 P.M. a boat was discovered on the starboard quarter, one hundred and fifty yards distant, moving up rapidly against the tide until abeam; then she turned and moved directly for the ship. The engines of the Wabash were started ahead, the chain slipped and the starboad battery and small arms opened fire upon the boat. Two round shot struck it, or near it when about forty yards distant from the vessel, and the boat was seen no more. The vessel cruised around the spot with men at the guns and marines ready with small arms, and signal was made to the blockading vessels of proximity of danger, but the boat was not seen by any of them.

The enemy not only used torpedo-boats with some success, but in the adjacent waters fixed torpedoes, which exploded on contact. By this means, in the St. John's River, fifteen miles above Jacksonville, on the 1st of April, the army transport Maple Leaf was sunk; and on the 10th of May, below the city, the transport Weed, and a third one later on. The navy steamer Harvest Moon, nearly one year later, was sunk in the same manner below Georgetown, and the Patapsco (monitor), particularly described hereafter, near Fort Sumter.

On May 23d, in an endeavor to aid army operations at Volusia, on the St. John's River, the tug Columbine, Ensign Sanborn, having an army detachment of 25 men on board, was fired upon, disabled, and run aground from the wheel-ropes having been cut by the shells, at Horse Shoe Landing, on her return from Volusia. Master's mate John Davis, "while nobly performing his duty," was killed; also 16 soldiers were killed or missing, and 5 wounded. The remainder were taken prisoners, and the vessel set on fire without removing the dead.

On June 3, 1864, the Water Witch, Commander Pendergrast, blockading in Ossabaw Sound, was boarded and captured, only one man (a "contraband") escaping. Seven cotton barges, carrying 150 men, approached the vessel, the night being dark and squally; they were, in fact, alongside almost as soon as discovered, and although boarding nettings were up, the vessel soon became a prize. The Water Witch lost 1 man killed, 13 wounded, and 2 missing. The Confederates lost their leader, Lieutenant Pelot of their navy, 8 or 10 killed, and 15 or 20 wounded.

Toward the middle of June Admiral Dahlgren received information from the Navy Department "that the enemy meditated a simultaneous movement on the blockade, inside and out, in order to cover the exit of a large quantity of cotton."

This led to some strategic movements on the part of the army along the Stono River, aided by a naval force in those waters. These operations were concluded on the 9th of July, after which General Foster returned to Port Royal. General Schimmelfennig, in command of the troops on James Island, in a letter to the admiral says : "I take pleasure in informing you of the excellent practice by your gunboats and monitors on Stono River yesterday. They drove the

enemy out of his rifle-pits, and prevented him from erecting
an earthwork which he had commenced."

Commander G. M. Colvocoresses commanded the sailing
sloop-of-war Saratoga, lying in Doboy Sound, Ga., blockading. He had received a copy of a newspaper published in
Savannah, and observed that a county meeting had been
called in his vicinity for the purpose of organizing a coast-
guard.

As he regarded himself and those under his command as
interested parties, he determined to attend, and for the purpose of holding a controlling majority, took with him 8 officers and 107 sailors and marines, supplied with bullets in lieu
of ballots, leaving the vessel on the afternoon of the 2d of
August. His party reached the mainland at 9 P.M., and the
boats with their crews were sent back to the ship, to meet
him the next day at the Ridge Landing, somewhat nearer
the ship. A skirmish line was thrown out, and the advance
begun. At midnight a house was reached, which was silently
passed, and the main road toward Savannah was taken.
Arriving at a bridge, the expedition was halted ; an officer
with seven men was detailed to guard it and to capture all
persons coming from the direction of the McIntosh County
Court House. At 11 A.M. on the following day the bridge
was to be burned, which would prevent a possible attendance also of some three hundred Confederate cavalry supposed to be encamped some miles beyond.

The vicinity of the court house was reached, the party
divided, Captain Colvocoresses taking half the force and Ensign Rogers the remainder, the one proceeding to the right,
the other to the left. "When they arrived at the building
they took to the neighboring woods, and lay there concealed
until the proper time for making the attack. At 11 the sig-

nal was made, and the parties charged at double-quick, and completely surrounded the meeting, only three persons escaping." The officer left at the bridge burned it, and soon after came up, with eleven prisoners and a number of horses and buggies.

The captain then explained his designs to the persons who were found at the county meeting, placed them between lines of sailors and took up a line of march for the Ridge landing. As they proceeded, the party was augmented by three others, who had been somewhat tardy in leaving home. Another bridge was passed over, and set on fire. A large encampment near the road, which was to have been occupied by a force under organization for coast defence, was also burned. The expedition reached the point of embarkation at sunset, with twenty-six prisoners and twenty-two horses. It was ascertained that several of the prisoners held important county offices. It is not stated whether he took them and the horses on board, or paroled them. The attendance of Captain Colvocoresses was certainly quite a surprise, and was doubtless regarded as an unwarranted interference.

On a subsequent occasion Colvocoresses made another descent in the same vicinity, and captured a lieutenant and 28 cavalry, with their arms and equipments, and burned their encampment. He also destroyed two large salt works, and a bridge on the main road to Savannah.

Returning to Charleston we find the monitor Patapsco destroyed a sloop on shore near Moultrie, setting her on fire on the morning of November 5th, by the use of 150-pounder shells.

On the 10th the enemy, finding the Pontiac within range, in an endeavor to pick up her anchor that she had previously slipped, she received a rifle-shell which struck her bows, killing 5 and wounding 7 men; it did serious damage also to the woodwork, and broke a bronze casting connecting the stem to the keel. For the time the vessel was disabled.

Late in November, 1864, General Foster asked navy cooperation "in an attack to assist the movement of General Sherman." For this purpose a force of 500 men was organized and placed under Commander George H. Preble. Four depleted companies of marines formed a part, and two navy howitzers with their complement of men.

On the evening of the 28th, this force at Port Royal was embarked on the Mingoe, Pontiac, and Sonoma, but the fog was too thick to permit a movement. At 4 A.M. it broke away partially, and the vessels got over the shoals into Broad River, the Pontiac ahead, with the only pilot on board, followed by eight other navy vessels. At eight o'clock the admiral found himself at Boyd's Landing, the point designated, twenty miles up the river, with the Pawnee, Mingoe, Pontiac, Sonoma, and Winona. The Wissahickon had grounded below and did not get up. The army transports had not yet arrived, but the transport with General Hatch came in sight very soon, followed by others, and the troops began to debark, as also the naval force before named organized for landing. General Foster arrived at 2 P.M., and army transports continued to arrive with troops and field artillery throughout the day.

The general and the admiral returned in the afternoon, the latter ordering back two or three vessels not required. No advance was made toward the railroad at Grahamsville until the 30th. The enemy had by this time collected in force. General Hatch, who commanded, found "further progress barred by a work which looked upon the road, and was covered on the flanks by heavy woods and other obstructions."

On the 4th of December General Gillmore made a reconnoissance up the Whale Branch to Port Royal Ferry, and the
admiral went into the Coosawhatchie River with the Pawnee
and Sonoma, where the enemy had placed two guns to bar a
passage. The stream was too narrow and winding to get
nearer than two thousand yards, and the enemy, after firing
a few shots retired to the woods. At the same time, General
Hatch pushed out a light column from his right, and the
Pontiac sent her boats up the creek from Boyd's Landing,
the affair being made to assume the appearance of a demonstration.

The general and the admiral determined to move the
force up to Tulifiny Creek with the expressed intention of
destroying the railroad above. On the 5th of December
(1864), the greater number of the troops and the naval
force on shore were embarked, leaving General Hatch with
a sufficient force to maintain his position, aided by the gunboat Pontiac. At 8 A.M. of the 6th, the vessels had reached
a landing on the right bank of the Tulifiny, but low water
prevented landing, except in boats, which was accomplished
with as much despatch as possible, and the whole force
moved up the single road lying between the river Coosawhatchie and the Tulifiny. The line of railroad, however, was
not reached, and if anything was effected by the movement,
it was in diverting a force from opposing the march of General Sherman to the sea.

On the 11th the admiral left the Tulifiny, and the following day reported the presence of General Sherman's troops
near Savannah. His occupation of that city on the 22d practically ended all naval operations that were not auxiliary to
the movements of the army, except that of blockade. Rainy
weather held the Union army fast until January 24th. General Sherman was then at Beaufort, S. C., with the right

7*

wing, which some time before had been sent in transports from Savannah. As the rains had ceased, and the roads were passable, he left for Pocotaligo, and the following day demonstrated on Salkahatchie. He requested that the admiral would fire heavy guns high up on the Edisto River, to make the enemy uneasy on that flank, and to develop whether they intended to hold fast both to Charleston and to Columbia.

During January there were constant night demonstrations of the monitors near the forts at the entrance to Charleston harbor, which led the Confederates to believe that it was intended to attempt an entrance. This caused the placing of sixteen torpedoes just without the line of rope obstructions on the afternoon of the 15th of January, and the loss of the monitor Patapsco through exploding one of them a few hours thereafter. She was on the advance picket line, attended by two tugs with several row-boats, dragging for torpedoes. She had drifted up with a strong flood-tide near the line of rope obstructions, and had already steamed out twice before, when in repeating this she struck a torpedo which exploded on the port side, under the fore-body of the vessel. The force was sufficiently great to raise the deck, through which the smoke issued. In fifteen seconds the vessel sunk in five fathoms of water, and very near the spot where she had been held on an obstruction for some minutes on April 7, 1863. An officer and sailor on the turret jumped at once to the falls of a boat, and barely succeeded in clearing them before the vessel went down with 62 of the officers and men. This occurred soon after 8 P.M. One man in the windlass-room, the engineer and firemen on watch, and one man, who rushed from the berth-deck through the fire-room, were the only persons who were below and escaped death. Five officers who were on deck at the time, and 38 men escaped, among whom were the Commander, Quackenbush, and Lieutenant William T. Sampson, the executive officer.

The Dai Ching was directed to proceed up the Combahee from St. Helena on January 26th, for the purpose of supporting an army force if required. In the vicinity of Tar Bluff the river is small and crooked, and when a battery opened on her the pilot left the wheel and she ran aground before Chaplin, who commanded, was aware of the fact. The tug Clover, which accompanied her, could not be brought up to get the vessel off, as her captain would not understand or obey signals. The vessel was defended for seven hours, when the carriage of the 100-pounder rifle was disabled by the fire of the enemy. She was then set on fire, the crew landed, and, with the exception of five, escaped to the tug, lying four miles below. Three of the officers and six men were wounded, and sent down in a boat. The armament of the vessel was, one 100-pounder rifle and two small guns.

The Pawnee, Sonoma, and tug Daffodil, lying in the waters of the North Edisto, on the 9th of February engaged three batteries of the enemy, respectively armed with six, four, and two guns. They were situated on Togado Creek, in such manner as to support each other against an attack from gunboats. In the evening the enemy ceased firing; the Pawnee had been struck ten times without serious injury, and the other vessels had received two hits each, without loss of life. Various other engagements occurred about the same time, and until the evacuation of Charleston. Naval forces made attacks of this kind for the purpose of keeping the troops of the enemy from concentrating, and to perplex him as to what were the actual movements of Sherman's army.

In order to aid an army diversion on Bull's Bay, eighteen miles north of Charleston, the admiral despatched, on the evening of the 11th of February, the Shenandoah, Juniata, Canandaigua, Georgia, Pawnee, Sonoma, Ottawa, Winona, Wando, and Iris to that point. A large number of army transports had arrived also, with troops under the command of General Potter. A preliminary to landing was to find a favorable depth of water and hard ground. It was only on the evening of the 17th that a satisfactory landing-place was found, and 750 men were disembarked under cover of howitzers in launches; the remainder of the force landed the following day, and took up its line of march for Charleston. As on the morning of the 18th that city was found evacuated, it does not seem necessary to note further than the return of the naval vessels and transports to Charleston.

Commander Belknap, in the monitor Canonicus, lying near Moultrie, reported heavy fires in Charleston and on James Island at 1 A.M. (18th), and heavy explosions were heard. At daylight haze and smoke shut out the view. At 8 A.M. he threw two heavy shells into Moultrie, and received no reply; the Confederate flag was, however, flying over it and Castle Pinckney, and the city of Charleston also, but no movement was visible. At this time a magazine blew up in Battery Bee.

The forts had been evacuated the previous night, and an army boat from Morris Island hoisted the flag over Moultrie. About 9 A.M. the Canonicus sent a boat and took possession of a small steamboat, a blockade-runner, under English colors, that had been on shore for several days near Fort Moultrie.

The admiral reports that upon the evacuation of Charleston, he found the ram Columbia, which had been ready for service on January 12th, and grounding coming out of dock, had been seriously strained through lying on uneven bottom. Her length was 209 feet; extreme beam, 49 feet, with a casemate 65 feet in length pierced for 6 guns, pivoting as before described in the Atlanta, captured in Wassaw Sound in 1863. She had two high-pressure engines, and was plated on the casemate with six inches of iron. A cigar-shaped steamer 160 feet long, supposed to be of sufficient capacity to carry from two hundred and fifty to three hundred bales of cotton, was also found.

Three torpedo boats fitted for service were found sunk in Cooper River. Two were raised, and one of them put in working order. Their length was 64 feet, diameter 5½ feet, and they had a speed of five knots. Six others were under repairs or being completed, and two ready for service.

Higher up in the Cooper River the rams Chicora, Palmetto, and Charleston, had been destroyed and sunk on the evacuation of the city. The fourth, Columbia, has already been described.[1]

After the fall of Charleston, under instructions from the Department, Admiral Dahlgren proceeded to gain information as to the character of the obstructions and defences within Charleston Harbor.

It was asserted by the Secretary of the Navy before the Joint Congressional Committee on the Conduct of the War that the water defences within Charleston harbor had been materially strengthened after the monitor attack of April 7, 1863. This does not seem to be supported by the testimony in Dahlgren's report.

Several persons, whose duties had been to make and plant torpedoes and to make and put down rope obstructions, were examined, and the following facts elicited:

Several months before the spring of 1863 a boom torpedo was placed between battery Bee and Sumter, but it was

---

[1] Admiral Dahlgren's report.

found to be impracticable, and a continuous rope netting was then tried, which was also swept out of position by the strong tides. The rope obstructions were then cut in lengths of one hundred feet and moored at one end, and three rows of them were then placed so as to swing with the tide, the intervals between them being about one hundred feet, and having about the same distances between the lines. A rope having a diameter of nearly two inches was secured to beer casks tarred, or to pine logs, to serve as floats at distances apart of fifteen feet. Over this rope were secured bights of smaller rope, each end being several fathoms in length. The movement of the water by a propeller, it was supposed, would draw these rope-ends within its influence, and thus foul the propeller.

A row of piles was driven across the middle ground and into the channel, just below Fort Johnson. This was intact in April, 1863, but by the autumn many of the piles had washed out.

In the Hog Island channel a heavy boom obstruction was maintained throughout the war, and several sets of torpedoes on inclined planes beneath the water, the frames resting on the bottom, having usually fifteen torpedoes on each frame.

All of the inferior channels and Cooper River were protected in like manner by torpedoes placed in sets on submarine inclined planes, upon which several of the Confederate vessels had been blown up at various times.

The main channel, leading up close under the guns of Fort Johnson, had three large boiler torpedoes, stated to be in good condition, and having one thousand or more pounds of powder within them. They were on range lines, and intended to be exploded by electricity.

At Fort Johnson and on the wharves of Charleston were a

great many barrel torpedoes fitted for placing in that chan-
nel-way and off Charleston with the least possible delay.
They were of the same construction as those which had sunk
three army transports in St. John's River, the monitor Patapsco off the harbor on January 15th, and the flag-ship Harvest Moon below Georgetown after the fall of Charleston.
These barrel torpedoes were held by their moorings some
eight feet below the ordinary surface of the water, and were
fitted so as to explode on contact.

On the wharf at Charleston was found one of these inclined frames ready for use, with thirty torpedoes fitted for
it; they also were constructed to explode by contact.

A boiler torpedo, probably of English fabrication, was
found on the wharf ready for charging, together with a large
quantity of insulated copper wire protected by a hemp wrap-
ping overlaid with wire.

The torpedoes made for the ironclads, or rams, as they
were called, and for the torpedo-boats, were elongated copper cylinders ten inches in diameter, with hemispherical
ends, thirty-two inches long, each having several screw sockets for eight fuses so as to present points of explosion widely
separated. The charge was one hundred and thirty-four
pounds of powder.

Another was of copper, barrel-shaped, tapering to points
on the ends; it had sockets for seven fuses on the upper
bilge, and contained one hundred and thirty-four pounds of
powder.[1]

During the autumn of 1863 reconnoitering boats were sent
almost nightly, when the weather permitted, into the mouth
of Charleston Harbor, and diverse reports were brought to
the admiral in respect to the character of the channel ob-

---

[1] Number 16, Professional Papers, Corps U. S. Engineers, contains full descrip-
tions of these harbor obstructions, etc.

structions. To settle this point as to the main ship channel, a commander on duty proposed making an examination, which met the approval of the admiral. To facilitate this examination General Terry placed a light on Cumming's Point, in order that a fixed point might be known. At midnight Commander Ammen left the New Ironsides in a six-oared boat, and after reaching the vicinity of the obstructions a small grapnel with ten fathoms of line was dragged within and around to the north of Sumter until the light on Cumming's Point was opened well out to the westward of Sumter. The boat was then directed outward further from the fort than when entering, and at the turn of the tide the black buoys sustaining one section of the rope obstructions were found in a cluster. This was partially cut away and taken out; the rope was considerably rotted. The admiral was informed as above, and that no difficulty whatever existed in clearing away these rope obstructions just previous to his entering whenever he had a force which he deemed sufficient.

It is well known that a month or so later the Navy Department hoped to send several monitors to strengthen the force off Charleston. On p. 419 of "Memoir of Admiral Dahlgren" is found the following:

"October 22d, 11 A.M. [1863].—I held a council of war in regard to entering the harbor of Charleston when the seven monitors were ready, which would be the second week in November.

"There were eight captains of ironclads and two staff officers. The object was not to have the advice for myself, but to comply with the request of the Secretary, who asked for the opinion of these officers. We began at eleven and finished at five. The four junior officers voted for an attack with seven ironclads. The six seniors were averse. The intelligence was largely with the latter. One of the juniors seemed hardly to know what he was about. So my views were sustained. The majority were for waiting till the reinforcements arrived in December."

The import of an ironclad or, more properly speaking, a monitor attack has not been fully understood by many intelligent persons. Had the absolute destruction of all the vessels entering been assured in the event of failure, and had there remained a sufficient reserve force of any character off the harbor to assure the maintenance of the blockade against the ironclads of the enemy within the harbor, probably every captain at the "Council of War" would have been in favor of entering, but with the chances of some of the vessels grounding, and of others being sunk in shoal water by torpedoes, and afterward raised and employed by the enemy, there was too much danger of losing control of the coast to make it desirable to take the risk. These considerations would naturally be controlling proportionately with the damage that might follow a lack of success in an attack, and would be quite independent of the loss of vessels and of men in making one with reasonable probability of success.

From pages 553 to 593 of "Memoir of Admiral Dahlgren" will be found the text of an official letter of the admiral to the Department, explanatory of the ironclad question in relation to the taking of Charleston. It is dated October 16, 1865, and as we are informed on the preceding page by the editor: "We hold the manuscript in our possession, thus endorsed by the admiral: 'Withdrawn November 8, 1865, *the Department objecting* to the introduction of Dupont and the opinions of officers, and to those parts where it is assumed, or seems to be so, that the Department did not send vessels enough.—J. A. D.'"

The editor of the "Memoir," adds: "In other words, the Department was too inimical and revengeful in feeling to Dupont *to be just*, or to be willing to have him relieved in any measure through any act of theirs, of any possible effect resulting from their continuous displeasure."

The pages preceding the quotations were written before
the perusal of the "Memoir." If the reader of this volume
labors under the idea that either Admiral Dupont or Admiral Dahlgren should have gone to Charleston or made the
attempt, the pages of the "Memoir" may enlighten him.

Bearing in mind that the Department did not think it
worth while to give publicity to a letter which it evoked in
May, 1863, signed by all of the commanders of ironclads in
those waters,[1] and that after the Civil War had ended, it had
declined to receive an able and perfectly proper letter concerning operations before Charleston during the period of
command of its writer, the Department seems to have wished
to spare the reading public the doubts and perplexities
which the Dutch judge avoided by not listening to the other
side of a case. He had heard the one side and declined
hearing the other, as he was then perfectly at rest in regard
to the merit of the question. If he heard the other side his
mind would be filled with perplexity and doubt. The Department had made its statement as to the invulnerability
and sufficiency of the monitors to take Charleston, and that
was all that the public should require or listen to, *even after
the war was over;* what the commanders of the ironclads
wrote about them, and what Admiral Dahlgren had to say
about going to Charleston, if given to the public, would only
cause doubt and perplexity.

On page 436 of the "Memoir" will be found the following
from the diary of Dahlgren: "January 12.—Mail came. . . .
Among the letters was one from the Secretary and one from
Fox, both prodigiously flattering, and asking for a good character to the monitors." Here is truly "food for reflection."

_____

[1] Captain John Rodgers and Commanders Daniel Ammen, George W. Rodgers,
D. M. Fairfax, and John Downes, were the signers, and the letter afterward seen
by Captain Drayton and Commander Worden was concurred in by them.

N O R T H
C A R O L I
ONSLOW BAY
78
77
36
35
Weldon
Winton
Enfield
Edwards' Fy.
Fishing Creek
Roanoke River
Hamilton
Tarboro
Williamston
Tar R.
Greenville
Contentnea Creek
Goldsboro
Kinston
Neuse River
NEWBERN
Trenton
Trent River
Kenansville
Onslow C.H.
New River
Holly Shelter Swamp
Bogue Inlet
New River Inlet
New Topsail Inlet
Old Topsail Inlet
WILMINGTON
Wrightsville
Masonboro Inlet
Brunswick
Sugar Loaf
Smithville
FORT FISHER
Federal Pt.
New Inlet
SMITH'S I.
Cape Fear
Bald Head Pt.

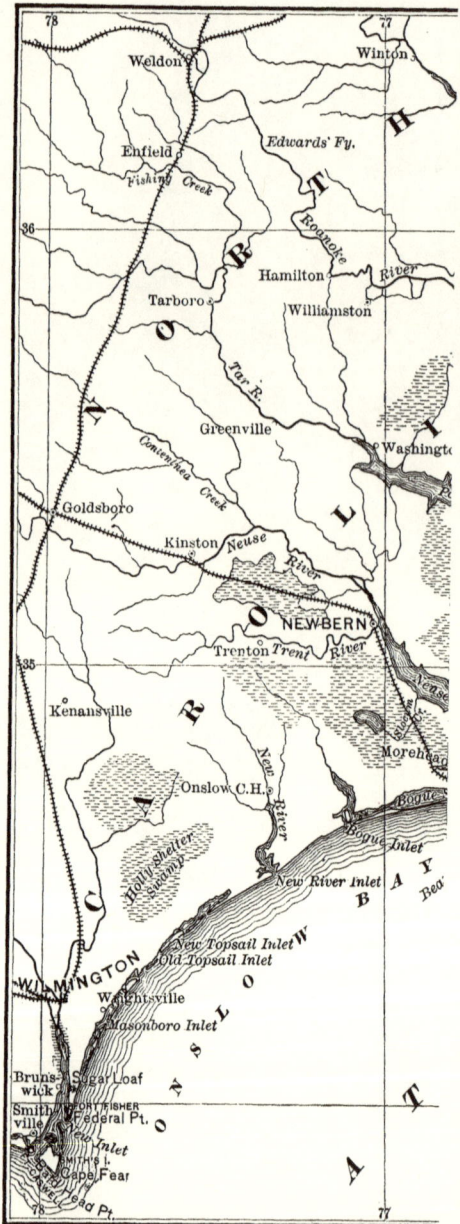

Elizabeth City

Perquimans R.

ertford

lenton

ALBEMARLE SOUND

36

outh

Red Stone Pt.

ROANOKE I.

Croton Inlet

Stumpy P.

L. Phelps

Loggerhead Inlet

Kinnakeet

EGG SHOAL

Cape Hatteras

Hatteras Inlet

Portsmouth

Ocracoke Inlet

35

Beaufort

Cape Lookout

PAMLICO SOUND

RALEIGH BAY

OCEAN

ATLANTIC

COAST AND SOUNDS
OF
NORTH CAROLINA.

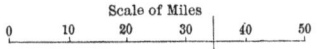

Scale of Miles

0   10   20   30   40   50

76

34

CHAPTER VIII.

THE reader who has examined the coast charts or maps of the United States is aware that low, long, sandy islets fringe almost the entire coasts of what are known as the Southern States. There are numerous inlets between these islets that have a certain degree of permanency, but many of them close for a series of years, and are found open again after some gale of unusual severity.

Between Cape Henry and Cape Hatteras are several of these ephemeral "inlets" or channels, between the sea and inland waters. Thirteen miles south of Cape Hatteras is Hatteras Inlet, and eighteen miles farther, Ocracoke, the bend of that coast from the cape being west-southwest and, looking toward Cape Henry, north by east.

Hatteras Inlet has more depth over the bar, and its regimen is more permanent than any of the other entrances into the sounds of North Carolina. It was the most convenient entrance for the distribution of supplies to the Confederate army in Virginia, and bordering the inland waters were produced in great abundance what are known as "naval stores." These, and considerable cotton grown in that region, gave ample cargoes for outward bound blockade-running vessels.

No sooner was the Civil War fairly begun, and the Navy Yard at Norfolk in the possession of the Confederates, than heavy guns were transported from that point, and the inlets at Hatteras and Ocracoke fortified.

From the Sounds of Albemarle and Pamlico through Hatteras and Ocracoke Inlets, small vessels made raids to capture vessels under the National flag that might be passing along the coast, and for a time these efforts were well rewarded.

The shoal water extending far out gave these entrances a certain amount of immunity to the raids of privateers and blockade-runners, and it was hoped would prevent a successful attack on the batteries designed to protect these entrances. Hatteras Inlet has on its bar, at ordinary high water, usually fourteen feet, the depth varying one or two feet more or less from the effects of gales and freshets on the inland waters. Within this outer bar, at a distance of nearly one mile, is what is known as the "bulkhead," a bank of sand separating the deeper waters of the sounds and those within the exterior bar. At ordinary high tide there is a depth of seven feet; when heavy southeast winds bank up the waters, as they do from time to time, nearly double this depth may be found temporarily on the "bulkhead." Once within the outer bar, by means of lighterage, easily effected in smooth water, vessels with cargoes can readily lessen their draught so as to cross the bulkhead; with vessels having batteries and fitted for war purposes, the difficulty of entering is much greater, and where the required depth is eight or nine feet, considerable delay occurs in awaiting the banking up of the waters.

The Navy Department, appreciating the importance of Hatteras Inlet, the principal one affording access to the magnificent sound with its wide ramifications, directed in 1861 the preparation and concentration of such naval force as was available, and invited an army co-operation for its capture.

The military importance of holding Hatteras Inlet was at that time quite unappreciated save by the Navy Department. The transport steamers were chartered by the navy and commanded by navy officers, and the detachment of troops "was to return to Fort Monroe after the expedition." "It was not intended that you (General Wood) should take any further action in relation to the expedition than to provide such troops for the same as on conference with Commodore Stringham should be found sufficient for the purpose. The expedition originated in the Navy Department, and is under its control." [1]

General Wool, at Fort Monroe, on the 25th of August, 1861, made a detail of 860 men under General B. F. Butler, who was directed to report, as soon as his troops were ready, to Flag-Officer Stringham. "As soon as the object of the expedition is attained, the detachment will return to Fort Monroe."

The following day, the transport steamer Adelaide, Commander Henry S. Stellwagen, and the Peabody, Lieutenant R. R. Lowry, took on board 500 of the 20th Regiment N. Y. Volunteers, Colonel Weber; 220 of the Ninth N. Y. Volunteers, Colonel Hawkins; 100 of the Union Coast Guard, Captain Nixon, and 60 of the 2d U. S. Artillery, Lieutenant Larned. With commendable alacrity they left the same day (26th of August) with the flag-ship of Stringham, the steam frigate Minnesota, Captain G. I. Van Brunt; steam frigate Wabash, Captain Samuel Mercer; Monticello, Commander John P. Gillis; Pawnee, Commander S. C. Rowan, and Revenue Cutter Harriet Lane, Captain John Faunce. The army tug Fanny, under the command of Lieutenant Peirce Crosby, of the navy, also accompanied the expedition.

---

[1] Letter of Assistant Adjutant-General, Rebellion Records, Vol. IV., p. 580.

The transports towed two schooners, having large, unwieldy iron surf-boats on board.

The same afternoon this force rounded Cape Hatteras and anchored off shore near the proposed point of debarkation, which was some three miles east of Hatteras Inlet. Surf-boats were hoisted out, and preparations made to facilitate debarkation early in the morning. At daylight on that day Major-General Butler left the flag-ship for the Harriet Lane with the company of marines on that vessel, Captain Shuttleworth, which augmented his command to 915 men.

Signal was made from the flag-ship to disembark troops, and the Pawnee, Monticello, and Harriet Lane to assist the work and cover the landing.

While this was in process of execution, at 8.45 A.M., the Wabash took in tow the sailing frigate Cumberland that had joined the force after arrival off the bar, and followed by the flag-ship Minnesota, led in to attack the batteries known to have been placed for the defence of the inlet.

Soon after, the steam frigate Susquehanna appeared and signal was made her to engage the batteries. The first object of attack was what was afterward known as Fort Clark, situated a half mile east from the principal work at the immediate entrance to the inlet. The vessels had opened fire beyond extreme range and the fort replied.

The Minnesota passed inside and ahead and with her consorts soon caused the battery of five guns, which was without a bomb-proof, to be deserted, the men passing through or around the shallow lagoon, to reach and take shelter in the principal work, which was also on the eastern side of the inlet and known as Fort Hatteras. Shortly after noon it was observed that no flags were flying on either fort, and, as seen from the flag-ship, the nearest work, Clark, was evidently abandoned.

In the meantime the attempt to land had been only partially successful. As the heavy iron surf-boats struck the beach they were thrown high upon it, there to remain, and two flat-boats landing troops were stove. In this manner 315 troops, including 50 United States Artillery, 55 marines, and 2 navy howitzers were thrown on shore without provisions or supplies of any kind, and much of their ammunition was wetted. The surf was heavy and increasing and further attempts to land were discontinued. A movement by the troops was made along the beach toward Fort Clark, and at 2 P.M. the Union flag was hoisted over it by them.

The firing from the fleet had been suspended since 12.30, from the supposition of an intended surrender, as the larger fort was not flying a flag, and was silent.

The Monticello was directed at 4 P.M. to effect an entrance to the inlet, and when well within the breakers Fort Hatteras opened on her and received at once the fire from the Minnesota, Susquehanna, and the Pawnee, which latter vessel had joined in the attack, and soon after was followed by the Harriet Lane with her battery of small rifled guns, effective at the long range then necessary to reach the fort. The Wabash at the time was employed in towing the sailing frigate Cumberland into an offing, as it was supposed the fort had surrendered.

The bombardment continued until sunset, for the most part ineffective, from too great a distance, when the larger vessels hauled off for the night, and the Pawnee, Monticello, and Harriet Lane went up the coast toward the cape and anchored close to the beach for the purpose of protecting the troops, they having withdrawn from the immediate vicinity of the forts.

On the following day (28th) at 5.30 A.M. signal was made to prepare for action and follow the motions of the flag-ship; the weather, which had been threatening, had become pleasant and the sea less rough.

While the heavier vessels led in to attack Fort Hatteras, the Monticello was directed to embark or provision the troops on shore, at the option of General Butler.

The landed troops had during the night thrown up a sand battery, placed their howitzers in it, and had opened on the vessels in the sound in communication with the fort, which seems to have materially disconcerted the enemy.

At 8 A.M. the Susquehanna, leading, opened fire on the fort, the Wabash following; the Minnesota then took position between the two. The vessels anchored, and maintained their fire, and were soon followed by the sailing frigate Cumberland, which anchored also in excellent position and commenced firing with effect. It was soon seen that the pivot guns did the principal part of the work, and this fact became the more apparent as the flag-officer reported "the enemy returned our fire throughout the engagement, but with no effect, their shot falling short," from the fact, doubtless, of not being able to obtain sufficient elevation. Half an hour before the end of the engagement the Harriet Lane, added the fire of her battery. The defenders, seeing that the fire from their guns was wholly ineffective, and having suffered considerable loss from the careful firing of the pivot guns in the fleet, hoisted a white flag at 11.10 A.M., when the firing ceased. The fire from the batteries on the ships' broadside had been suspended soon after going into action, the fort being in range only by giving great, if not extreme elevation to the guns. The plunging effect of the shells from the heavy pivot guns on the bomb-proof was very great, threatening breaking through; one shell had found its way through a ventilator, and the safety of the magazine was imperilled.

On the appearance of the white flag the troops on the beach marched toward the fort, the army transport and the tug Fanny, with General Butler on board, passed the bar and anchored within the inlet, and the Harriet Lane, in an attempt to do so, grounded, and did not succeed in getting off for some days. Three steamers and several schooners of the enemy that were within the sound watching events, and prepared to throw in reinforcements, left when a shell was thrown at them from the Fanny.

In this engagement not a single casualty occurred to the National forces. In Fort Clark two killed were found, and from Fort Hatteras several killed and a number of wounded were known to have been taken previous to the surrender— 13 wounded were among the prisoners.

The guns of the attacking vessels numbered one hundred and fifty-eight; the pivot guns, ten in number, were the most effective, to which may be added the five small rifled guns of the Harriet Lane. The character of the forts and the batteries captured will appear hereafter.

Articles of capitulation were signed between Flag-Officer Stringham and General Butler on the one part, and Samuel Barron, commanding naval force, Colonel Martin, commanding land forces, and Major Andrews, commanding Fort Hatteras: "It is stipulated and agreed by the contracting parties on the part of the United States Government, that the officers and men shall receive the treatment due to prisoners of war." Six hundred and fifteen prisoners were taken, among whom were several who some months before had been officers in the National navy. It is known that a certain number of the garrison escaped previous to the capitulation, some of whom were wounded.

Flag-Officer Barron, in his report to the Confederate Navy Department, states that he arrived at Hatteras Inlet early on

II.—8

the 28th, in the steamer Winslow, accompanied by Colonel
Bradford, Chief of Ordnance of North Carolina, and Lieutenants Murdaugh and Sharpe of the Confederate navy. He
found Colonel Winslow, in command of Fort Hatteras, very
much exhausted from exposure and hard fighting the previous day. He says : " The garrison had hoped for the arrival
of a regiment from Newbern the previous night, which would
have been employed in an attempted assault of Fort Clark,
held by the Union troops, the appearance of bad weather
having caused the protecting vessels to seek an offing. Early
in the morning the fleet again stood in, took positions and
opened fire, and in addition the Union troops had, during
the night, erected a battery of rifled field-guns near to Fort
Clark, which also opened on us.

"During the first hour, the shells from the ships fell
short, the fort only firing occasionally to get range, to reserve the very limited supply of ammunition until the vessels
might find it necessary to come nearer in ; but they, after
some practice, got the exact range of the IX-, X-, and XI-inch
guns, and did not find it necessary to alter their positions,
while not a shot from our battery reached them with the
greatest elevation we could get. . . . Several hours had
thus passed, without the ability to damage our adversaries,
and just at this time, the magazine being reported to be
on fire, a shell having fallen through the ventilator of the
bomb-proof into the room adjoining the principal magazine,
a white flag was ordered to be shown, when the firing ceased,
and the surrender was made."

A very succinct report of General Gatlin, Commander-in-
Chief in North Carolina, will be found on p. 573, Vol. IV., of
the "Rebellion Records," published by the Government. It
concludes as follows : "I may be permitted to conclude this
rapid sketch by stating that we failed to make timely efforts

to maintain the ascendancy on Pamlico Sound, and thus admitted Burnside's fleet without a contest; we failed to put a proper force on Roanoke Island, and thus lost the key to our interior coast; and we failed to furnish General Branch with a reasonable force, and thus lost the important town of Newbern."

On consultation with Flag-Officer Stringham and Commander Stellwagen, General Butler determined to leave the troops and hold the fort until he could get some further instructions from the Government.

He adds : "The importance of the point cannot be overrated. When the channel is buoyed out any vessel may carry fifteen feet of water over it with ease. Once inside, there is a safe harbor and anchorage in all weathers. From there the whole coast of Virginia and North Carolina, from Norfolk to Cape Lookout, is within our reach by light-draught vessels, which cannot possibly live at sea during the winter months. From it offensive operations may be made upon the whole coast of North Carolina to Bogue Inlet, extending many miles inland to Washington, Newbern, and Beaufort. In the language of the chief-engineer of the rebels, Colonel Thompson, in an official report, 'it is the key of the Albemarle.' In my judgment, it is a station second in importance only to Fortress Monroe on this coast. As a depot for coaling and supplies for the blockading squadron it is invaluable. As a harbor for our coasting trade, or inlet from the winter storms or from pirates, it is of the first importance." Future events fully confirmed the opinion of General Butler as to the value of Hatteras Inlet in a military point of view, and no less in respect to all of the advantages so clearly expressed.

Twenty-five pieces of artillery, one thousand stand of arms, a large quantity of ordnance stores, provisions, three valuable prizes, two light-boats, and four stands of colors were captured.

From the 25th of June to the capture of Hatteras Inlet, on the 28th of August, one bark, seven brigs, and eight schooners had been captured by "privateers" or Confederate cruisers, and had been brought into the inlet.

The flag-ship proceeded to New York on the 30th with the prisoners on board; the Pawnee and Monticello remained at the inlet, the remainder of the vessels proceeded to different points of blockade, the company of regulars returned to Fortress Monroe, and the other troops remained as a garrison until further orders. Hatteras Inlet became a depot of supplies for coal and the other wants of vessels blockading, and in the coming months a centre of operations. As soon as necessary surroundings were satisfactorily arranged, Commander Rowan, of the Pawnee, became active.

On the 16th of September he sent Lieutenant Maxwell to the fort commanding Ocracoke Inlet, situated on Beacon Island, some twenty miles distant. He was in command of the army tug Fanny, and carried 61 men belonging to what was known as the naval brigade, commanded by Colonel Hawkins.

The launch of the Pawnee was in tow, manned by 22 sailors and 6 marines, armed with a 12-pounder howitzer, commanded by Lieutenant Eastman. The fort was situated on the sea face of Beacon Island, and was found deserted. It was octagonal, having in the centre a bomb-proof one hundred feet square, with the magazine within, and four large water-tanks directly over it. Twenty platforms for guns were partially destroyed by fire; the gun-carriages had been burned, four VIII-inch navy shell-guns, and fourteen heavy 32-pounders were found; two guns had been carried away the previous day. The men were landed without delay, the trunnions of the guns broken off, and at the same time the launch went to the town of Portsmouth near by, where three VIII-inch navy guns were found lying on the beach and one mounted on its carriage. The attempt to make a battery had been abandoned in consequence of the taking of the forts at Hatteras Inlet. The town, which had some five hundred inhabitants before the attack on the Hatteras Inlet forts, was nearly deserted; those remaining said they were Union men, and expressed their gratification at seeing their old flag again. "Lieutenant Eastman assured them that they would not be molested by the Government, and that they might return to their usual occupations." He then destroyed the guns and returned to the Fanny. The combustible material had been placed within and around the bomb-proof of Fort Ocracoke, which was supported by heavy pine timbers and logs. It was destroyed by fire, after which the expedition returned to the Pawnee.

Either with or without competent authority, soon after the occupation of Hatteras Inlet, the Twentieth Regiment of Indiana volunteers, Colonel Brown, was sent to occupy Chicamicomico, near the northern end of Hatteras Island, some twenty-five miles north of the lighthouse. Within this sand-spit the water is quite shoal for two miles or more, and this speedily led to the capture of the army tug Fanny, and a considerable quantity of army stores.

The proximity of Roanoke Island and the presence of a large number of Confederate troops fortifying it, made the bait of a regiment too tempting to be resisted, so on the 4th of October there appeared ten transports and seven steamers, including the captured tug Fanny, a cotton barge, and two flat-boats laden with troops. A part of this force was landed north of the Indiana regiment, and the remainder was taken south to cut off the retreat.

The troops retreated in haste, and favored by the delay of the enemy in getting his forces on shore from the shoal water extending so far out, all save twenty or more stragglers had passed the point of debarkation when it had been effected. The retreat was continued to Hatteras lighthouse, the Confederates pursuing to within a short distance of it. Here the Union troops were reinforced by a regiment from Hatteras Inlet, and here was also found the steam frigate Susquehanna as close to the shore as moderately bold water would allow. The retreat had been hasty and laborious, and the troops were greatly in want of food and water; their necessities were soon relieved, and when the morning dawned the Confederates took up their line of retreat to some point where a comparatively near approach to the long sand-spit upon which they were would enable them to re-embark. The Monticello, commanded by Lieutenant D. L. Braine, arrived at the lighthouse on the sea face, and was directed to pursue the enemy in retreat. At 1.30 P.M. of the 5th she came up with a considerable force at Kinekeet, moving north with many stragglers in the rear; two small Confederate steamers were in the inland waters, following as near the island as the depth of the water would allow. A heavy fire of shells from three guns on board of the Monticello was maintained with great effect, which caused the men to scatter in haste to a clump of trees, beyond which, in the sound, were several of their steamers, upon which the fugitives were taking refuge by means of boats. The Monticello continued her firing for two hours, when two men were discovered on the beach making signals; a boat was sent near the beach, and one man belonging to the Twentieth Indiana was rescued; the other was unfortunately drowned in the surf.

The Monticello was in three fathoms, as near the beach as the roughness of the water would permit, and guided by the

information obtained, resumed throwing shells, which was
continued until near sunset—nearly four hours—with little
intermission.

Commander O. S. Glisson, in the Mount Vernon, sent two
armed boats on the night of December 31, 1861, to destroy a
lightship formerly anchored on Frying Pan Shoal, and then
secured under the guns of Fort Caswell. No one was found
on board of the vessel ; she had been fitted for the reception
of eight guns, to aid, it was supposed, in harbor defence.
The combustible material found on board, saturated with the
turpentine brought for the purpose, soon made a blaze sufficient to attract the attention of the men in the fort, whose
cry of alarm was heard by the boats' crews. The fort opened
fire soon after in the supposed direction of retreat of the
boats. The lightboat was speedily burned.

The reader is reminded of the magnitude of the struggle
in progress and of its geographical extent on land and sea.
Considering the waters only, the Potomac River and the
water within the Capes of Virginia presented no inconsiderable field of operations ; then again, as soon after the capture of Hatteras Inlet as a force could be got together,
followed a much larger expedition for the capture of
Port Royal and further operations east of Cape Florida.
The coasts bordering on the Gulf of Mexico and upper
waters of the Mississippi were no less theatres of armed contention.

Important as was the possession of Hatteras Inlet, it need
not be a subject of wonder that nothing further grew out of
it for the time. The Confederates set to work with earnest-
ness with their limited means, after the capture of the inlet,
to fortify Roanoke Island, which was still a key to the greater
part of the inland waters, but even after a lapse of intervening months, when the preparations of the co-operative Union

forces had been completed and were within Hatteras Inlet, they had not yet perfected their defences.

On that coast of storms in winter, neither the "vessels of war," as they were somewhat inaptly termed, if compared with vessels built for the purpose, nor the transports for the troops, often unseaworthy, stood on the order of their coming. Happily for them, Hampton Roads was only one hundred and fifty miles distant, but on arriving off the inlet vessels that had been chartered not to draw more than twelve feet were found of heavier draught, and some of them hammered to pieces on the bar, and many of the naval vessels were of extreme draught for crossing the bulkhead. They came as they could, crossed the bar into the inlet as soon as possible, then awaited exceptional banking of the waters to cross the "bulkhead."

Rear-Admiral L. M. Goldsborough, who was in command of the naval forces, and General A. E. Burnside, who commanded the troops, arrived on January 13th. Owing, however, to a lack of water for days before, few or none of the vessels had crossed the bulkhead; on the 15th, however, the naval vessels, having least draught in general, began crossing, and by the 23d all of them that had arrived up to that time were over the bulkhead. The Whitehall, in getting across the outer bar, or within the inlet from the sea, was so injured that she had to be sent to Hampton Roads for repairs.

Not before the 22d of January had General Burnside made any considerable progress in getting the army transports over the bulkhead, and from the facts above stated, the last naval vessel was delayed until the 28th of January, and the last of the army transports until February 5th. For the time being, the river steamer Philadelphia was the flag-ship of Rear-Admiral Goldsborough; the naval vessels intended for action were as follows: Stars and Stripes, Lieutenant-Commanding Reed Werden, and flag-ship of Commander S. C. Rowan; Louisiana, Lieutenant-Commanding A. Murray; Hetzel, Lieutenant-Commanding H. K. Davenport; Underwriter, Lieutenant-Commanding Wm. N. Jeffers; Delaware, Lieutenant-Commanding S. P. Quackenbush; Commodore Perry, Lieutenant-Commanding C. W. Flusser; Valley City, Lieutenant-Commanding J. C. Chaplin; Commodore Barney, Acting-Lieutenant R. T. Renshaw; Hunchback, Acting Volunteer Lieutenant-Commanding E. R. Colhoun; Southfield, Acting Volunteer Lieutenant-Commanding C. F. W. Behm; Morse, Acting-Master Peter Hayes; Whitehead, Acting-Master Chas. A. French; Lockwood, Acting-Master G. W. Graves; Brincker, Acting-Master, John E. Giddings; I. N. Seymour, Acting-Master F. S. Wells; Ceres, Acting-Master John McDiarmid; Putnam, Acting-Master W. J. Hotchkiss; Shawsheen, Acting-Master Thos. G. Woodward, and Granite, Acting-Master's Mate E. Boomer.

The army transports were forty-six in number, armed with forty-seven guns of small calibre, and carried in round numbers 12,000 troops. They formed not an inconsiderable part of the attacking force, and were under Commander Samuel F. Hazard, U.S.N.

Flag-Officer Goldsborough reports, February 18th: "During our detention at the inlet we resorted to every means in our power to get accurate information of the enemy's position and preparations, and we obtained enough to enable us to arrange our programme of attack, which, in substance, was as follows: The naval division was to lead from the time of starting up to that of encountering the enemy.

"Early on the morning of the 5th, the necessary general signals for a move were thrown out from the Philadelphia, and as soon afterward as could be expected for so large a

8*

number of vessels, all were under way, with the naval division as prescribed, arranged in three columns, commanded respectively by Lieutenants-Commanding Werden, Murray, and Davenport. Although the weather favored us, our progress was unavoidably slow."

At sundown the vessels arrived and anchored in line off Stumpy Point, within ten miles of the marshes. "A certain individual" was sent for, who lived near by, whose services were deemed important, and he was brought on board of the flag-ship Philadelphia. The following morning, Flag-Officer Goldsborough, with his staff, consisting of Commander Case, Captain's Clerk Fisher, as signal officer, and Lieutenants T. R. Robeson and N. S. Barstow went on board of the Southfield, which for the time became the flag-ship. The vessels were again under way with two light-draught steamers, Ceres and Putnam, a mile or so in advance. About 9 A.M. the weather, which had been thick, partially cleared, and the vessels of the enemy were seen at anchor, apparently close in with the shore, between Pork and Wier Points. At 10.30, when within a couple of miles of the marshes, it became thick, rainy, and windy, and the vessels again anchored in line. In the afternoon, one of the steamers of the enemy approached the marshes for the purpose of reconnoitring, and was not molested, as the flag-officer "was not unwilling that she should accomplish her wishes."

The day following, February 7th, gave evident signs of good weather. At nine, general signal was made to get under way. The Underwriter was also put in advance as a lookout, the Ceres and Putnam to keep only one-fourth of a mile in advance of the flag-ship. The channel through the marshes is so narrow as not to admit of more than two vessels abreast, and that was the order of steaming until the much wider waters of Croatan Sound were reached. The vessels having IX-inch guns were then "closed up around the flag-ship." At 10.30, eight vessels of the enemy were seen drawn up behind an extensive obstruction formed by a double row of piles and sunken vessels stretching well across the sound and between the forts on Pork and Wier Points. One of them fired a heavy gun, to announce, perhaps, the impending attack. In less than an hour, the Underwriter, in advance, having shelled Sandy Point, made signal that it was not fortified. This omission on the part of the enemy favored the landing of troops at Ashby's Harbor, as arranged.

Not long after this announcement the naval division, commanded as above given, accompanied as previously arranged by the army division, composed of the Picket, Captain T. P. Ives; Huzzar, Captain F. Crocker; Pioneer, Captain C. E. Baker; Vidette, Captain I. L. Foster; Ranger, Captain S. Emerson; Lancer, Captain M. B. Morley, and Chasseur, Captain John West, in close order, had approached sufficiently near the enemy to attack, and to employ their heaviest fire against the battery on Pork Point, a battery between Pork and Wier Points, and another on Redstone Point, all of which had opened fire on the advancing vessels. At noon the action became general; at 1.30 the barracks behind Pork Point had been set on fire by shells and burned furiously for an hour. At this time the vessels were hotly engaged.

Toward 3 P.M. the troops, embarked on board of light-draught steamers and boats, started to land at Ashby's Harbor. It was guarded by a large body of the enemy's troops, with a field battery, but the Delaware, with the division flag of Commander S. C. Rowan, having very judiciously taken up a flanking position to the southward of Pork Point, opportunely turned her guns on the enemy, enfilading Ashby's Harbor and scattered the troops with IX-inch shrapnel.

At 4.30, Pork Point battery and the one next to the northward ceased firing for a time, and five of the enemy's steamers, apparently injured, went behind Wier's Point, and the
troops landed. At 5 P.M., the batteries and the enemy's

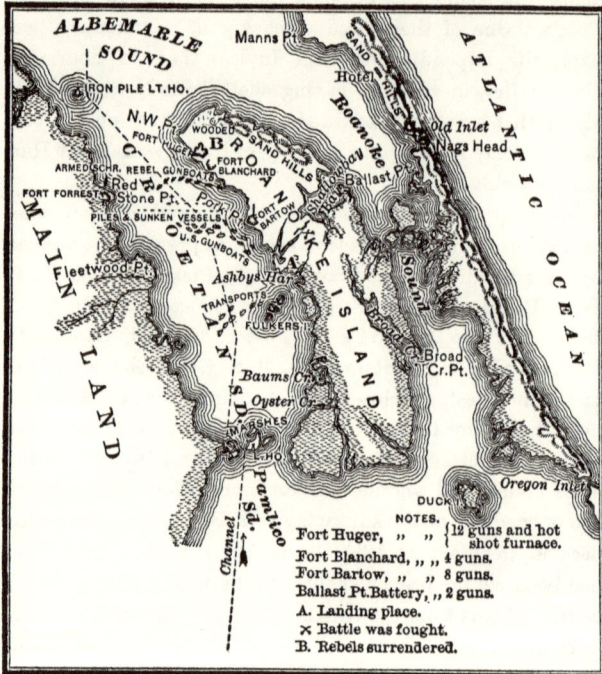

ALBEMARLE SOUND
Manns Pt
IRON PILE LT.HO.
N.W.
FORT
WOODED
SAND HILLS
FORT BLANCHARD
ARMED SCHR. REBEL GUNBOATS
FORT FORREST
Red Stone Pt.
PILES & SUNKEN VESSELS
FORT BARTOW
U.S. GUNBOATS
Fleetwood Pt.
Ashbys Har.
TRANSPORTS
FULKERS
Baums Cr.
Oyster Cr.
MARSHES
LT.HO.
Channel
Pamlico Sd.
MAIN LAND
ROANOKE ISLAND
Roanoke River
Hotel
SAND HILLS
Old Inlet
Nags Head
Ballast
Shallow Bay
Sound
Broad Cr.Pt.
Oregon Inlet
ATLANTIC OCEAN
DUCK
NOTES.
Fort Huger, ,, ,, { 12 guns and hot shot furnace.
Fort Blanchard, ,, ,, 4 guns.
Fort Bartow, ,, ,, 8 guns.
Ballast Pt. Battery, ,, 2 guns.
A. Landing place.
× Battle was fought.
B. Rebels surrendered.

Roanoke Island.

steamers again opened fire. In forty minutes these vessels
were compelled to retire; one of them in a disabled condition took refuge under Redstone battery. At six, only Pork
Point battery was active, and to avoid wasting shells, signal
was made to cease firing. In the course of the afternoon

Midshipman B. J. Porter landed with six navy howitzers, "to assist the army in commanding the main road and its two forks during the night," and to assist in more active operations the following morning."

The direction from which the rattle of musketry on the land proceeded gave assurance that the Union troops were not in the line of fire, and the gunboats were again moved up and engaged the forts. This continued until the firing of small arms slackened, and then signal was made to cease firing, as it was supposed that the Union troops were approaching the rear of the batteries. At that time, however, the enemy were replying with only one gun.

At 1 P.M. the Underwriter, Valley City, Seymour, Lockwood, Ceres, Shawsheen, Putnam, Whitehead, and Brincker, were ordered to clear away the double line of piling, which was effected soon after 4 P.M. About the time our vessels had removed the obstructions, the National flag had been hoisted by the Union troops, and a few minutes later the enemy had set on fire the works at Redstone, and the steamer Curlew. Both blew up in the early part of the evening, and Roanoke Island was then in the undisputed possession of the National troops.

Pork Point batteries, known to the Confederates as Fort Bartow, was found to be a heptagon, mounting eight 32-pounders and one 68-pounder rifled gun. In its rear was a field battery of three guns, designed to protect it against the advance of troops. The six howitzers from the fleet under Midshipman Porter rendered essential service in the reduction of this work. A mile and a half north of Fort Bartow was Fort Blanchard, mounting four 32-pounders, and one mile beyond that Fort Huger, on Wier's Point, mounting two 68-pounder rifles and ten 32-pounders. Fort Ellis, on the eastern side of the island, was a four-gun battery, intended to prevent the debarkation of troops. On the mainland, nearly opposite Fort Bartow (Pork Point), was Fort Forrest. This was placed on hulks sunk in the sand, and to enfilade vessels that might attempt to remove the double row of piles beyond which the eight Confederate vessels were placed. It was stated in a post return, made ten days previous to the attack, that the defence for Roanoke Island was forty 32-pounders, seven rifled guns, and five days' ammunition.

The naval casualties, including the howitzer battery of six guns operating with the army, were 6 killed, 17 wounded, and 2 missing.

Flag-Officer Goldsborough speaks in terms of great commendation of all under his command, and especially of officers commanding vessels. He adds, " It is really difficult for me to state in adequate terms how largely I feel indebted to Commanders Rowan and Case for their constant and signal services throughout, from the very inception to the consummation of the achievement in view."

This victory was most important; the proximate result left no ports or inlets unoccupied by our forces along the entire North Carolina coast except Wilmington. Including what was soon after achieved by Flag-Officer Dupont, on the coast of Georgia and Florida, Charleston and Wilmington were the only entrances unclosed from Cape Henry to Cape Florida.[1]

With untiring labor and zeal we find that at 3 P.M. of the day following the surrender of the Confederate forts, Commander Rowan had taken on board all of the ammunition

---

[1] The army followed the scattered forces of the Confederates, and on the northern part of the island received the surrender of a considerable number, making a total of 2,677, including the wounded. A considerable number had effected their escape at Nag's Head. The army loss was 41 killed, and 181 wounded. The loss of the enemy was considerably less, as he was well protected.

obtainable, which was only twenty rounds per gun, and had
entered Albemarle Sound for the purpose of destroying the
seven Confederate war vessels that had escaped after the fall
of Roanoke Island. His pennant was on board the Delaware, Commander Quackenbush, and was followed by the
Louisiana, Hetzel, Underwriter, Commodore Perry, Valley
City, Morse, Seymour, Whitehead, Lockwood, Ceres, Shawsheen, Brincker, and Putnam.

As this force passed into the sound the smoke of the two
Confederate steamers was seen on the further shore, apparently heading for the Pasquotank River. Signal was made
to chase, and the course changed to cut them off if possible,
but without success. The flotilla steamed up the Pasquotank to within ten miles of Fort Cobb, where it anchored at
8 P.M.

The officers commanding vessels were assembled on board
of the flag-ship and informed by Commander Rowan that
the vessels of the enemy would be found either drawn
up behind the Cobb Point battery, or they had escaped
through the canal to Norfolk. "Calling their attention to
the fact that there were only twenty rounds of ammunition
per gun, the vessels would be organized for a reconnoissance
in force, to be converted into an attack if it was deemed
prudent. No firing would be admissible until the order
was given, and in order further to economize ammunition,
each vessel as she approached the enemy should run him
down and engage hand-to-hand. With this understanding
these noble spirits returned to their respective ships to await
the events of the morrow." [1]

At daylight of the 10th, the flotilla weighed anchor and
formed in the order prescribed, the Underwriter, Perry,

---

[1] Commander Rowan's Report.

Morse, and Delaware in advance, with the Ceres on their right flank. The remainder of the force, led in order by the Louisiana, and the Hetzel, Valley City, and Whitehead being ordered, if the attack was made, to leave the line as soon as the battery was passed, and attack it in reverse. The flotilla proceeded at moderate speed up the river.

At 8.30 the enemy's steamers were seen drawn up, as anticipated, behind the battery, which mounted four heavy 32-pounders, and was commanded by Commodore Lynch in person, and supported by the schooner Black Warrior, moored on the opposite shore, armed with two guns of the same class. The vessels of the enemy were drawn up on a diagonal line, the right resting on the Cobb Point battery. When within long range, battery and vessels opened fire with 80-pounder rifle and other guns; when within three-quarters of a mile signal was made, "Dash at the enemy," and fire was opened by the flotilla with telling effect. This quite demoralized the enemy; the Black Warrior was set on fire and abandoned; the fort was abandoned when the head of the column passed it, and the vessels designated dashed at the vessels of the enemy. The Perry, under command of Flusser, struck the flag-ship Sea Bird and sunk her, and took the officers and crew prisoners; the Underwriter cut off the retreat of the Beaufort, and the Ceres ran ahead and took possession of the Ellis, whose crew deserted and endeavored to escape to the shore; the Delaware boarded the Fanny, that had been set on fire and deserted by the enemy. His defeat was sudden and overwhelming. "Three or four of the flotilla proceeded at once to Elizabeth City and ran alongside of the wharves. A battery of field artillery fled from the principal street. An armed party from the flotilla came suddenly on a mounted officer of the 'Wise Legion,' who, in obedience to orders from General Henningsen, was compelling the de-

fenceless people to set fire to the houses." Several were
set on fire before he was arrested and brought to Commander
Rowan. A curious incident, truly, in war, when the enemy
becomes the protector against the senseless injuries inflicted
by pretended friends.

The armed men were recalled to their respective vessels.
"No other houses were destroyed besides those set on fire
under the direction of Lieutenant Scroggs of the Wise Legion." [1]

The Confederate steamer Forrest, which had been disabled
in the engagement at Roanoke Island on the 7th, a gunboat
on the stocks, and another vessel with lighter frame had been
set on fire at the shipyard by the enemy. Competent persons
were sent on shore to destroy boilers and machinery and
ways ; this done, the vessels withdrew to Cobb's Point. Unsuccessful efforts had been made by other vessels of the flotilla to extinguish the fires on board of the Fanny and the
Black Warrior. The latter vessel had on board a large
amount of provisions and stores for the Confederate vessels,
all of which were burned. The machinery of the Fanny and
Sea Bird was destroyed and the armament of those vessels
was in part recovered. The fort at Cobb's Point was destroyed, after removing powder, powder tanks, and projectiles, and some of the vessels were then despatched to further
thwart the designs of the enemy. Nothing more brilliant in
naval "dash" occurred during the entire civil war than
appears in this attack.

Lieutenant-Commanding Murray, in the Louisiana, accompanied by the Underwriter, the Perry, and the Lockwood,
went to Edenton on the 12th. After a reconnoissance of the
entrance, the smallest vessel in advance passed up to the

---

[1] Rowan's Report.

town. A company of mounted artillery precipitately fled and many of the inhabitants had left the town. Eight cannon and one schooner were destroyed.

The vessels were visited by the town authorities and other persons "who professed sentiments of loyalty to the Union."

Lieutenant-Commanding Jeffers proceeded on the 13th, in the Lockwood, accompanied by the Shawsheen and Whitehead, with two schooners in tow, to the mouth of the Chesapeake and Albemarle Canal. Two small steamers and three small schooners were about a mile and a quarter distant, and the entrance was obstructed. A picket stationed near fired to give the alarm, and a large body of men got under cover.

From a point near the entrance to the canal, three shells were thrown by the vessels, when the whole body of the enemy fled. A sunken schooner, supported by piles and logs, was found fifty yards within the canal, which formed a complete barrier. A body of fifteen armed men were thrown out, and at the distance of half a mile a second row of piles was found obstructing the canal. A fine dredging-machine that had been in use sunk at that moment. The enemy had destroyed the machinery and set the upper works on fire. The two schooners in tow were then sunk in the mouth of the canal, supplementing as it were the work already done by the enemy.

Commander Rowan, in the Delaware, returned to Elizabeth City at five P.M. of the 18th, and ordered the Louisiana, Perry, Morse, Lockwood, and Whitehead to follow. Going up Croatan Sound, he found the Barney at anchor as prearranged; another vessel, the Hunchback, with a battalion of the Ninth New York on board, had grounded; the remainder of the regiment was on board of the Barney.

The vessels anchored to await the arrival of the Hunchback. On the morning of the 19th the gunboats moved to the head of the sound, and Lieutenant-Commanding Murray was sent in the Lockwood to make a reconnoissance of Plymouth. In the meantime the Hunchback with the remainder of the troops came up and anchored. Leaving the force off the mouth of the Roanoke to await Murray's return in the Lockwood, with the Delaware and Perry, Rowan proceeded to Winton "for the purpose of communicating with the Union men said to be in arms at that place."

On the return of Murray the vessels awaiting him followed Rowan. Being desirous to reach Winton at an early hour the Delaware and Perry proceeded at full speed. At 4 P.M they came in sight of the wharf and houses at the landing; the town itself was hidden by a high bluff covered with oak trees.

"Ranging up past the wharf and bluff, where a negro woman stood, apparently to assure us that no danger need be apprehended, suddenly a small armed force and two batteries of light artillery opened a heavy fire on the vessels." The artillery overshot their mark; the Delaware was too near to bring her battery to bear, and was obliged to steam ahead. She turned with some difficulty in the narrow channel, and opened fire on the enemy; the Perry from a position more favorable opened at once with shrapnel. The vessels moved down the river some seven miles and anchored to await the arrival of the expected reinforcement.

At early daylight on the 20th the flotilla moved up to Winton, the leading vessels throwing a few shrapnel on shore to cover the landing of the troops, which was speedily effected. In a few minutes Colonel Hawkins's force, accompanied by two navy howitzers, had possession of the bluff and passed over to the town without opposition. A quantity of military stores, tents, arms and knapsacks, and the quarters occupied by the troops of the enemy were destroyed. The troops were re-embarked, and the force withdrew to the sound. The Perry and Whitehead were despatched to watch Elizabeth City.

The sounds were patroled by the flotilla until the army had made its preparations and the vessels had received an abundant supply of ammunition, indispensable stores for the work before them.

CHAPTER IX.

REDUCTION OF NEWBERN—THE ALBEMARLE.

ROWAN left Hatteras Inlet with the flotilla under his command, at 7.30 A.M. of the 12th of March, 1862, accompanied by the army transports carrying twelve thousand troops intended to be employed against the works of the enemy. At sunset of the same day the flotilla anchored off Slocum's Neck, fifteen miles distant and within sight of the city of Newbern.

The following vessels composed the attacking force; Delaware, Lieutenant-Commanding L. P. Quackenbush, and flag-ship of Commander S. C. Rowan; Stars and Stripes, Lieutenant-Commanding Reed Werden; Louisiana, Lieutenant-Commanding Alexander Murray; Hetzel, Lieutenant-Commanding H. K. Davenport; Commodore Perry, Lieutenant-Commanding C. W. Flusser; Valley City, Lieutenant-Commanding J. C. Chaplin; Underwriter, Lieutenant-Commanding A. Hopkins; Commodore Barney, Lieutenant-Commanding R. T. Renshaw; Hunchback, Lieutenant-Commanding E. R. Colhoun; Southfield, Lieutenant-Commanding C. F. Behm; Morse, Acting-Master Peter Hayes; Brincker, Acting-Master J. E. Giddings; and Lockwood, Acting-Master G. W. Graves.[1]

---

[1] The reader will find the armaments of these vessels in the Appendix, and has doubtless already perceived that they are generally the same vessels that five weeks earlier had acted so effectively in the capture of Roanoke Island.

At 8.30 A.M. on the 13th the vessels shelled the woods near the proposed place of landing, under cover of which part of the troops were disembarked and moved up the beach at 11.30 A.M., and in the meantime the remainder were landed as rapidly as possible. Six navy howitzers with crews, under command of Lieutenant R. S. McCook, were also landed. As the troops marched the gunboats moved parallel, throwing shells into the woods in advance of them. No Confederate force opposed the troops during the day. At 4.15 P.M. the first of the enemy's batteries opened fire at long range on the leading vessels of the flotilla, which was returned. At sundown the firing was discontinued and the vessels anchored in position to protect the flanks of the land force.

At daylight of the 14th the report of a field piece was heard. The fog was too dense to make signal; the Delaware, Hunchback, and Lockwood were got under way, the latter ordered to follow the land down and order up the vessels that had been stationed along the shore. The Delaware, Hunchback, and Southfield moved up to open fire on Fort Dixie. They were soon joined by the heavier vessels from below. Receiving no response from the fort, a boat was sent on shore and the American flag hoisted over it. The force then passed up and opened on Fort Ellis, which was returned until the magazine was blown up. At this time the troops were pressing on the rear intrenchments of Fort Thompson. Signal was made to the vessels to advance in line abreast; the force closed up to the barriers, and opened fire on that work. General Burnside informed Commander Rowan that his shells were falling to the left and near our own troops.

Fort Thompson having ceased to return the fire, signal was made to follow the motions of the flag-ship, and that vessel passed through the obstructions, followed by the

others in "line ahead." As the vessels were passing
through, the co-operating troops appeared on the ramparts

SKETCH SHOWING THE ROUTE TO NEWBERN, Pursued by the Burnside Expedition, March 13th and 14th, 1862.

NOTE.
J. Anchorage on night of March 12th, 1862.
A. Landing place of the troops, March 13th, 1862.
B. Deserted entrenchments.
✗ Battlefield, March 14th, 1862.
C. Line of obstructions.
D. Line of Yankee Catchers.

of Fort Thompson, waving the Union flag. Shells were
then thrown into Fort Lane, next above, without response.
The Valley City was directed to hoist the flag over the re-

maining forts and the flotilla passed rapidly up the river. On opening the Trent River two deserted batteries, mounting two guns each, were seen on the wharves in front of the city.

The vessels passed up the Neuse River, the Delaware opening fire on steamboats that were attempting to escape up the river, one of them having a schooner in tow. One of the steamers was run on shore and burned, and two others were captured, together with a schooner laden with commissary stores.

At noon the Delaware went alongside the wharf and the inhabitants were informed that it was not intended to injure the town. At this time fires broke out in several parts of the city, probably caused by a similar action to that of Lieutenant Scroggs of the "Wise Legion" at Elizabeth City. A floating raft in the Trent River that had been prepared to send down on the fleet was also set on fire, and drifting against the railroad bridge, destroyed it.

The Louisiana and the Barney were sent to the Trent side of the town to secure such public property as might be found there. Several hundred stand of arms, other munitions of war, a large amount of naval stores, and a three-masted schooner fell into their hands. At 2 P.M., our victorious troops appearing on the opposite side of the Trent, the work of transportation commenced, and at sundown the army was in full occupancy of the city.[1]

Commander Rowan describes the obstructions passed through as "formidable, and had evidently been prepared with great care." The lower barrier was composed of a series of piling driven securely into the bottom and cut off below the water; added to this was another row of pointed

---

[1] Rowan's Report.

and iron-capped piles, inclined to an angle of about forty-five degrees down stream. Near these was a row of thirty torpedoes, containing about two hundred pounds of powder each, and fitted with metal fuses connected with spring percussion locks, with trigger-lines attached to the pointed piles. The second barrier was quite as formidable, about one mile above the first, and abreast of Fort Thompson. It consisted of a line of sunken vessels closely massed and of chevaux de frise, leaving a very narrow passage close to the battery. The Perry in passing through carried away a head of iron on the piling; the Barney had a hole cut in her, and the Stars and Stripes was also injured; but fortunately the torpedoes failed to serve the enemy's purpose.[1]

The forts, six in number, exclusive of those on Trent River, were well constructed earthworks, varying in distance apart from half a mile to a mile and a half, and mounting in all thirty-two guns, ranging from 32-pounders to 80-pounders, rifled, all *en barbette*, with the exception of one casemated fort, mounting two guns.

It may well excite surprise that not a single casualty occurred on board of the flotilla. Of the navy force on shore with six howitzers, under Lieutenant McCook, 2 men were killed, 11 wounded, and one howitzer disabled.

The force of the enemy was about equal in number to the Union troops. Only 200 were captured, but a very large amount of army equipage and supplies were found at Newbern. Our casualties were 88 killed and 352 wounded. Those of the Confederates are not known.

On the 25th of April the Union troops then in Beaufort, N. C., with breaching batteries, which they had established, opened fire on Fort Macon; before sunset the fort surren-

---

[1] Rowan's Report.

II.—9

dered. Lockwood in command of the Daylight, Armstrong in the Georgia, Bryson in the Chippewa, and Cavendy in the Gemsbok, took part in the bombardment for several hours, when the sea grew too rough to manage their guns.

In order to secure the forces on the sounds from an attack from Norfolk, Flusser was directed to block additionally the Chesapeake and Albemarle Canal. For this purpose he left Elizabeth City, on the 23d of April, with the Whitehead, Lockwood, and Putnam, and at the mouth of the river met the Shawsheen with a schooner in tow filled with sand. The vessel was sunk near the entrance of the canal, and some fifty yards in length was filled in with trunks of trees, stumps, and brushwood. On his return he assisted Colonel Hawkins in destroying Confederate commissary stores on the Chowan, which was effected on the 7th of May.

Lieutenant William B. Cushing had been given command of the steamer Ellis and was employed in blockading New River Inlet, which he entered on the 23d of November, 1862, with the object of going to Jacksonville, destroying any salt works found, and capturing such vessels as he might find. Five miles up he sighted a vessel with a cargo of cotton and turpentine, which was on fire and abandoned by the enemy. At 1 P.M. he reached the town, thirty-five miles from the mouth of the river, where twenty-five stand of arms, a large mail, and two schooners were captured. At 2.30 P.M. the Ellis started down the river; at five an encampment was seen near the banks and thoroughly shelled. At the point where the vessel was burned as he ascended the enemy opened fire with rifles, but was soon silenced. The two pilots on board agreed that high water and daylight were essential to take the Ellis out of the inlet. She was anchored, the prizes brought alongside, and preparation made to repel attack. At daylight the Ellis was got under way, and at the worst part of the channel was opened upon by two field pieces. In an hour the enemy was driven from his guns and from the bluff, and the vessel passed within one hundred yards of it without molestation. Five hundred yards farther down the pilots mistook the channel and the Ellis got hard and fast aground; it was found, moreover, that she was in a pocket with shoaler water all around.

A party was sent on shore to carry off the abandoned artillery, but in the meantime the enemy had removed it. At dark one of the prize schooners was taken alongside and everything taken out of the Ellis except the pivot gun, some ammunition, two tons of coal, and a few small arms. But steam and anchor planted to haul her off were ineffective. It was quite certain that the Confederates would come in overwhelming numbers and capture the vessel; therefore Cushing called all hands to muster, and told the crew that they could go aboard the schooner. Six volunteers were asked to remain on board and fight the remaining gun.

The officer in charge of the schooner was directed to drop down the channel out of range from the bluffs and await results. At daylight the enemy opened on the Ellis from four points with rifled guns. It was a destructive cross-fire; the engine was soon disabled and the vessel much cut up; in the meantime the pivot gun was used with as much effect as possible. The contest was hopeless; the Ellis was set on fire in five places, and Cushing and his six comrades took to their small boat and pulled for the schooner, at anchor a mile and a half below. On reaching the schooner sail was made and the vessel forced over the bar, although she struck several times. The magazine of the Ellis blew up soon after the schooner had crossed the bar.

At daylight on February 23d, at the western entrance to Cape Fear River, a blockade-runner was seen from the

Dacotah, one of the blockading vessels. It was supposed that the blockader was aground, but when the Monticello and Dacotah went in and opened on her she moved up the river. The vessels were opened on from Fort Caswell, mortally wounding Master's Mate Henry Baker on board of the Monticello.

At daylight on the morning of March 14th a large Confederate force attacked Fort Anderson (opposite Newbern, N. C.), on the river Neuse. It was an unfinished work, garrisoned by 300 men. Its defence was aided by the gunboats Hetzel and Hunchback, and some guns on a schooner. The enemy evidently was informed as to the contents of a telegram, and counted upon a literal compliance with the request of General Foster, made four days previously, "to send *all* the light gunboats to aid the expedition to Hyde County." The enemy supposed all had gone and made his first attack here.[1] He opened on the fort from a two-gun battery on the south bank, and on the Hunchback and the schooner. Those vessels commanded the point and its approach, and the Hetzel enfiladed from below. The latter vessel, as well as the Shawsheen, were undergoing repairs and had to be towed into position.

At six o'clock the firing ceased, "when signals from the fort said that the enemy gave them thirty minutes in which to surrender." This demand was made, it was supposed, to get fourteen pieces of artillery into position. At 6.30 this battery, within two hundred and fifty yards of the fort, opened upon it again, and the two-gun battery on the opposite shore fired on the Hunchback and the schooner. The action was very fierce for thirty minutes, when the Hetzel in tow of a tug got into position "and threw IX-inch shells

---

[1] Murray's Report.

among the enemy, causing him to withdraw immediately, leaving one disabled 30-pounder Parrott gun on the field."

At 10.08 the Hunchback, which had previously grounded, was again afloat. An hour later, the revenue cutter Agassiz, the Shawsheen towed by a tug, and the Ceres were in position, but the enemy had withdrawn beyond the reach of the guns. Two light-draught gunboats followed the enemy ten miles up the river, picking up stragglers who wished to desert.

Colonel Belknap, Eighty-fifth New York, wrote to the senior naval officer present as follows : "When, on the 14th of March, General Pettigrew, with eighteen pieces of artillery and more than 3,000 men, made his furious assault upon Fort Anderson, an unfinished earthwork, garrisoned by 300 men of my command, the capture or destruction of the brave little band seemed inevitable. But the gunboats under your command—the pride of loyal men and the terror of traitors—came promptly to the rescue. Your well-directed fire drove the enemy from the field, covered the landing of the Eighty-fifth New York, sent to the relief of the garrison, and the repulse of the rebel army was complete."

The Confederate forces invested Washington, N. C., on the 30th of March, and maintained the siege eighteen days, reoccupying their old works seven miles below. On March 31st they opened 'fire from Rodman's Point, a mile and three-quarters below, on the Commodore Hull, which had been stationed there to prevent the occupation of the point. After a spirited action of an hour and a half, the vessel grounded in an endeavor to change position, and remained so until 8 P.M., exposed to a continuous and accurate fire, cutting up but not vitally injuring her.

On the morning of the 15th Major-General Foster passed Hill's Point battery in the Escort, returning from Washington.

The next night the enemy withdrew. Few casualties resulted from this lengthy siege.

Lieutenant-Commanding Cushing, who lost the steamer Ellis in November, was soon after assigned to the command of the steamer Shokokon, and, ever active, made a reconnoissance of New Topsail Inlet in a boat on the 12th of August, but was driven out by four pieces of artillery. He had seen within the inlet a schooner which he determined to destroy. With this view, on the evening of the 22d, the Shokokon was anchored close to the beach, five miles south of the inlet, and two boats were sent on shore. The men shouldered the dingy (smallest boat carried by a vessel of war) and carried it through the thickets across the neck of land, half a mile in width, which divides the sea from the sound.

The boat being launched in the inland waters, Ensign Cony "started with orders to capture or destroy anything that might be of use to the enemy."

A Confederate 12-pound howitzer was stationed near that locality, and Captain Adams, in charge, had come down to the schooner with it, having seen the smoke-stack of the Shokokon over the thicket. A lookout at the masthead of the schooner was peering toward the sea entrance, while the Shokokon's boat came in the opposite direction. The men landed within fifty yards of the vessel without being discovered ; one of the dingy's crew crawled into the camp, counted the men, and returning, made his report. "A charge was ordered and our seven men bore down on the enemy with a shout." Ten prisoners were secured, among whom were Captains Adams and Latham, one 12-pounder army howitzer, eighteen horses, one schooner, and the salt works. Two men were thrown out as pickets, two detailed to guard the prisoners, and with the aid of the other two men Ensign Cony burned the vessel and salt works.

The object of the expedition accomplished, the ensign was unable to distinguish the officers from the privates, and as his boat would only carry three additional persons, he took those who seemed most intelligent and good-looking, *who turned out to be privates.* Cushing reports, " The manner in which my orders were carried out is highly creditable to Mr. Cony, who is, I beg leave to state, a good officer, seaman, artillerist, and navigator." The schooner destroyed had cleared from New York for Port Royal, and was once towed outside the line of blockade by a gunboat.

Owing to extraordinary army operations on or near James River, and a co-operation where practicable of naval forces which were withdrawn from North Carolina, an unwonted quiet prevailed for months within the sounds and on the coasts of that State, broken only by very frequent captures of blockade-runners.

An account of a " Confederate victory " was published in the newspapers, the report of Colonel Griffin, commanding. It was as follows : "January 30, 1864, engaged the enemy with a force of 200 men and a mounted rifle piece. After a fight of two hours, in which we engaged 1,200 of the enemy and three pieces of artillery, the Yankees were driven from Windsor, N. C., to their boats. We lost six men ; the loss of the enemy is not known."

In relation to this, Flusser says : "The report is false from beginning to conclusion. I planned the affair, and we would have captured the entire party had we been ten minutes earlier.

" I had 40 sailors and one 12-pounder howitzer, and there were about 350 infantry. We marched about sixteen miles. There was no fight and nothing worth reporting ; the rebels ran. I fired three or four times at them at long range. We held the town of Windsor several hours, and marched back eight miles to our boats without a single shot from the enemy."

This will remind the older reader of the very many "victories" of like import that came daily, and filled the columns of the newspapers, taxing credulity to the utmost. It is only fair to say that the narrators were quite as frequently of the National as of the Confederate forces.

Cushing, commanding the Monticello, blockading the western entrance to Cape Fear River, on the night of the 29th of February visited Smithville with two boats manned by twenty men. His object was to capture the commanding officer, and to carry out any vessel that might be at anchor near by. He landed directly in front of the hotel, captured some negroes to gain information, after which, accompanied by Ensign Jones, Mate Howarth, and one seaman, proceeded to General Herbert's headquarters, across the street from the barracks, supposed to contain a thousand men. Cushing says: "The party captured the chief-engineer of these defences, but found the general had gone to Wilmington the same day. The adjutant-general escaped from the door after severely wounding his hand; but thinking that a mutiny was in progress, took to the woods with a great scarcity of clothing and neglected to turn out the garrison." The boats were within fifty yards of the fort, and within the same distance of a sentinel. Cushing brought off his prisoner and was abreast of Fort Caswell before signal was made that boats were in the harbor.

On April 18, 1864, in command of the Miami, at Plymouth, N. C., Flusser reported as follows: "We have been fighting here all day. About sunset the enemy made a general advance along our whole line. They have been repulsed. . . . The ram [Albemarle] will be down to-night or to-morrow. I fear for the protection of the town. I shall have to abandon my plan of fighting the ram, lashed to the Southfield. The army ought to be reinforced at once. I think I have force enough to whip the ram, but not sufficient to assist in holding the town as I should like. . . . If we whip the ram the [Confederate] land force may retire."

Flusser died bravely in action, fighting his formidable antagonist, at 4 A.M. the day following.

On the morning of the 18th, between three and five, the enemy tried to carry Fort Gary by storm, but were repulsed. In the afternoon heavy artillery opened fire upon the town and breastworks. Then the fight became general. Up to this time the gunboats Southfield and Miami were chained together in preparation to encounter the ram. They were then separated. The Southfield, moving up the river, opened fire over the town. The Miami, moving down the river, opened a cross-fire upon the enemy, who were charging upon Fort Williams. The firing being very exact caused the enemy to fall back. After three attempts to storm the fort, at nine o'clock the firing ceased from the enemy, they having withdrawn from range.[1]

General Wessels, who commanded the troops, said of this naval co-operation: "The fire from the naval vessels was very satisfactory and effective—so much so that the advancing columns of the enemy broke and retreated." He desired that the Miami might be kept below the town to prevent a flank movement by the enemy. At 10.30 P.M. the Southfield came down and anchored near. At 12.20 A.M. April 19th the Southfield came alongside to rechain the two steamers, as speedily as possible, the ram having been seen by Captain Barrett, of the Whitehead, and reported by him as com-

---

[1] Report of Wells, commanding the Miami.

9*

ing down the river. At 3.45 the gunboat Ceres came down, passing near, stating that the ram was close upon her.

Commander Flusser was informed of this fact, immediately came on deck, and ordered both vessels (which were lashed together) to steam as fast as possible to run the ram down. The order was instantly obeyed; the chain was slipped, and "bells rung to go ahead fast." The vessels were moving up the river to meet the ram, and it was making for the vessels.

Within two minutes the ram struck the Miami on the port-bow without serious injury. At the same time the South-field was pierced nearly to her boilers and sank rapidly. As soon as the batteries of the two vessels could be brought to bear on the ram, they opened on her with 100-pounder rifles and IX-inch guns. The guns had been loaded with shells. "Flusser fired the first shots personally from the Miami, the third being a 10-second Dahlgren shell. It was directly after that fire that he was killed by pieces of shell." [1]

Several of the guns' crews were wounded at the same time; the bow-hawser had parted, and the Miami swung around to starboard. The after-hawser was then either cut or parted, and the Southfield sank directly, while the engines of the Miami had to be reversed to keep her off the bank. The ram again made for the Miami, and the officer then in command, says in his report: "From the fatal effects of her prow upon the Southfield, and of our sustaining injury, I deemed it useless to sacrifice the Miami in the same way." Certainly he was not wrong in keeping out of the way of the ram, at least until he determined how to attack her effectively.

When running into the two vessels the ram had made use

---

[1] Wells' Report.

of small arms, but not her heavy guns. It was only after the Miami moved off that two shells were fired at her.

The writer is at a loss to understand the *rationale* of lashing two vessels together, and then running bows on to a vessel of such construction as the Albemarle, by which name she will be called hereafter. Had Flusser reserved his attack until daylight the result might have been different.

In reporting the death of Commander Flusser, Admiral Lee says: "This brave officer was a native of Maryland and a citizen of Kentucky. His patriotic and distinguished services had won for him the respect and esteem of the navy and the country. He was generous, good, and gallant, and his untimely death is a real and great loss to the public service." In appearance, so fine a specimen of physical, intelligent manhood is rarely seen; he had too all the requisite qualities to have made him distinguished as an officer.

The Ceres, on picket duty above the town, on the 17th had been fired on by the field batteries of the enemy, by which 2 men were killed and 4 officers wounded.

The army force under General Wessels had no longer the support of the vessels, and overwhelmed by numbers surrendered on the 20th, the Albemarle thereafter occupying the river until her destruction the October following.

On the 21st of April, Rear-Admiral Lee sent instructions to Commander Davenport as to a plan of attack on the ram. He expresses the opinion that the Albemarle must be weak, and quite slow. "The great point is to get and hold position on each side of the ram. Have stout lines with small heaving lines thereto, to throw across the ends of the ram, and so secure her between two of our vessels. Her plating will loosen and bolts fly like canister, and the concussion will knock down and demoralize her crew if they keep their ports down, as in the late attack."

After the Albemarle had come down an inquiry was made as to why she had not been destroyed when under construction at Edwards Ferry, forty miles above Rainbow Bluffs on the Roanoke River.

On the 8th of the preceding June Lieutenant-Commander Flusser had sent a sketch of her cross-section. He stated further that "she was built on the plan of the Merrimac." On the 8th of the following August Admiral Lee reported to the Department that the ironclad building at Edwards Ferry was considered by Flusser "as a formidable affair, though of light draught." The information elicited was to the effect that the depth of water would not permit the gunboats to ascend to Edwards Ferry in shoal and narrow channels, in the face of several formidable batteries, and the army did not attach enough importance to her construction to send a sufficient force to destroy her.

The Navy Department ordered Captain Melancton Smith, an officer of ability and experience, to the sounds of North Carolina to destroy the "ram" at all hazards, if possible.

Admiral Lee, in an official letter to Captain Smith, alludes to his former instructions and adds: "Entrusted by the Department with the performance of this signal service, I leave (with the expression of my views) to you the manner of executing it" (the destruction of the ram).

Some of the vessels assigned were still without the sounds, but the full moon gave promise of high tides, and we soon find them ready for operating.

Captain Melancton Smith hoisted his flag on board of the "double-ender" Mattabesett, Commander Febiger, and on the 2d of May had arranged his order of battle: "The steamers will advance in the third order of steaming, the Miami leading the second line of steamers. The Mattabesett, Sassacus, Wyalusing, and Whitehead formed the right column, and the Miami, Ceres, Commodore Hull, and Seymour the left.

"The proposed plan of attack will be for the large vessels to pass as close as possible to the ram, without endangering their wheels, delivering their fire and rounding to immediately for a second discharge.

"The steamer Miami will attack the ram and endeavor to explode her torpedo at any moment she may have the advantage, or a favorable opportunity. Ramming may be resorted to, but the peculiar construction of the sterns of the double-enders will render this a matter of serious consideration with their commanders, who may be at liberty to use their judgment as to the propriety of this course when a chance shall present itself."

On May 5th at 1 P.M. the Miami, Commodore Hull, Ceres, and army transport Trumpeter left their picket station off Edenton Bay for the mouth of Roanoke River to lay several torpedoes within it.

When near the buoy at the mouth of the river, the Albemarle was seen coming out with the Cotton Plant, having troops on board, and towing a number of launches or scows, and the Bombshell, as afterward known, laden with provisions and coal, and having on board thirty-three persons including the crew ; the Bombshell had received injuries from shells above Plymouth on the 18th, and reaching that place had sunk. After the enemy took the town on the 20th she was raised and put into service by the Confederates.

The report of the senior officer on picket duty, who commanded the Miami, states that he despatched the Trumpeter in haste to inform the squadron of the approach of the Albemarle. No mention is made of that vessel by Captain Smith, or in the several reports of the different commanding officers. The Miami, Hull, and Ceres followed the

Trumpeter and kept out of the range of the guns of the Albemarle.

It appears that as soon as the commanding officer of the Albemarle became aware of the force with which he had to contend, he despatched the Cotton Plant to a place of refuge, with her scows in tow, and made a face of advance for a time with the Bombshell. At 3.10 the squadron was fairly under way, and in position in two columns, line ahead, or the column of small vessels was soon after completed, as the squadron advanced to meet the Albemarle. At 4.20 the Miami, then heading the line of the port (left) column, advancing, made signal "Enemy is retreating." No other report mentions the fact that the Albemarle was in retreat when the vessels were advancing to make the attack.

The attacking vessels by their superior speed were coming up with the Albemarle. At 4.40 that vessel opened fire on the Mattabesett, leading the right column. The shell wounded several of a gun's crew and destroyed the launch. This was soon followed by another, doing less damage. The Albemarle had the general construction described in the ram Atlanta, and was armed with two 100-pounder rifles, one a Brooke, the other a Whitworth. These guns could pivot on either side, or ahead and astern.

The Mattabesett and vessels in line continued their advance ; the Albemarle then put her helm aport, "with an evident intention to ram the Mattabesett ; " that vessel put her helm astarboard to avoid being run into, and that threw the antagonists farther apart than intended by the last named. At 4.45, when a little abaft the port beam of the Albemarle, the Mattabesett delivered her broadside of two rifled guns and four IX-inch guns at a distance of one hundred and fifty yards from the Albemarle. At about the same time the

Sassacus had sheered to starboard, and when nearly abeam delivered her port broadside into the Albemarle, and keeping her helm hard aport to avoid being rammed, described a circle, and passing the stern of the Albemarle, was again in line following the Mattabesett. That vessel passing ahead, had fired her forward rifle and howitzers into the Bombshell, when she surrendered, and was ordered to follow in the wake ; the Sassacus coming up, fired a broadside into the Bombshell also, in the belief that she had not surrendered, and when informed of the fact, directed her to pass astern and anchor ; the Wyalusing then coming up, was on the point of running her down, not knowing that she had surrendered (as was afterward seen), and backed barely in time to prevent injury. The Mattabesett, followed by the Sassacus and the Wyalusing, passed ahead of the Albemarle, delivering their fire as they could, and found themselves in the line of fire of the left column and of the Whitehead ; that vessel, owing to inferior speed, had reached the Albemarle when the Bombshell had fallen back to anchor as ordered.

Here the three forward vessels of the right line reversed their engines to keep out of the fire of the other vessels, and as the Albemarle drew ahead the Mattabesett was on her starboard quarter, the Sassacus on her beam, and the Wyalusing on her bow. The Sassacus pointed fair, and at a distance of from two to three hundred yards, with open throttles, thirty pounds steam pressure, and making twenty-two revolutions when striking, ran head on to the Albemarle, striking her nearly at right angles, just abaft the casemate on the starboard side, at a speed estimated by her commanding officer of ten knots, and by Captain Smith on board of the Mattabesett at half that velocity. On being struck, the Albemarle heeled considerably, the water washing over the deck on the starboard side abaft the casemate. The Sassacus steamed heavily, in the hope of forcing the vessel under. As the Sassacus came in contact, the Albemarle fired a rifle shell, which passed through both sides near the bow of the Sassacus. While in that position three solid shot from a 100-pounder rifle were fired into the Albemarle and were shattered, coming back in fragments on the deck of the Sassacus. At the moment of the third discharge the vessel had swung so as to permit the after gun of the Albemarle to bear from a broadside port, and a shell was sent into the Sassacus which passed longitudinally through her starboard boiler. The vessel was then filled with steam and dropped astern. The report of her commanding officer says : "In the meantime the engine was going, as no one could do anything below ; some sixteen men being scalded. I then put the helm hard aport, headed up the sound, and around to the land, in order to clear the field for the other boats." After the explosion of the boiler the signal-books were thrown overboard, but no reason is given therefor. While dropping out of action the guns continued to play on the Albemarle.

The flag of the Albemarle was shot away about the time the Sassacus was disabled, and it was not hoisted again during the action. As her firing was interrupted from some cause it was thought she had surrendered, and until she resumed the use of her guns she was spared the fire from her adversaries.

The attacking force at that time (5.15 P.M.) was in great confusion ; the vessels so surrounded the Albemarle as in a great degree to prevent any effective fire against her. "Our attention was turned to getting them [the vessels] into line. At 5.20 signal was made to the Miami to pass within hail, and when she did so she was ordered to "go ahead and try her torpedo." [1] At 5.30 signal was made to "keep in line," and fifteen minutes later it was repeated. At 5.55 signal was made to the Wyalusing to "cease firing," that vessel being still on the starboard bow of the Albemarle. At that time "the remainder of the vessels (with the exception of the Sassacus) were taking position on the port quarter of the enemy." At 6.05 signal for "close order" was made, and again at 6.45 "signal to the Wyalusing to cease firing, she at the time coming round to take position. Soon after, hailing her with an order to go ahead of the line and pass close to the Albemarle, in reply she reported herself sinking, and at 6.55 made signal ' sinking,' but still going ahead, finally took position." [2]

Finding that the line was gradually edging off, the Mattabesett steamed ahead inside, delivering her fire as rapidly as possible when on the quarter and abeam of the enemy, and after passing ahead attempted to lay a seine in the course of the Albemarle for the purpose of fouling her propeller, but it was torn and lost before getting into the desired position. The Mattabesett was then rounded to port, and the port battery usèd ; when nearly abeam of the Albemarle a VI-inch rifle-shot from that vessel fatally wounded two men and did considerable damage to the vessel. At 7.30, growing quite dark, signal was made to cease firing, and to anchor, with the exception of the Commodore Hull and the Ceres, those vessels being directed to follow and watch the movements of the enemy.

The commanding officer of the Whitehead states : "The rebel steamer Cotton Plant, with a number of launches in tow, having succeeded in making her escape, my attention was directed to the ram, upon which I opened fire with the

---

[1] Febiger's Report.   [2] Report of commander of the Mattabesett.

100-pounder rifle, using solid shot, first at a distance of one thousand, but soon lessened it to four hundred yards." No other mention is made of the Cotton Plant having launches in tow, or of that vessel, except by the Miami, when on picket duty, that the Cotton Plant came out.

Josselyn, commanding the Hull, reported his part in the engagement, and states that the Hull crossed the bows of the Albemarle and " paid out a large seine for the purpose of fouling her propeller, but though encompassing the ram, it did not have the desired effect."

The batteries, expenditures of ammunition, and casualties of the different vessels engaged will be found in the Appendix.

No accounts whatever are found among the Confederate archives in Washington of this engagement, of injuries sustained, or of the purposes for which the Albemarle and her two consorts went out. Captain Smith reports the appearance of the vessel again on the 24th of May, near the mouth of the Roanoke River, with a row-boat dragging for torpedoes. The Whitehead fired a shell which fell near, and the Albemarle steamed up the river. Refugees and others from Plymouth stated that the plating of the Albemarle had been much injured, four of the shot had penetrated the armor, and during the engagement the concussion was so great as to put out lights burning in the casemate. One of the two guns with which the vessel was armed was rendered useless by the muzzle being broken off.

On the night of May 7, 1864, an armor-plated vessel, known as the ram North Carolina, came out of New Inlet at the mouth of Wilmington River, and exchanged shots with the steamers Mount Vernon, Kansas, Howqua, Nansemond, and Britannia. She did no serious damage to any of the vessels, but put a rifled shell of large size through the smoke-stack of the Howqua at an estimated distance of a mile and a half. She never made her appearance again ; her consort, the Raleigh, was found, later on, "wrecked" below Wilmington, from what cause is unknown.

In June Lieutenant William B. Cushing had received permission to attempt the destruction of the Raleigh in Wilmington River. He was then in command of the Monticello, aiding in the blockade. He thought it prudent to make a thorough reconnoissance to determine the position of the Raleigh.

On the night of the 23d he left his command in a ship's boat, taking with him Ensign Jones, Master's Mate Howarth, and 15 men, crossed the west bar, passed the forts, then the town and batteries of Smithville, and pulled swiftly up the river undiscovered. He was within the river some two days, visited the wreck of the Raleigh, and coming out effected his escape with his usual gallantry and cleverness.

As auxiliary again to proposed army operations, Commander Macomb, on July 28th, accompanied the army transports Collyer and Massasoit up the Chowan. The objects of the expedition were attained, and at Gatesville the Confederate steamer Arrow was captured.

On October 30th, Lieutenant Cushing wrote as follows : " I have the honor to report that the rebel ironclad Albemarle is at the bottom of Roanoke River." The means by which this was accomplished were a steam launch and a torpedo on the end of a pole, fastened to the bow. On the night of the 27th, he proceeded up the Roanoke River toward Plymouth, where the ram was made fast to a wharf, and for her protection against torpedoes " booms " were secured twenty or thirty feet from her broadside. The newspapers had gratuitously furnished the enemy with information for weeks before of the daily progress of Cushing with

his launch, from New York to the sounds, as well as the
avowed object of destroying the Albemarle.   The reader may
well imagine the increased difficulty of effecting the object.

The party consisted of 15 officers and men in the launch,
and 2 officers and 11 men in the cutter which was in tow. The
distance from the mouth of the river to the object of attack
was eight miles, the average width of river two hundred
yards, and shores picketed. In case of being hailed in passing the Southfield, a mile below the Albemarle, on which a
gun was supposed to be mounted, to command the bend,
the cutter was to cast off and attack the men on the sunken
steamer.

The launch and cutter passed along within twenty yards
of the Southfield without discovery, indeed, until hailed by
the lookouts on the ram. "The cutter was then cast off and
ordered below, while the launch made for the enemy under
a full head of steam. The enemy sprung rattles, rang the
bell, and commenced firing, and at the same time repeating
their hail ; the light of a fire ashore showed me the ironclad,
made fast to the wharf, with a pen of logs around her about
thirty feet from her side." Passing close to the Albemarle
in order to ensure coming squarely on the logs to press them
in, the launch performed nearly a circle, running at first
directly from her intended prey. " By this time the enemy's
fire was very severe, but a dose of canister, at short range,
served to moderate their zeal and disturb their aim." At
this time coming head on to the Albemarle, Paymaster Swan,
by Cushing's side, was wounded, " but," he says, " how
many more I know not. Three bullets struck my clothing,
and the air seemed full of them. In a moment we had struck
the logs just abreast of the quarter port, breasting them in
some feet, and our bows resting on them. The torpedo
boom was then lowered, and by a vigorous pull I succeeded

in driving the torpedo under the overhang, and exploded it at the same time that the Albemarle's gun was fired. A shot seemed to go crashing through my boat, and a dense mass of water rushed in from the torpedo, filling the launch and completely disabling her."

The enemy within a few yards continued their fire at the men and demanded their surrender. Cushing ordered them to "save themselves," divested himself of shoes and coat and swam with others into the middle of the stream. "Master's Mate Woodman I met in the water half a mile below the town, and assisted him as best I could, but failed to get him ashore." [1]

Cushing reached the shore "completely exhausted, too weak to crawl out of the water until just at daylight," when he went into the swamp near the fort for the night and a part of the following day. Exhausted as he was, he walked miles through swamps, and at length found a boat in which, by eleven o'clock the next night, he found his way to the Valley City. He says : "Master's Mate Howarth showed as usual conspicuous gallantry," and he expresses the hope that Howarth and Engineer Stolesbury will be promoted when exchanged.

A more heroic picture can hardly be conceived than Cushing, standing in the bows of his launch, running head on to the Albemarle, the glare of the fire on shore throwing its lights and shadows on the doomed ram, and illuminating the man, who pushed on, placed the torpedo by his own hand where he desired, exploded it, and received at the same time, at the cannon's mouth, the blast of a 100-pounder rifle. He was at that time twenty-one years of age.

The reader may be interested in the personal appearance

---

[1] The quotation marks are in Cushing's words.

of Cushing. He was perhaps six feet in height, and slender, resembling greatly an engraving of the poet Schiller when he was young. The attentive reader will not fail to see in his despatches a poetic vein, at times of great humor. He will see, too, that within his sphere of action he was a man of consummate plan and courage.

The cutter that was in tow and cast off when the launch was hailed, proceeded to the wreck of the Southfield and secured four prisoners. No gun was mounted as supposed.

On the 8th of December, 1864, the army asked a co-operative movement on the part of the navy for the purpose of reducing Confederate batteries at Rainbow Bluffs, on the Roanoke River, some sixty miles above Plymouth. As agreed upon, Commander Macomb left Plymouth in the Wyalusing, followed by the Otsego, Valley City, tugs Belle and Bazley, and picket boat No. 5. At 10 P.M. the force had arrived at a sharp bend just below Jameston, at which point they were to meet an army force. The vessels were about anchoring when the Otsego exploded a submerged torpedo under her port side forward, and almost immediately another under the forward pivot gun, which was thrown over. The vessel settled on the bottom at once, making a depth of three feet of water over the spar-deck. In a torpedo net which the vessel carried as a protection were found two others. The following morning the tug Bazley, in making preliminary preparations to execute orders, was also blown up in the same manner, and sank at once, two men having been killed by the explosion.

The 10th and 11th were spent in dragging for torpedoes, and six were found. No army force appeared. Commander Macomb asked instructions of the admiral as to further action, and as then the preparations for an attack on Fort Fisher was the engrossing object, nothing further is to be found in the published official papers of this " co-operative movement."

For a long period the only ports or inlets that remained to the Confederates admitting a vessel of twelve feet draught were Charleston and Wilmington ; the latter, however, had two entrances far apart, which made practically a double blockading force necessary. It was of the greatest importance to prevent the arrival of supplies, and however many blockade-runners were destroyed, it was not to be denied that many vessels arrived at and departed from those ports, and would continue to do so until the National forces actually held the entrances.

The usual blockade force off Charleston numbered twenty vessels. Preceding the bombardments of Fort Fisher, thirty to forty vessels blockaded the two entrances to Wilmington, yet, with the utmost vigilance on their part, a great number of vessels got in and out.   Hence the great anxiety of the Navy Department to gain possession of the entrances to those harbors. An official letter to Rear-Admiral Farragut, dated September 5, 1864, appointing him to the command of a naval force designed to attack the defences of Cape Fear River, states that since the winter of 1862 the Navy Department had endeavored " to get the consent of the War Department to a joint attack upon the defences of Cape Fear River, but they had decided that no troops could be spared for the operation.   Lieutenant-General Grant had, however, recently given the subject his attention, and thought an army force would be ready to co-operate on the 1st of October."

For strategic purposes the force was to assemble at Port Royal, and in addition to the force to assemble through the direct order of the Department, the admiral was authorized to bring with him all such vessels and officers as could be spared from the West Gulf Squadron without impairing its necessary efficiency.

The condition of the health of Admiral Farragut did not permit his acceptance of the command, and on the 22d of the same month Rear-Admiral D. D. Porter was detached from the command of the Mississippi Squadron, and directed to proceed to Beaufort, N. C., and relieve Acting Rear-Admiral S. P. Lee in command of the North Atlantic Blockading Squadron.

On the 28th of October the Secretary of the Navy sent to President Lincoln a memorandum of the following import: The President was aware that because of the shoal water at the mouth of Cape Fear River, a purely naval attack could not be made against Wilmington. Two months prior, an attack had been arranged to be made on October 1st, postponed to the 15th; the naval force was ready, and at the time of writing, "one hundred and fifty vessels of war now form the North Atlantic Squadron. . . . The detention of so many vessels from blockade and cruising duty is a most serious injury to the public service; and if the expedition cannot go forward for want of troops, I desire to be notified, so that the ships may be relieved and dispersed for other service."

The tone of the above indicates potential influences, either to further delay the expedition or cause its abandonment. The vessels, for the most part of the largest size and heaviest batteries, were yet north of Cape Hatteras; those that could enter Beaufort Harbor were there, and the smaller ones actually in face of the entrances, blockading. They all, however, found their way to the outer anchorage off Beaufort, and there remained awaiting a detachment of troops to co-operate in the taking of Fort Fisher.

In composition the force was as extraordinary as was ever

assembled. The Ironsides, a fair specimen of an early iron-clad ship, a double-turreted monitor, and three monitors of single turrets, old steam frigates, "double-enders," merchant-ships converted into vessels of war, and vessels of war proper, but the force was not embarrassed by a sailing vessel.

On the 10th of December Rear-Admiral Porter issued a General Order "with chart plan of the proposed attack on the batteries at New Inlet." He says: "It is first proposed to endeavor to paralyze the garrison by an explosion, all the vessels remaining twelve miles out from the bar, and the troops in transports twelve miles down the coast, ready to steam up and be prepared to take the works by assault in case the latter are disabled. At a given signal all the bar vessels will run off shore twelve miles, when the vessel with powder will go in under the forts. When the explosion takes place all the vessels will stand in shore in the order marked on the plan."

The New Ironsides was to bring the flag-staff on Fort Fisher southwest by west half west, and anchor in three and a half fathoms of water, and open fire without delay; the monitors to anchor astern one length apart, directly in line along the shore.

"The large ships to anchor in five fathoms of water, in line of battle to the eastward of the ironclads, and heading parallel with the land (south half west). The Minnesota, leading this line, on signal to take position will go ahead slowly and anchor about one mile from Fort Fisher, open-ing fire when she passes the Ironsides, and anchoring when her after guns firing on Fisher will clear the range of the Ironsides; the Mohican, next in line, will then anchor ahead of the Minnesota, Colorado next ahead of her, and all of the line thus when anchored in reverse of order of sailing."

"The Seneca, Shenandoah, and six other vessels will take

II.—10

their positions between and outside the different vessels as marked on the plan.

"After the vessels above designated have got into position, the Nyack, Unadilla, Huron, and Pequot will take up position outside and between the monitors, keeping up a rapid fire when the monitors are loading.

"The following vessels will then take their positions as marked on the plan : Fort Jackson, Santiago de Cuba, Tacony, Osceola, Chippewa, Sassacus, Maratanza, Rhode Island, Monticello, Mount Vernon, Montgomery, Cuyler, Quaker City, and Iosco, anchoring in reverse as before.

"It is not desirable that the vessels should be seen by the enemy prior to the time of attack. A rendezvous, twenty-five miles east of New Inlet, is given. Commanders of divisions will get their divisions in line and keep them so. When signal is made to form line of battle, every vessel will take her position, the first division forming first.

"As low steam will suffice in going into action, those vessels that can move and work handily with half-boiler power will do so, having full boilers without steam next the enemy. Slow deliberate firing will be made."

In accordance with this programme, the Louisiana, an old vessel designed for "a torpedo on a large scale," was towed from Norfolk by the Sassacus to a remote part of Beaufort Harbor, there anchored and filled with powder, with carefully studied arrangements for firing many centres at the same moment. The vessel was disguised as a blockade-runner, and her preparation for service was assigned to Commander Rhind, aided by Lieutenant Preston, Second Assistant Engineer Mullan, and Master's Mate Boyden, with seven men.

CHAPTER X.

FORT FISHER.

PREPARATIONS having been completed, at noon on the 18th of December the largest fleet that had ever sailed under the Union flag formed lines in accordance with instructions, and proceeded to the rendezvous, twenty-five miles east of Fort Fisher, a distance of fifty miles from Beaufort Roads. There was a good deal of awkwardness in forming lines with vessels that had never acted together, and there were several officers in command not well versed in the matter, simple enough, had the leading vessels steamed slowly on their course and thus permitted their followers to fall into the positions assigned in line. The appearance was not promising; there was much room for improvement; but when under the fire of the enemy the vessels took up their positions with less disorder and more celerity than in forming the first order of sailing, or "line ahead," at distances of two ships' lengths apart. The fleet reached the rendezvous and anchored after a run of ten hours, and found the transports at anchor, having on board the command of General Butler. The weather was not regarded as favorable for landing troops, and the vessels remained at anchor. On the 20th a heavy southwest gale set in, and the army transports being short of water, and many of them not well adapted to ride out a gale at anchor, a number of them made for Beaufort. The depth of water where the vessels anchored was seventeen fathoms with sandy bottom ; the seas rolled in unbroken by land for hundreds of miles. Many of the vessels dragged for miles, and some occasions were presented where seamanship was necessary to prevent them fouling each other. When the gale was over the fleet was widely scattered, but as soon as the weather moderated vessels that had dragged steamed into line again and anchored.

After the gale the wind changed to the westward, off the land, the sea became smooth, and as it was necessary to avail himself of the good weather, although the transports with the troops had not returned, the admiral determined to go in and attack the batteries. Mr. Bradford, of the Coast Survey, had previously made a night examination of the depth of water near Fort Fisher, and found that a vessel of seven feet draught could be placed right on the edge of the beach. At 10.30 P.M. of the 23d, the powder-boat Louisiana, Commander Rhind and the officers before mentioned, was taken in tow by the Wilderness, Master Arey in command, and Lieutenant Lamson, commanding the Gettysburg, on board to take her into position.

The Louisiana, though having steam, was towed in and piloted by the Wilderness to near her station, when she was cast off. Lieutenant Lamson, Mr. Bradford, of the Coast Survey, and Mr. Bowen, bar-pilot, were of the "greatest service in perfecting arrangements and carrying out the plan successfully." The officers and crew of the Wilderness "shared whatever of risk or danger attended the enterprise." At 11.30 the Wilderness cast off her tow, and the powder-boat (Louisiana) steamed in until she reached a point east by north, half north, from Fort Fisher, within three hundred yards of the beach. There was a light wind off shore; the anchor was let go, the fires hauled, the men put in the boat, and Commander Rhind and Lieutenant

Preston proceeded to light the fuses and the fires; the latter had been arranged by Engineer Mullan. The officers then got in the boat, and they reached the Wilderness precisely at midnight; her anchor was slipped, and she steamed at full speed a distance of twelve miles, and then hove to. At 1.40 the powder-boat blew up; the shock was hardly felt, and four distinct reports were heard. The fuses were set by the clocks to one hour and a half, and the explosion did not occur until twenty-two minutes later. Commander Rhind says: "The zeal, patience, and endurance of officers and men were unsurpassed, and I believe no officer could have been better supported."

At the anchorage, twenty-five miles from the powder-boat, there was the appearance of distant lightning on the horizon; then came, after a lapse of time, a dull sound, and after a couple of hours a dense powder-smoke that shut out the view and was an hour in passing.

At daylight the different divisions of the fleet stood in at low speed. At 11.30 A.M. the signal was made to engage the forts, the Ironsides leading, and the Monadnock, Canonicus, and Mahopac following. The Ironsides took her position in the most beautiful and seamanlike manner, got her spring out, and opened deliberate fire on the fort, which was firing at her with all available guns.

The Minnesota then took her position in handsome style, closely followed by the Mohican, which ranged ahead and anchored; a few shells gave the range, and then they opened fire rapidly and with precision *on the guns in the fort*, receiving at the same time their fire. There was a considerable gap in the line, and some fifteen minutes elapsed before the Colorado passed in and ahead, anchored, opened on the fort, and was followed by the other vessels of the line. The other lines then got into position with a moderate degree of success, and the works of the enemy were alive with the bursting shells. The fort maintained an indifferent fire from the more distant guns, and but little, if any, from the parts of the work within range of the shell-guns of the fleet.

At signal made by the admiral to "fire slowly," the firing from the vessels became veritable target practice at particular guns of the fort, with officers in the tops to mark the ranges; from the inner line and from the ironclads and gunboats near them the firing was also accurate. The outer lines were somewhat too distant, and many shells from them were observed to fall short.

Two service magazine explosions occurred in the forts, and several buildings were set on fire and burned. The admiral's report says: "Finding that the batteries were silenced completely, I directed the ships to keep up a moderate fire, in the hopes of attracting the attention of the transports and bringing them in. At sunset General Butler came in, in his flag-ship, with a few transports, the rest not having arrived from Beaufort. Being too late to do anything more, I signaled the fleet to retire for the night for a safe anchorage, which they did without being molested by the enemy." With the exception of a boiler explosion on board the Mackinaw by a shell, the casualties were entirely from the bursting of 100-pounder Parrott rifled guns, and they were serious. These occurred on board of the Ticonderoga, 8 killed, 11 wounded; Yantic, 2 killed, 3 wounded; Juniata, 5 killed, 8 wounded; Mackinaw, 1 killed and 1 wounded, and Quaker City.

Some of the fleet were somewhat damaged by shells. The Osceola received "a shell near her magazine, and at one time was in a sinking condition; but her efficient commander stopped up the leak, while the Mackinaw fought out the battle notwithstanding the damage she received."

On the 25th the transports generally had arrived, and General Weitzel, chief-of-staff, went on board of the flag-ship "to arrange the programme for the day. It was decided that the fleet should attack the forts again, while the army landed and assaulted them, if possible, under our heavy fire."[1] Seventeen gunboats, under command of Captain O. S. Glisson, were sent to cover the landing, and assist with their boats; it was perceived that the smaller vessels kept too far from the beach, and the Brooklyn was despatched to set them an example. An addition of perhaps twenty vessels was sent to aid in the debarkation of the troops, the aggregate number of their boats being one hundred; the army had boats probably better adapted to the purpose than those belonging to the ships.

The admiral made signal for commanders of vessels to go on board the flag-ship, and determined to form his lines as near the forts as a close examination of the depth of water by boats sounding in advance would permit. The Minnesota was held off until the soundings were made, and then took up position, and the main line was soon in very effective position, and previously "the Ironsides took position in her usual handsome style, the monitors following close after her, all the vessels followed according to order, and took position without a shot being fired at them, excepting a few shots fired at the four last vessels that got into line."

The firing was slow at intervals, and was directed actually at the guns as at target practice; the parapets and the traverses of huge proportions were dug into and so changed in appearance by the craters made from heavy shells that these enormous piles seemed likely to be relegated to fellowship with the neighboring "dunes" or natural sand-hillocks.

---

[1] Admiral Porter's Report.

The admiral in his report says : "I suppose about 3,000 men had landed, when I was notified they were re-embarking. I could see our soldiers near the forts reconnoitring and sharpshooting, and was in hopes an assault was deemed practicable. General Weitzel in person was making observations about six hundred yards off, and the troops were in and around the works. One gallant officer, whose name I do not know, went on the parapet and brought away the rebel flag we had knocked down. A soldier went into the works and led out a horse, killing the orderly who was mounted on him and taking the despatches from his body. Another soldier fired his musket into the bomb-proof among the rebels, and eight or ten others who had ventured near the forts were wounded by our shells. As the ammunition gave out the vessels retired from action, and the ironclads and Minnesota, Colorado, and Susquehanna were ordered to open rapidly, which they did with such effect that it seemed to tear the works to pieces. We drew off at sunset, leaving the ironclads to fire through the night, expecting the troops would attack in the morning, when we would commence again. I received word from General Weitzel, informing me that it was impracticable to assault." [1]

The bombardment of this day was of about seven hours' duration. A few guns near the Mound battery kept up a fire on the vessels, and at intervals there was some firing from

---

[1] Extract of letter of General Butler to Admiral Porter, dated December 25, 1864 : " Admiral—Upon landing the troops and making a thorough reconnoissance of Fort Fisher, both General Weitzel and myself are fully of the opinion that the place could not be carried by assault, as it was left substantially uninjured as a defensive work by the navy fire. We found seventeen guns protected by traverses, two only of which were dismounted, bearing up the beach, and covering a strip of land, the only practicable route, not more than wide enough for a thousand men in line of battle. . . . I shall therefore sail for Hampton Roads as soon as the transport fleet can be got in order. My engineers and officers report Fort Fisher to me as substantially uninjured as a defensive work."

guns nearer the ironclads and line of frigates. "Everything was coolly and systematically done," and the admiral adds, "I witnessed some fine practice."

The weather had grown threatening and a heavy swell rolled in, which toward night put an end to the re-embarkation of the troops. In relation to this the admiral states in his report: "Seven hundred men were left on the beach by General Butler when he departed for Fortress Monroe, and we had no difficulty in protecting them from the rebel army said to be in the background, which was a very small army after all." The men were not re-embarked until the noon of the 27th, owing to the surf, when the transports left for Fortress Monroe.

In an official letter of December 31, 1864, commenting upon the letter of General Butler, Admiral Porter says: "General Butler mentions in his letter to me that he had captured Flag-pond battery with sixty-five men, and Half Moon battery with two hundred and eighteen men and seven officers. This is making capital out of very small material.

"Flag-pond battery was some loose sand thrown up, behind which the rebels used to lie with field pieces and fire at our blockaders when they chased runners ashore. It does not deserve the name of a work. Sixty-five or seventy rebels in it came forward and delivered themselves up to the navy and were taken on board the Santiago de Cuba. The men in Half Moon battery (which is no work at all and exactly like the other) came forward and delivered themselves up to the army. They could easily have escaped had they desired to do so."

The fact that these men were taken prisoners is significant. They could have reached the cover of an adjacent wood and gone toward Wilmington entirely unmolested. This does not comport with the report of Major-General Whiting of

10*

the Confederate service herein quoted, as to the spirit animating the garrison of Fort Fisher, or with the fact that some of our skirmish line carried off a Confederate flag, killed a courier, and carried off his horse actually behind the curtain, and left without injury or molestation save from the shells of the bombarding vessels.

General Whiting paid a visit to Fort Fisher, under the command of Colonel Lamb, reaching the fort just before the close of the first day's bombardment. He says : "The bombardment of the second day commenced at 10.20 A.M., and continued, with no interruption or apparent slackening, with great fury from over fifty ships till dark. During the day the enemy landed a large force, and at 4.30 P.M. advanced a line of skirmishers on the left flank of the sand curtain, the fleet at the same time making a concentrated and tremendous enfilading fire on the curtain.

"The garrison, however, at the proper moment, when the fire slackened to allow the approach of the enemy's land force, drove them off with grape and musketry ; at dark the enemy withdrew. A heavy storm set in, and the garrison were much exposed, as they were under arms all night." [1]

---

[1] General Whiting, in answer to inquiries by General Butler, states that the garrison was 667 men on the 18th. On the 23d, 110 veteran artillery, 50 sailors, and 250 junior reserves were added. Total, 1,077. On the 24th the fleet disabled five guns ; on the 25th four guns, two of them being on the left, looking up the beach, and nineteen in position, and mines (for explosion) undisturbed. He doubts the success of an assault at that time. In the official report of General Whiting, dated December 30th, is found the fact that the "Junior Reserves" and others had to be coaxed out of the bomb-proofs, one might say, on the 25th, to repel a possible assault. This report concludes as follows : "Whatever the power of resistance of the fort, and it is great, no doubt, the delay due to the heavy weather of Wednesday and Thursday after the arrival of the fleet was its salvation. . . . But we cannot always hope for such aid from weather, or the blunder of the enemy, manifest here for his not landing and occupying the work before the commencement of his bombardment, and I trust the lesson will not be lost." The reader can now form his own conclusion whether General Butler could or could not have taken Fort Fisher.

The vessels not engaged on the blockade were withdrawn to Beaufort, to get a full supply of ammunition and shells, and to await further instructions. The results of the bombardment were not satisfactory to either side, but doubtless more so to the Confederates than to their opponents. It was heralded that this great fleet had been driven off, when in fact surprisingly little injury had been inflicted upon it, save through the bursting of rifled guns.

On December 29th the Secretary of the Navy, in a letter to Lieutenant-General Grant, said : " Ships can approach nearer the enemy's works at New Inlet than was anticipated. Their fire can keep the enemy away from their guns. A landing can easily be effected upon the beach north of Fort Fisher, not only of troops, but all their supplies and artillery. This force can have its flanks protected by gunboats. The navy can assist in the siege of Fort Fisher precisely as it covered the operations which resulted in the capture of Wagner. . . . Rear-Admiral Porter will remain off Fort Fisher, continuing a moderate fire to prevent new works from being erected, and the ironclads have proved that they can maintain themselves in spite of bad weather. Under all these circumstances, I invite you to such a military co-operation as will ensure the fall of Fort Fisher, the importance of which has already received your careful consideration." He added that the telegram was sent at the suggestion of the President.

On the 31st of December the Secretary of the Navy wrote Admiral Porter as follows : " Lieutenant-General Grant will send immediately a competent force, properly commanded, to co-operate in the capture of the defences on Federal Point."

On January 14, 1865, Admiral Porter reports that he had been busily employed since his withdrawal from Fort Fisher in filling the ships with ammunition and coal. The large vessels had no harbor, and these operations outside were attended by extreme difficulties. It was a season of gales upon which the enemy relied to break up operations against him. " We will see ; we have gone through the worst of it, have held on through gales heavy enough to drive anything to sea, and we have sustained no damage whatever."

In a subsequent report he informs the Department that Major-General Terry arrived at Beaufort, N. C., on the 8th of January, in command of a co-operating army force, and a plan of operations had been agreed upon that had resulted in success.

Heavy weather set in about the time of Terry's arrival, which lasted for forty-eight hours, although the large vessels of war lying off the harbor were exposed to its full force ; with furious seas setting in on a lee shore, they rode out the gales without accident ; some of the heavier transports, with troops, were also lying with them ; ammunition and coal had been taken on board, notwithstanding all of the difficulties, and on the 12th of January the fleet had sailed in three columns, accompanied by the transports.

The Brooklyn led the first line, followed in order by the Mohican, Tacony, Kansas, Yantic, Unadilla, Huron, Maumee, Pequot, Pawtuxet, Seneca, Pontoosuc, and Nereus, thirteen vessels.

The Minnesota led the second line, followed in order by the Colorado, Wabash, Susquehanna, Powhatan, Juniata, Shenandoah, Ticonderoga, Vanderbilt, Mackinaw, and Tuscarora, eleven heavy vessels.

The Santiago de Cuba led the third line, followed in order by the Fort Jackson, Osceola, Sassacus, Chippewa, Cuyler, Maratanza, Rhode Island, Monticello, Alabama, Montgomery, and Iosco, twelve vessels.

The Vance led the reserve division, followed in order by

the Britannia, Tristram Shandy, Lillian, Fort Donelson, Wilderness, Aries, Buckingham, Nansemond, Little Ada, Eolus, and Republic, the two last being despatch boats, twelve vessels.

The lines above form a total of forty-eight vessels, the ironclads, not yet mentioned, being five in number. The reader will bear in mind the very effective broadside battery of the Ironsides (seven XI-inch shell-guns and one VIII-inch rifle), and that the Monadnock with her two turrets was equivalent in force to two monitors such as the Canonicus, Saugus, and Mahopac, of more recent construction than the Passaic class, and possessed more power of resistance to projectiles.

The fleet, accompanied by numerous army transports, anchored during the night some twelve miles east of Fisher. In the morning, the Ironsides and her consorts proceeded at once to get under way toward Fort Fisher, and following in on their former range lines anchored as near that work as the depth of water would permit. This brought the Ironsides within one thousand yards, and the nearest monitor within seven hundred yards of the nearest guns, that were vigorously firing upon them as they anchored. The vessels proceeded to get ranges, and then to make effective practice at the guns in the fort, which, however, "replied vigorously until late in the afternoon, when the heavier ships coming into line soon drove them into their bomb-proofs." [1]

At daylight lines one, two, and three proceeded also to execute the duties assigned them, and soon after sunrise were anchored in lines near the beach at Half Moon battery, four miles north of Fort Fisher. Boats were at once sent to the transports, and although there was considerable swell,

---

[1] Belknap's Report.

the work of debarkation went on vigorously and effectively.
Preceding this, vessels on line No. 1 had shelled the woods
back of the beach, and hundreds of cattle that had doubtless
been brought there for the supply of the garrison of Fort
Fisher rushed wildly to the beach and delivered themselves
over, opportune food for the army.

At 2 P.M. 6,000 men and twelve days' provisions had been
landed, and one hour later the whole force was in front of
Fort Fisher, or prepared to go. At 3.30 line No. 1 was signalled to get under way and attack Fort Fisher, and half an
hour later line No. 2 followed under like instructions ; the
vessel to lead, Minnesota, was detained for an hour by a
hawser fouling the propeller, and joined the line during the
bombardment. Line No. 3 remained during the day to debark artillery and whatever might still be afloat, which was
fully accomplished the next day.

With the ironclads in position serving as guides, Line No.
1 soon anchored, and at 4.35 P.M. opened fire, and with this
line in position, line No. 2, composed of heavier ships, was
soon after at anchor, and delivering broadsides which " soon
drove the enemy to their bomb-proofs."

As the sun went down, and the shadows fell over the
waters, the spectacle was truly grand ; the smoke rose and
partially drifted off, permitting glimpses now and then of
the earthwork, and the fitful yet incessant gleams from the
hundreds of shells bursting on or beyond the parapet illuminated, like lightning flashes, the clouds above and the
smoke of battle beneath.

At 5.50 it was too dark to fire with precision. All the
wooden vessels were signalled to withdraw and anchor in
line to seaward, and the ironclads to maintain a slow fire on
the works throughout the night.

The admiral observed that the fire had already damaged

some of the guns of the enemy, and he determined that before
the army went to the assault there should be no guns within
the reach of the fleet to arrest progress ; he saw, too, that
within, near Mound battery, heavy guns were brought to
bear, and therefore changed the plan of bombardment on
the next day.

On the 14th, all of the small gunboats carrying XI-inch
pivot guns were sent into positions commanding the north
face of Fisher to dismount the guns bearing along the intended line of assault by the army; line No. 1 at the same
time delivering a rapid fire on the fort to keep the enemy in
his bomb-proofs. The vessels were fairly in position at
1 P.M., and all of them actively employed until long after
dark, and during the whole night this gunboat fire was added
to that of the slower fire of the ironclads. The guns far up
in the line of works alone replied to this attack, and in doing
so hit the gunboats occasionally, cutting off the mainmast of
the Huron and doing other damage.

In the evening, General Terry visited the flag-ship Mal-
vern to arrange final plans. His troops on the night after
landing had effected a lodgment and thrown up defences
across the peninsula, some two miles north of Fort Fisher.
They had recovered from the effects of the sea voyage and
from the drenching received when landing in the surf, and
were prepared to make the assault, and gallantly indeed was
it done the following afternoon.

It was determined that the entire fleet should go into
action at an early hour the following day, and continue a vigorous bombardment until the hour of assault. The admiral
"detailed 1,600 sailors and 400 marines to accompany the
troops in the assault, the sailors to board the sea face while
the troops assaulted the land side." The order sent to
commanders of vessels was as follows : "The sailors will be

armed with cutlasses, well sharpened, and with revolvers. When the signal is made to man the boats, the men will get in but not show themselves. When the signal is made to assault, the boats will pull around the stern of the monitors and land right abreast of them, and board the fort on the run in a seamanlike way. The marines will form in the rear and cover the sailors. While the soldiers are going over the parapets in front, the sailors will take the sea face of Fort Fisher." This was more easily said than done, as we shall presently see.

At 9 A.M on the 15th signal was made for the fleet to bombard as per plan. The last of the vessels got into position by 11 A.M., but the heads of some of the lines were in action very promptly. The reader will bear in mind that the ironclads remained where they had first anchored, and were supplied with ammunition brought alongside during the night. On signal from the flag-ship the vessels sent their quotas of men on shore some time in the early forenoon, for making the assault. At 2 P.M. the admiral was in expectancy of the signal from the general for "vessels change direction of fire." The sailors landed under command of their officers, who had no previous knowledge to whom they should report, or who was to lead them in the assault. Fleet-Captain K. R. Breese, a very gallant and competent officer, had gone to arrange details with General Terry, and he was absent for that purpose. Until his return it was not known to all who was to lead the assault.

Lieutenant-Commander Parker, the executive officer of the Minnesota, commanded the detail, 240 men, from that vessel. He says : "We were huddling there together like a flock of sheep, and pretty soon the enemy got the range with sufficient accuracy to satisfy me that a formation of some kind must be made if we expected to do anything."

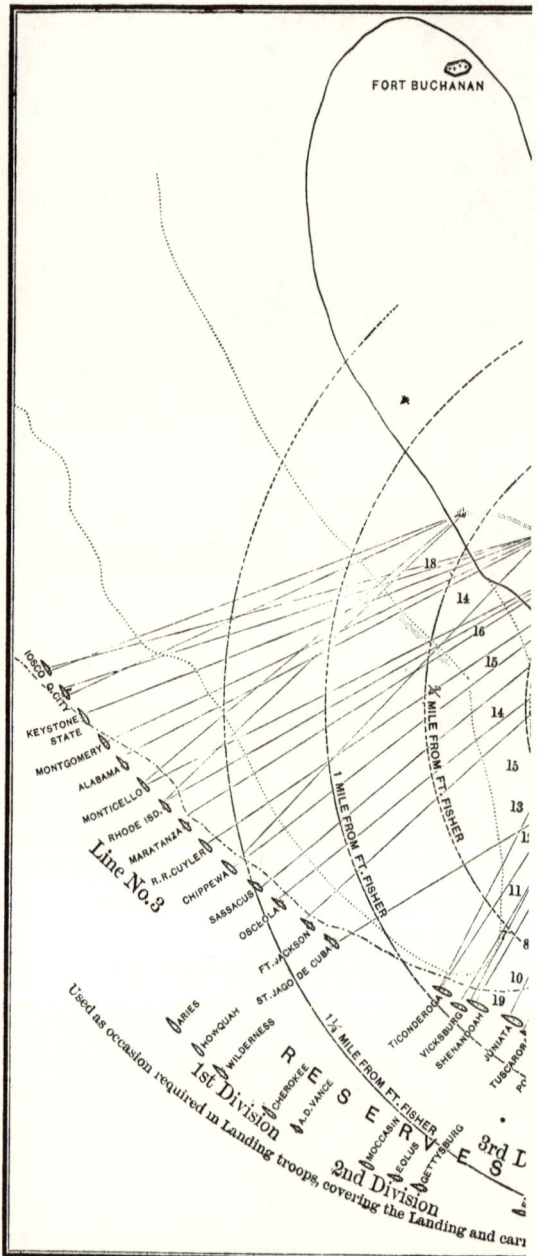

FORT BUCHANAN

18
14
16
15
14
15
13
1
11
8
10
19

1 MILE FROM FT. FISHER

1 MILE FROM FT. FISHER

IOSCO CITY

KEYSTONE STATE

MONTGOMERY

ALABAMA

MONTICELLO

RHODE ISD.

MARATANZA

R.R. CUYLER

CHIPPEWA

SASSACUS

OSCEOLA

FT. JACKSON

ST. JAGO DE CUBA

Line No. 3

ARIES

HOWQUAH

WILDERNESS

CHEROKEE

A.D. VANCE

TICONDEROGA

VICKSBURG

SHENANDOAH

JUNIATA

TUSCARORA

PO

1¼ MILE FROM FT. FISHER

MOCCASIN

AEOLUS

GETTYSBURG

1st Division

2nd Division

3rd L

R E S E R V E S

Used as occasion required in Landing troops, covering the Landing and carr

SECOND ATTACK
UPON
FORT FISHER
BY THE U. S. NAVY UNDER
REAR ADMIRAL D. D. PORTER.
Jan. 13, 14, 15, 1865.
Showing the Position of Vessels and Line of Fire.

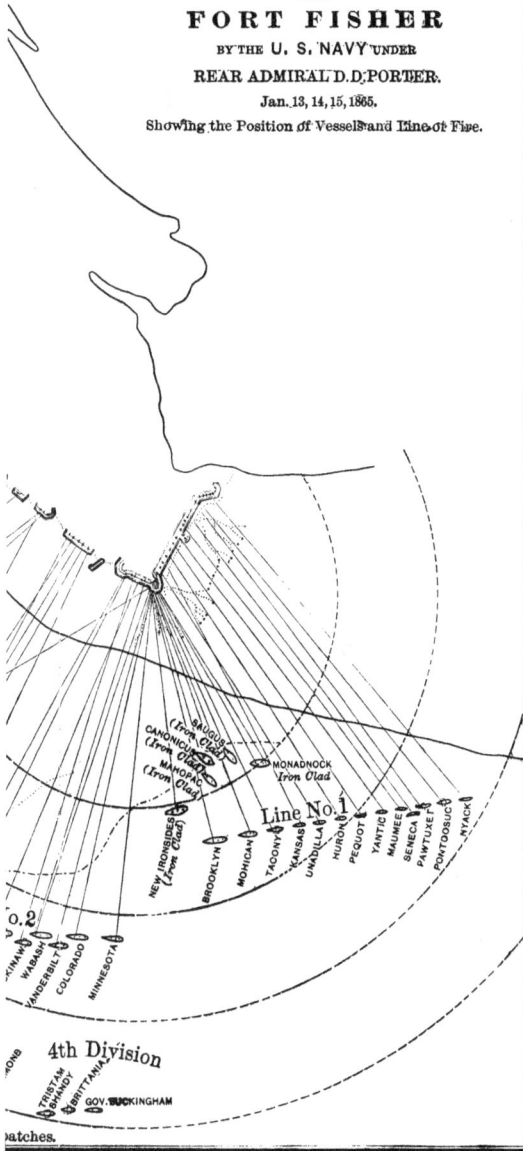

SAUGUS
(Iron Clad)
CANONICUS
(Iron Clad)
MAHOPAC
(Iron Clad)
MONADNOCK
Iron Clad
NEW IRONSIDES
(Iron Clad)
BROOKLYN
MOHICAN
TACONY
KANSAS
UNADILLA
HURON
PEQUOT
YANTIC
MAUMEE
SENECA
PAWTUXET
PONTOOSUC
NYACK

Line No. 1

No. 2
KINAW
WABASH
VANDERBILT
COLORADO
MINNESOTA

4th Division

ONB
TRISTAM
SHANDY
BRITTANIA
GOV. BUCKINGHAM

atches.

He was the senior officer ashore, and therefore directed the commanding officers of detachments from the different ships to report to the senior lieutenant-commander of that division of the fleet to which their respective vessels belonged, and that they should be formed in line of battle, first division in front and second and third following. Cushman was in command of the first division, Parker of the second, and Selfridge of the third.

These preparations were completed when Lieutenant-Commander Breese came in haste from General Terry. He had with him two sailors, one of whom bore the admiral's flag. On meeting Parker, the last named asked who was to command, and Breese produced a letter from the admiral stating that he [Breese] was to represent the admiral in the assault. With praiseworthy zeal Parker assumed the role of an inferior rank, in deference to the admiral's flag, and the columns actually in movement were proceeding by the flank under the shelving beach, which afforded partial protection from the enemy's fire.

In his report, in reference to preliminary arrangements, Fleet-Captain Breese says : " Lieutenant Preston with a detail of men from the vessels, threw up, within six hundred yards of the fort, a well-protected breastwork, and from that gradually advanced to within two hundred yards a succession of rifle-pits, which were most promptly occupied by a line of skirmishers composed of marines under Lieutenant Fagan. The manner in which this was done reflects most creditably upon Lieutenant Preston." He states further that four lines of assault were intended, the first of marines, Captain L. L. Dawson ; the second of sailors from the first and fourth divisions of the fleet, under Cushman ; the third, sailors from the second division, under Parker ; the fourth, the sailors from the third division of the fleet, under Selfridge.

"It was intended that the men should assault in line, the marines acting as sharpshooters, and the different lines were to charge over them; but from the difficulty I had of informing myself of the time when the army was to assault, which was to guide our movements, that moment found us too far off to move to the attack unless under cover." [1]

"At three o'clock the signal came, the vessels changed their fire to the upper batteries; all the steam-whistles were blown, and the troops and sailors dashed ahead, nobly vying with each other to reach the top of the parapet. . . . The sailors took to the assault by the flank along the beach, while the troops rushed in at the left [right?], through the palisades that had been knocked away by the fire of our guns." [2]

Fifty steam-whistles from the vessels, blown long and loud, and the sound of shells bursting far beyond the near faces of Fort Fisher, upon which assaulting columns were advancing, gave notice within every bomb-proof of a movement. The army force, managed dexterously, had been placed under cover close to the land face of the fort. It advanced rapidly, gained and held the western end of that parapet and between the traverses, but the sailors and marines had nearly half a mile before them, along a line, too, enfiladed by low and more distant guns that swept the ground with grape and shells. The enemy swarmed the bastion and delivered deadly volleys at distances at which the cutlasses and revolvers in the hands of the sailors were quite inoperative, and yet many of the assailants reached, and some of them passed through the line of palisades that remained in part, and now afforded them partial protection, and the only one, from certain death; others farther away, and

---

[1] Captain Breese's Report.   [2] Admiral Porter's Report.

still advancing, seeing that to press on would simply end in measuring their length upon the sand, turned, fled in haste up the beach, and sought the cover of the pits and trench dug some hours before, too distant to enable even the marines with their arms to return an effective fire. A doubt may be ventured whether any troops, however armed, could have effected an advance on this line of assault at that time.

"When it was discovered that the army column was moving to attack, the navy columns were ordered to advance by the flank along the beach, with the hope of forming them for the assault under cover of the marines ; but exposed to a galling fire of musketry, only four hundred yards distance, threw a portion of the marines into the first line, and the rest of them did not take position as they should.

"The second and third lines came along and the heads of the three lines joined and formed one compact column, which filing up to the sea face of Fort Fisher, assaulted to within fifty yards of the parapet, which was lined by one dense mass of musketeers, who played sad havoc with our men. Although exposed to a most severe fire from the enemy, the men were rallied three times under the personal encouragement and exposure of their commanding officers, but failed to gain much ground." [1]

Captain Breese mentioned the gallantry of many officers, among whom was his senior, Lieutenant-Commander Parker, who led the third line of assault, if the columns advancing as above described can be called lines of assault.

In fact, the palisades, a shelving sea-beach, the rifle-pits, some small sand-hills, and the trench before mentioned served partially to protect the survivors of the heads of columns from the fire of the small arms on the bastion until the

---

[1] Captain Breese's Report.

heavy guns of the fleet again opened on that part of the fort, and made it necessary for the Confederates to look to their safety.

In the meantime, the National troops having gained the parapets on their front, had carried seven of the traverses most to the west, without serious loss, attacked the traverses more toward the sea, one after the other, and the vessels farthest in, especially the Ironsides and the monitors, resumed a fire of heavy shells between the traverses in advance of the troops, as they carried traverse after traverse, most obstinately defended as they were by the Confederates. But the odds were against them. They had to face as gallant men pressing onward as the Confederate defenders, who were flanked by a destructive fire of heavy shells ; they had, in fact, either to abandon traverse after traverse or be killed where they stood. By nightfall the bastion was carried and some of the traverses on the sea face.

As opportunity offered, officers and men of the navy who had been held fast under their imperfect cover, found their way around the palisades into the army lines or went within them higher up. Lieutenant Cushing, who was wounded, organized the sailors and took charge of a line of breastworks to protect the rear from a Confederate attack from the north along the sandspit, and thus released additional troops, who joined those already within the fort.

But while the battle raged hot in the fort and its defenders looked for relief from Hoke's division along the peninsula, and have upbraided General Bragg because it did not advance, the half dozen gunboats placed close along the beach north of General Terry's lines, defended by General Paine's brigade, about 4 P.M. saw from their mast-heads Hoke's skirmish line advancing, and with shells exerted a restraining influence. Had assaulting columns followed the skirmish line, they certainly would have reached General Terry's intrenchments in bad plight, and admitting that line had been carried, the Confederates would not have been formidable after a march of two miles toward Fort Fisher on an open sandspit under the fire of gunboats.

Shortly after ten o'clock resistance in Fort Fisher ceased, the Confederates retreating, as is stated by Colonel Lamb, without ammunition, to the innermost point, from whence such of them as had the means of transportation escaped. Lieutenant Chapman and others of the Confederate Navy are known to have done so, but the whole number that fled is not ascertainable. When the sound of fire-arms had ceased, and it was known the enemy had surrendered, the sky was illuminated by hundreds of rockets from the fleet, and the remote works for the defence of the entrances to Cape Fear River were thus incidentally apprised that their defenders had the alternative in prospect to surrender or to precipitately retreat.

In the Appendix will be found the list of the vessels engaged, by whom commanded, the batteries, and the casualties in the fleet.

Among the killed in the assault were Lieutenants Preston and Porter, both of them young officers of great ability and admirable qualities; also Assistant-Surgeon Longshaw and Ensign Wiley, and by the explosion of the magazine, Paymaster Gillett and Ensign Leighton. There were wounded in the assault, Lieutenant-Commander Allen, Lieutenants Bache, Lamson, and Baury; Ensigns Evans, Harris, Chester, Bertwistle, O'Connor, Coffin, and Wood; Acting-Master Louch, and Mates Green, Simms, and Aldridge.

In relation to Flag-Captain Breese, who led the assault, Lieutenant-Commander Parker said in his report: "He led the advance to the palisades, and when he saw the rear de-

laying, endeavored, sword in hand, to bring them forward to
our support. Failing to accomplish this, he returned, under
a shower of bullets directed at him alone, to the sand-hills
at 'C,' and when it seemed no longer useful to remain
there coolly followed the retreating mass. How he escaped
death is a marvel."

In relation to Lieutenant-Commander Daniels, he says:
"He came ashore in command of the party from his vessel.
Although fitter for the sick-bed of a hospital than for the
field, he persisted in going to the assault. He started with
us, marched until his strength gave out, and his weak body
was unable to carry his brave heart forward, when, by my
orders, he went into the trench thrown up by Lieutenant
Preston's party." An interesting letter from Colonel Lamb
to Parker is given in the foot-note.[1]

In his report, the fleet-captain attributes "the failure of
the assault to the absence of the marines from their position,
as their fire would have enabled our boarders to use their

---

[1] NORFOLK, VA., January 15, 1879.

CAPTAIN JAMES PARKER:

Dear Sir—In reply to your recent letter, I would state that I was colonel in
command of the Confederate garrison of Fort Fisher, North Carolina, upon the
occasion of its assault and capture by the United States forces on this day fourteen
years ago. The attacking column of the army was hid and protected by the river
bank as it approached the left flank of the work, but the naval column came up
the open beach upon our centre. As its success would have been disastrous, I
concentrated all available guns upon this column, and met its assault with the
larger portion of my men, posting them upon the ramparts so as to fire down
upon the sailors and marines. I particularly noticed in the assault an officer who
seemed to lead the column, and who was almost recklessly brave, and directed my
men to pick him and other officers off, to discourage the assailants. When we
afterward met on board the steamship California, at Old Point Comfort (where
you had come to see if you could be of service to me in my wounded condition),
you can imagine my surprise, after I had described this officer's dress to you, to
learn that you were he, and the pleasure it gave me to know that so brave and
gallant a foe had escaped.

With best wishes, yours very truly,

WILLIAM LAMB.

PLAN AND SECTIONS
OF
FORT FISHER,
CARRIED BY ASSAULT
BY THE
U.S.FORCES
MAJ. GEN. A. H. TERRY
Commanding.
January 15th, 1865.
After three days' bombardment by
U. S. Fleet,
REAR ADMIRAL D. D. PORTER,
Commanding.

ATLANTIC OCEAN

CAPE FEAR RIVER

Section on a-b

Section on c-d

Section on e-f

0 32 64 96 128 ft.
1:768

LINE OF RIFLEPITS

LINE OF RIFLEPITS

MOUND BATTERY

10" Columbiad Rifle

10" Columbiad
10" Columbiad

TELEGRAPH STA.

6⅜" Rifle
7" Rifle Brooks

10" Columbiad
10" Columbiad

150 Pdr. Armstrong

8" Rifle

6⅜" Rifle
6⅜" Rifle

8" Columbiad
7" Rifle Brooks
8" Columbiad
8" Columbiad
8" Columbiad
8" Columbiad

HEADQUARTERS

10" Colum...
10" Columbiad
6⅜" Rifle
10" Columbiad
8⅜" Rifle Blake

PALISADES

8" Mortar

Smooth Bore

10" Columbiad

Place of Explosion

ELECTRIC WIRES

LINE OF TORPEDOES

5½" Mortar
5½" Mortar
4½" Rifle Parrot
8" Smooth Bore
8" Rifle
10" Columbiad
10" Columbiad

5½" Mortar
6⅜" Rifle
6⅜"
6⅜"
6⅜"
6⅜"
6⅜"
6⅜" Rifle
6⅜" Rifle.Brooks
6⅜" Rifle
Smooth Bore
Columbiad
Smooth Bore

cutlasses and pistols most effectively. By this I would imply the lack of proper organization, it being impossible in the short space of time, on account of so many small squads of men from the different vessels in one mass, lacking proper company formations, and wholly unacquainted with each other, to secure such organization. This led to the confusion exhibited, for it was not due to any want of personal valor on the part of the officers or men."

A more thorough organization, and a studied preparation with proper arms in the hands of the sailors instead of cutlasses, would have made the gallantry displayed by many serve a more effective purpose, and, indeed, would probably have transformed putative cowardice into effective endeavor. There are few men so stupid or so sublimated as to march on an enemy when the palpable result is simply to be shot. Had parallel lines of trenches been dug during the night on the line between the ironclads and the northeast bastion, extending them to the sea at such distances from the fort as might have been found practicable, and the sailors been properly armed, that bastion might not have proven so popular a point of defence as it evidently was, as seen from the fleet. No reflection is intended on the defenders of the fort, who certainly in the second attack exhibited throughout the utmost pertinacity and courage.

The morning following the fall of the defences of New Inlet, as soon as a channel could be found and buoyed, the light-draught gunboats were taken over the outer bar as fast as possible, and as there is a shoaler one within, similar to the "bulkhead" at Hatteras Inlet, it was only on the forenoon of the 20th that all of the gunboats assigned for operations were within the river proper. Commander Truxton, of the Tacony, reported as follows: "In Fort Lamb was a galvanic battery in good working order, connecting with copper wires, which I this morning [19th of January] caused to be under-run, and which I found led directly across the river to the magazine in Fort Fisher. This, I believe, will fully account for the mysterious explosion on the 16th instant, by which over two hundred gallant men lost their lives."

In reply to a letter of General Bragg, published in Vol. X., "Southern Historical Society Papers," Colonel Lamb in the same volume, p. 360, indignantly denies that the troops under his command just after the fall of Fort Fisher were drunk. He says : " I had no liquor for distribution to the garrison, and what remained in the hospital bomb-proof was captured by some sailors from the fleet, who becoming intoxicated with it, entered the reserve magazine the morning after the battle seeking plunder, and caused its explosion, which resulted in the death and wounding of nearly two hundred brave men."

Colonel Lamb seemed at the time to be either indifferent to or ignorant of the report of Truxton. The existence of the insulated wire and galvanic battery could hardly be unknown to him, and would seem a more reasonable explanation of the cause of the explosion of the magazine than drunken sailors, in relation to whom we have no other accounts than the one above given.

Admitting the existence of the appliances establishes the existence of a purpose in an eventuality to blow up the magazine. If executed, as seems altogether probable, by a Confederate, with or without orders, the perpetrator had sooner or later the knowledge that he had destroyed quite as many of his former comrades as his foes. Whatever the cause, the magazine in Fort Fisher was blown up soon after sunrise on the morning of the 16th, the day following the surrender of the fort.

Fort Fisher had a northern or land face of 480 yards and mounted on it 21 guns, and a sea face of 1,300 yards, upon which were mounted 17 guns. The heavy calibres and character of the guns will appear in the Appendix or in the plan of the work. The parapets were 25 feet thick and an average of 20 feet in height; traverses ten feet higher, sloping back on their tops, were 8 to 12 feet thick. The traverses were generally bomb-proofed for men or magazines. Thirty bomb-proofs and magazines had a superficial area of 14,500 feet, not including the main magazine, which was exploded.

In all the works defending the two entrances of Cape Fear River were found one hundred and sixty-nine pieces of artillery, nearly all of which were heavy, and two thousand stand of small arms.

In common with his comrades afloat, the writer would fail in his duty were he to omit an expression of the universal sentiment of admiration of the ability and courage shown by General Terry, his Chief-of-Staff, General Comstock, and of General Ames, who led the assaulting columns, and of their gallant comrades, the living and the dead, who achieved this gallant work. Nothing could exceed the devotion and the courage shown by them.

The army losses in killed and severely wounded in the assault are given as 700. When the work accomplished is considered the losses are light, which show the true merit of the soldier. They met and conquered not less than 2,500 men in the best constructed earthwork known; 112 officers and 1,971 enlisted men were taken prisoners.

The night of the 16th and 17th was lurid with burning forts and barracks on Smith's Island, Fort Caswell, and elsewhere, and from time to time the explosions of powder magazines "vexed the dull ear of night." As soon as possible, after getting into the river, Admiral Porter pressed on

II.—11

with unabated energy and zeal with the gunboats within the river, which was filled with torpedoes. The work of dragging for them was painfully slow and laborious. The army was pressing onward also on both banks of the river to Wilmington.

The march of General Sherman had been delayed by rains; a considerable force under Bragg opposed the progress of the comparatively small one under General Terry, who could well afford to move cautiously, as the end was inevitable and could not be far off.

For the reduction of Wilmington General Schofield advanced from Smithville on the 17th of February. At the same time Admiral Porter attacked Fort Anderson, situated on the river, nearly half way to Wilmington, the monitor Montauk close to the works, and the gunboats Pawtuxet, Lenapee, Unadilla, and Pequot at some distance; the river had been previously dragged for torpedoes. The attacking force was limited, by reason of the difficulty of having more vessels in position. The following day (18th), in order to get more batteries to bear, at 8 A.M. the monitor Montauk led, followed by the Mackinaw, Huron, Sassacus, Pontoosuc, Maratanza, Lenapee, Unadilla, Pawtuxet, Osceola, Shawmut, Seneca, Nyack, Chippewa, and Little Ada. They anchored in position and maintained a heavy fire during the day. At 3 P.M. the fort no longer replied, but the fire was maintained by the fleet until after dark, and throughout the night with diminished intensity.

Aware that General Schofield was on the point of cutting off their retreat, the garrison abandoned the work during the night, carrying away six field pieces. Ten heavy guns were found in the fort. The casualties during the day in the attacking force were 3 killed and 4 wounded.

On the 20th and 21st the boats of the fleet were employed

in dragging for torpedoes in the waters over which the gunboats had to pass to attack the batteries higher up. While
thus employed a torpedo exploded under the bow of a boat
of the Shawmut, killing two men and wounding an officer
and one man.

On the 22d Admiral Porter reports that Wilmington had
been evacuated and was in possession of the Union troops.
On the evacuation of Fort Anderson the gunboats had pushed
up as far as the depth of water would permit, an army force
pushing up on both sides of the river, on the hard ground,
more or less distant from intervening marshes. At Big
Island the channel was sounded and buoyed, the gunboats
moved up, and fire was opened on Fort Strong, the work
commanding the principal obstructions ; the fire soon drove
the enemy from the fort. During the engagement a shell
struck the Sassacus below the water-line, causing her to leak
badly ; she received several other shots.

During the night of the 20th, not having further use for
them, as they intended to evacuate Wilmington, the enemy
sent down two hundred floating torpedoes, which for the
most part were sunk by musketry fire ; one that lodged in
the wheel of the Osceola blew the wheelhouse to pieces and
knocked down bulkheads inboard, but did not damage the
hull. The following morning fishing-nets were spread across
the river above the vessels to intercept torpedoes. The army
had also engaged Fort Strong. The admiral closes by saying
that he had the pleasure of hoisting the Union flag over it,
and that day being the anniversary of the birth of Washington, at noon would fire a national salute. No hostile gun
was thereafter fired between Wilmington and the sea, but
higher up, where the army of General Sherman was yet to
pass, the war was not yet over.

Some of the smaller vessels of the navy ascended the river

as a supporting force as high as Fayetteville, and found sunk, as a channel obstruction, the Confederate privateer Chicka- mauga. A national salute, reverberating over the navigable waters of Cape Fear River, now restored to national author- ity, seemed a fitting close to nearly four years of civil war.

CHAPTER XI.

CONCLUSIONS.

THE Navy Department had an immense work to perform in the civil war. Except so far as the purchase abroad of vessels of war was concerned, it had the markets of the world to supply its wants without impediment, and it had money without stint. That millions of dollars should have been wasted was a probable, not to say an inevitable result of a lack of preparation, and of empiricism, as shown in the construction of the Chimo and her twenty counterparts, known as the "totally submerged class of monitors." The defect of the latter was radical; no professional doctors could cure or even better them; their office was "to lie in cold obstruction and to rot." All that appears in these pages relating to them is given in the language of the Department, without comment.

To build and purchase vessels more or less adapted to war purposes; to fit, arm, officer, man, and provision them, and to keep up their supplies over a coast line of three thousand miles, with hundreds of inlets to blockade, and to provide fleets here and there to bombard, as at Fort Fisher, required great energy on the part of the Navy Department and its subordinates; and these onerous requirements were fulfilled with a reasonable degree of success and with an immense outlay of money.

There are teachings that seem to belong to war exclu-

sively. Officers learned to anchor vessels anywhere off the
Southern coast, where they rode out with safety the heaviest
gales that swept those waters during four years, and they
learned to appreciate the advantage of carrying a heavy
kedge on the quarter, ready to let go instantly when operating in narrow waters.

They learned, too, what was new then, the power of rifled
guns at long distances against brick or stone forts, and also
that wooden vessels armed with heavy spherical shell-guns,
aided by a few ironclads, can smother and control the fire
from an earthwork when brought within sixteen hundred
yards of it, or better at two-thirds that distance ; and further,
that if vessels attack an earthwork there should be no cessation until the troops advance to the assault.

To the general, as well as the professional reader who
has followed the writer through these pages, a few ideas are
ventured in connection with the civil war.

Accepting the political conditions as existent facts presented by the late Alexander H. Stephens in his remarkable
address at Milledgeville, Ga., on November 14, 1860, the
reader is lost in wonder that a sanguinary war of four years'
duration could have followed, without other inciting causes
than those so fairly and clearly stated by him. Hundreds of
thousands of men perished in battle or by disease through
exposure ; hundreds of thousands of men, women, and children, many of them former slaves, died from violence, exposure, and want. Thousands of millions of dollars were spent
in war, by the North and by the South, and when the forces
of the latter laid down their arms, they were absolutely without resources ; many of the inhabitants in various sections
would have suffered greatly, or actually perished, had not the
gratuitous private charity of the North supplied shiploads
of provisions immediately after the cessation of hostilities.

No one can deny the fact that the South commenced and continued the war with the utmost intensity of purpose, worthy of a sense of the most poignant wrongs. It is most difficult to reconcile this fact with the plain statements of Stephens, which were not, and never can be, fairly controverted.

In view of all this, does it not appear that the civil war was the result of prejudices, of obliquity, and misconceptions, the output of a long-continued material prosperity? Mankind after a time regard this as a normal condition, which is far from the fact. With the Jews of old the image of the Golden Calf seems but the symbol of great material prosperity, bringing in its train woes and repentance in sackcloth and ashes.

Eighteen years have passed since the Confederate forces laid down their arms and returned to their homes unharmed, nor has a human being been held to accountability for all the wretchedness and misery produced by the civil war ; and yet we find that prejudices, unfounded and without reason, are still paraded as facts, and as justifications of a long and sanguinary struggle. May we not say, as a rational deduction, that the prejudices of men far outweigh their reason?

These reflections grew out of a conversation with a lifelong friend that has lately passed away. He had been a large slave-owner, and a kind and considerate one ; the comfortable cabins and the happy faces of the occupants, and the attention given them in sickness and in health could not fail to be observed. The gentleman referred to was opposed to secession, yet when the many around him insisted on war, he took up arms, and bravely did his part. When the war was over he was broken down in fortune and no longer young, but his courage did not forsake him, and he bravely

and honestly struggled to supply the necessities that existence imposes.   Sitting in the gloam of the evening, a few
years ago, he said : "Had we succeeded in our efforts, our
troubles would have but begun.   South Carolina on the one
side, and Florida on the other, would have seceded from
Georgia, and we would have been a dismembered people."
In sadness and in toil he had passed many succeeding years,
and these were his final reflections.   May we not properly—
nay, can we do other than give to such men our entire sym-
pathy, and, in all sincerity, extend the hand of fellowship?
He was a man of thought, of courage, of action, and of purpose ; it is not given to the vulgar to be possessed of such
qualities, whether it be the rich or the poor vulgar, whether
it be the educated or the uneducated vulgar.   With them
thought and reason are as nothing; with them appetites,
selfishness, and prejudices are everything.

APPENDIX.

I.—*Names of Vessels, Character of Armament, and Officers Command-
ing them in the Attack on Port Royal, November 7, 1861.* FLAG-
OFFICER FRANCIS S. DUPONT *and* CAPTAIN CHARLES H. DAVIS,
CHIEF OF STAFF, *with flag on board of the Wabash.*

Name of vessel.	Name of officer commanding.	Battery.
Wabash	Commander C. R. P. Rogers.	28 IX-in., 14 VIII-in., 2 X-in. pivots.
Susquehanna..	Captain J. L. Lardner.......	15 VIII-inch guns.
Mohican......	Commander S. W. Godon ...	2 XI-in. pivots, 4 32-pounders.
Seminole	Commander John P. Gillis ..	1 XI-in. pivot, 4 32-pounders.
Pocahontas...	Commander Percival Drayton	1 XI-in. pivot, 4 32-pounders.
Pawnee.......	Lieut.·Com'g R. H. Wyman .	8 IX.-in. pivot, 2 12-pounder rifles.
Unadilla......	Lt.-Com'g Napoleon Collins..	1 XI-in. pivot, 1 20-pdr. rifle, 2 24-pdr. howitzers.
Ottawa.......	Lt.-Com'g T. H. Stevens	1 XI-in. pivot, 1 20-pounder rifle, 2 24-pounder howitzers.
Pembina	Lt.-Com'g J. P. Bankhead...	1 XI-in. pivot, 1 20-pounder rifle, 2 24-pounder howitzers.
Seneca	Lt.-Com'g Daniel Ammen...	1 XI-in. pivot, 1 20-pounder rifle, 2 24-pounder howitzers.
Vandalia (sailing sloop)...¹	Commander F. L. Haggerty..	4 VIII-in., 16 32-pounders.
Isaac Smith...	Lt.-Com'g J. W. A. Nicholson	1 30-pdr. rifle, afterward 8 VIII-in.
Bienville......	Commander Chas. Steedman.	8 32-pounders.
Augusta	Commander E. G. Parrott...	8 32-pounders.
Penguin......	Lieut.-Com'g T. A. Budd....	4 32-pounders.
Curlew	Lt.-Com'g P. G. Watmough..	6 32-pounders, 1 30-pounder rifle.
R. B. Forbes..	Lt.-Com'g H. S. Newcomb ..	2 32-pounders.

¹ The vessels above the line were built for war purposes, those below it were
purchased.

11*

II.—Ironclad Attack on Fortifications of Charleston Harbor, April 7, 1863.[1]

Name of vessel	Kind and calibre of armament	Projectiles fired.		Nearest approach to Sumter or Moultrie.	Times hit.	Remarks.
		Shot.	Shell.			
New Ironsides	2 150-pdr. rifles	1	...	1,000 yards.	Not stated.	Confederates say the New Ironsides was hit 65 times.
	14 XI-inch	7	...			
Montauk	1 XV-inch	10	1	700 yards.	14	
	1 XI-inch	16	9			
Passaic	1 XV-inch	2	2	880 yards, or less.	35	One gun temporarily disabled.
	1 XI-inch	...	11			
Weehawken	1 XV-inch	...	15	Not given.	53	One gun temporarily disabled.
	1 XI-inch	...	5			
Patapsco	1 XV-inch	...	5	600 yards.	47	Rifle temporarily disabled.
	1 150-pdr. rifle	...	10			
Catskill	1 XV-inch	...	12	600 yards.	20	
	1 XI-inch	...	3			
Nantucket	1 XV-inch	...	12	750 yards.	51	One gun temporarily disabled.
	1 XI-inch	...	...			
Nahant	1 XV-inch	3	4	500 yards.	36	Turret disabled for one day; not in good order for one month.
	1 XI-inch	4	4			
Keokuk	2 XI-inch	...	3	550 yards.	90	Totally disabled; sunk next day off Morris Island.

Vessels, 9; guns in action, 23; fires, 139; range, from 500 to 2,100 yards; fuses for shells cut for flights of from 3¼ to 15 seconds; charges: XV-inch, 35 pounds; XI-inch, 15 to 20 pounds; rifles, 46 pounds. Moultrie received 12 shots, Wagner 2, Sumter the remainder, which was struck 55 times.

Note.—Colonel Rhett, commanding Fort Sumter, reports that no monitor approached nearer than 1,000 yards; the Keokuk to within 900 yards: Ironsides, 1,700 yards. Beauregard reports that the fleet did not come nearer than 1,100 yards to outer batteries, save the Keokuk, which drifted to within 900 yards of Sumter. Engineer Echols reports nearest approach of monitors, 900 yards; of Ironsides to Moultrie, 1,700 yards, and to Sumter, 2,000 yards.

[1] Table compiled from official reports.

III.—*Return of Guns and Mortars at Forts and Batteries in Charleston Harbor engaged with the Ironclads, April 7, 1863, together with Return of Ammunition Expended, and Statement of Casualties.*

Fort or Battery.	X-in. Columbiad.	IX-in. Dahlgren.	VII-in. Brooke rifle.	VIII-in. Columbiad.	42-pounder, rifled.	32-pounder, rifled.	32-pdr., smooth.	X-in. mortars.	Grand total.
Fort Johnson	..	..	..	..	..	..	..	1	1
Fort Sumter	4	2	2	8	7	1	13	7	44
Fort Moultrie	..	..	..	9	..	5	5	2	21
Battery Bee....	5	..	..	1	..	..	..	..	6
Battery Beauregard	..	..	..	1	..	1	..	..	2
Battery Cumming's Point	1	1	..	..	..	..	..	..	2
Battery Wagner.....................	..	..	..	..	..	1	..	..	1
Total........	10	3	2	19	7	8	18	10	77
Ammunition—Shot	385	80	86	731	140	321	343	..	..
Shell	..	..	..	5	..	45	..	93	..

Total shot and shell............................ 2,229
Total pounds of powder..........................21,093
Casualties in action...............3 killed, 11 wounded.
Number of shots fired by fleet..................... 151
Number of shots struck vessels 520
Of shots fired by fleet, all but 24 were directed at Sumter.

NOTE.—This information is compiled from reports of General Beauregard, May 24, 1863; General Ripley, April 13, 1863; Colonel Rhett, April 13, 1863; Major Harris, Chief Engineer, dated April 28, 1863; Major Echols, Engineer, dated April 9, 1863; General Trapier, dated April 13, 1863; and from tabulated statements accompanying the reports of General Ripley and Major Echols.

IV.—*Extract from "Table of Effect of Projectiles on the Walls of Fort Sumter," Report of* MAJOR WILLIAM H. ECHOLS, *Confederate States Engineer, transmitted to* MAJOR D. B. HARRIS, *Chief Engineer of the Department, with his Report, dated April* 9, 1863.

No.	Projec- tile.	Penetra- tion.		Remarks.
	Inches.	Ft.	In.	
3	....	2	3	Embrasure "A." Exterior concrete keystone and interior embrasure arch knocked out; masonry cracked.
4	15	0	9	Assisted No. 3; spent.
5	11	1	0	Penetrated concrete and new masonry facing.
9	3 shots.	2	6	One 15-inch, two others not known; parapet wall cracked 25 feet in length; serious damage, perhaps by exploding shell.
10	15	2	3	Interior arch of embrasure "B" dislocated; masonry between piers and embrasure badly shaken and projecting.
12	15	1	6	Shook masonry.
15	....	1	6	Interior embrasure "C" arch broken; masonry cracked.
18	....	1	6	Masonry shaken.
19	....	3	0	Exploding shell on pier; not much internal injury.
21	....	1	6	Masonry around embrasure "D" badly cracked and projecting inside.
22	15	5	0	Penetrated, striking head of arch and thrown upward, tearing away a quantity of masonry, not seriously damaging body of masonry; exploded in casemate.
23	11	5	0	Same effect as No. 22; destroyed embrasure "E."
24	....	2	6	Not seriously damaging body of masonry.
25	15	5	0	Same effect as No. 22; destroyed embrasure "F;" exploded in parade.
27	... .	1	4	No serious damage.
29	....	2	4	Serious damage; wall not much cracked.
31	15	1	0	Knocked off one foot of angle.
35	....	1	6	Shook masonry.
36	15	1	3	Broke and projected in sole of embrasure "G."
41	....	2	1	Exploding shell.
48	....	2	4	Exploding shell cracked parapet wall.
49	....	......		Knocked out iron embrasure slab 1 foot wide, 6 inches thick, 3 feet long; indented it 1½ inches, and broke it in three pieces; shook masonry.
52	....	......		Entered western quarters and exploded, damaging walls.
54	....	......		Demolished 10-inch columbiad carriage and chassis in southwest angle.

NOTE.—Three shots in all struck or entered quarters. A sketch by Major Echols, showing the effect of these shots, will be found in Volume XIV. of Official Records of War of the Rebellion.

V.—*Abstract from Return of the United States Military Forces Serving in the State of North Carolina, from January, 1862, to February, 1865. Compiled from Original Returns.*

Command.	Present for duty.	Aggregate present.	Commanding general.
January, 1862	12,786	13,451	Brigadier-General A. E. Burnside, from January 13, 1862, to July 6, 1862.
February, 1862	12,700	14,143	
March, 1862	11,322	13,468	
April, 1862	14,054	16,528	
May, 1862	14,508	16,794	
June, 1862	14,371	16,718	
July, 1862	6,403	7,947	Major-General John G. Foster, from July 6, 1862, to July, 1863.
August, 1862	1,226	1,555	
September, 1862	6,642	8,647	
October, 1862	8,967	11,415	
November, 1862	12,872	15,569	
December, 1862	18,463	21,917	
January, 1863	25,023	28,194	
February, 1863	15,806	18,548	
March, 1863	14,672	17,105	
April, 1863	13,962	15,920	
May, 1863	16,643	19,715	
August, 1863	7,699	10,402	Major-General I. N. Palmer, from July, 1863, to August 14, 1863.
September, 1863	7,794	10,923	Major-General John J. Peck, from August 14, .1863, to April 19, 1864.
October, 1863	6,276	8,343	
November, 1863	9,411	12,245	
December, 1863	7,239	9,028	
January, 1864	9,095	11,111	
February 29, 1864	11,213	13,506	
March, 1864	11,772	14,208	
April 30, 1864	6,335	7,069	
May, 1864	6,041	7,623	
June, 1864	6,350	7,846	Major-General I. N. Palmer, from April 19, 1864, to February 9, 1865.
July 31, 1864	5,788	7,436	
August, 1864	5,556	7,505	
September, 1864	5,794	7,946	
October, 1864	6,093	8,920	
November, 1864	6,837	8,891	
December, 1864	6,282	8,117	
February, 1865	6,726	8,439 [1]	

[1] Besides which there were at this time serving in North Carolina the Twenty-third Army Corps and Provisional Army Corps, the aggregate of which was 23,954 men.

VI.—*Abstract from Returns of the Confederate Military Forces Serving in the State of North Carolina, from the close of the year 1861, to February, 1865. Compiled from Original Returns now in the War Department, Washington, D. C.*

Date.	Present for duty.	Aggregate present.	Commanding general.
September, 1861, Dist. of Pamlico..	9,016	10,743	Brigadier-General R. C. Gatlin, to March 19, 1862.
October 31, 1861, Newbern	......	8,239	
January 31. 1862, in North Carolina	6,290	12,095 [1]	
March 31, 1862, in North Carolina..	10,372	24,300	
April 19, 1862, in North Carolina...	17,947 [2]	22,068	Brig.-Gen. Joseph R. Anderson, from Mch. 19. 1862, to May 25, 1862.
April 30, 1862, in North Carolina ..	16,255	19,822	
July 15, 1862. in North Carolina and Southeast Virginia..............	17,505	21,196	Major-General T. H. Holmes, from May 25, 1862, to July 17, 1862.
December 20,1862,in North Carolina	11,074	12,207	Major-Gen. D. H. Hill, from July 17, 1862, to July 1, 1863.
January, 1863, in North Carolina..	26,958	31,273	
February 20,1863, in North Carolina	15,904	19,894	
March 1, 1863, in North Carolina...	......	20,733	
April 10, 1863, in North Carolina. .	7,501	8,385	
May 10, 1863, in North Carolina....	4,851	6,590	
May 31, 1863, in North Carolina ...	22,149	26,838	
June 30, 1863, in North Carolina...	18,601	22,822	
July 30, 1863, in North Carolina...	8,556	9,900	
August 31, 1863, in North Carolina.	7,391	8,867	Major-Gen. W. H. C. Whiting, from July 14, 1863, to October 16, 1863.
September 30, 1863, Defences of Wilmington	3,866	4,618	
October 31, 1863, Defences of Wilmington................	5,271	6,251	
November 30, 1863, Defences of Wilmington	5,830	6,669	
December 31, 1863, Defences of Wilmington	6,485	7,299	Major-Gen. George T. Pickett, from October 16, 1863, to April 21, 1864.
January 31, 1864, Defences of Wilmington......................	5,430	6,181	
February 29, 1864,in North Carolina	12,703	15,252	
March 30, 1864, District of Cape Fear	6,921	7,866	
April 30, 1864, District of Cape Fear	4,987	5,593	Gen. G. T. Beauregard, from April 21, 1864, to November, 1865.
June 10, 1864, in North Carolina...	12,592	17,130	
September 1, 1864, Dept. of Southeast Virginia and North Carolina.	22,005	26,678	
January 31, 1865, Dept. of Southeast Virginia and North Carolina.	11,548	13,164	Gen. Braxton Bragg, from November,1865, to end of the war.
February 10, 1865, Dept. of Southeast Virginia and North Carolina.	11,200	12,769	

NOTE.—The returns of Confederate troops are very incomplete, and it is impossible in many cases to distinguish those serving in Southeastern Virginia and Petersburg from those in North Carolina.

[1] Total enlisted men.   [2] " Effective total."

VII.—*Abstract from Returns of the United States Military Forces Serving in the Department of the South, from January, 1862, to January, 1865. Compiled from Original Returns.*

Date.	Present for duty in department.	Aggregate in South Carolina and Georgia.	Aggregate present in Florida.	Aggregate present in department.	Commanding general.
January 31, 1862....	14,197	16,284	....	16,284	Gen. T. W. Sherman, of the Expeditionary Corps, to March 31, 1862.
February 28, 1862...	16,495	17,875	....	17,875	
March 31, 1862......	16,495	15,257	2,721	17,978	
April 30, 1862.......	15,000	15,795	1,194	16,989	Major-Gen. D. Hunter, from March 31 to Sept. 5, 1862.
May 20, 1862........	19,219	15,878	7,412	23,290	
June 30, 1862	18,745	16,531	5,099	21,630	
July 31, 1862	13,249	11,170	5,029	16,199	
August 31, 1862.....	10,487	10,424	2,317	12,741	
September 30, 1862..	9,925	9,093	3,478	12,571	Bg.-Gen. J. M. Brannan, from Sept. 5 to Sept. 15, 1862.
October 31, 1862	10,190	10,530	2,307	12,837	Bg.-Gen. O.M.Mitchell, from Sept.15 to Oct. 27, 1862.
November 30, 1862..	10,811	11,056	2,390	13,446	Bg.-Gen. J. M. Brannan, from Oct. 27, 1862, to Jan. 20, 1863.
December 31, 1862 ..	10,875	11,056	2,723	13,370	
January 31, 1863....	22,567	23,089	2,697	25,786	
February 28, 1863...	21,612	21,763	3,308	25,071	Major-Gen. D. Hunter, from Jan. 20, 1863, to June 12, 1863.
March 31, 1863....	20,117	22,171	1,214	23,385	
April 30, 1863.......	17,680	19.223	1,396	20,619	
May 31, 1863........	15,745	17,687	1,320	18,997	
June 30, 1863.......	16,761	20.410	923	21,333	
July 31, 1863....	12,922	17,632	905	18,537	
August 31, 1863.....	21,193	28,462	943	29,405	
September 30, 1863..	19,750	27,996	965	28,961	
October 31, 1863	21,562	28,513	1,468	29,981	Brig.-Gen. Q. A. Gillmore, from June 12. 1863, to May 26, 1864.
November 30, 1863..	24,427	20,281	2,301	32,582	
December 31, 1863 ..	26,123	29.779	2,268	32.047	
January 31, 1864....	26,143	31,335	2,195	33,530	
February 29, 1864...	22,350	15.092	12.553	28,645	
March 31, 1864......	23,241	26,190	4,017	30,207	
April 30, 1864.......	15,861	14,234	4,959	19,193	
May 31, 1864	16,529	15,110	4,959	20.069	
June 30, 1864.......	16,138	16,244	3,366	19,610	
July 31, 1864	15,346	15.578	3,948	19,526	
August 31, 1864....	10,312	9,932	2,919	12,851	Maj.-Gen. J. G. Foster, from May 26, 1864, to Feb. 9, 1865.
September 30, 1864..	10,964	10,519	2,996	13,505	
October 31, 1864	11,501	11,101	2,970	14,071	
November 30, 1864 ..	11,322	10,613	3,285	13,898	
December 31, 1864 ..	7,518	7,773	1,766	9,539	
December 31, 1864 ..	4,818[1]	5,603	....	5,603	
January 31, 1865....	11,657	12,781	1,780	14,561	
January 31, 1865....	4,061[1]	4,737	....	4,737	

[1] At Devaux's Neck and Pocotaligo, South Carolina.

VIII.—*Abstract from Returns of the Confederate Military Forces Serving in the Department of South Carolina, Georgia, and Florida, from close of year*, 1861, *to January*, 1865. *Compiled from Original Returns now in the War Department, Washington, D. C.*

Date.	Present for duty.	Aggregate present in S. Carolina and Georgia.	Aggregate present in Florida.	Aggregate present in whole Department.	Commanding general.
Dec., 1861, in Florida .	3,518	....	3,972	......	Brig.-Gen. J. H. Trapier.
Oct , 1861. in Georgia..	4,805	⎫	⎧	5,497	Brig.-Gen. A. R. Lawton.
Nov. 19, 1861, in South		⎬ 18,597	⎨		
Carolina.............	....	⎭	⎩	13,100	Brig.-Gen. G. T. Beauregard.
March 31, 1862........	29,029	34,426	....	34,426[1]	
April 30, 1862........	26,471	32,783	....	32,783[1]	
May 31, 1862, in South				⎧	Major-Gen. J. C. Pemberton, from March 4, 1862, to Sept. 24, 1862.
Carolina..........	⎫ 18,135	30,490	.... ⎨	22,325	
May 31, 1862,in Georgia	⎭		⎩	8,165	
June 30, 1862	23,433	29,841	....	29,841[1]	
July 31, 1862..........	18,932	24,549	....	24,549[1]	
August 31, 1862.......	16,281	21,616	....	21,616[1]	
September 30, 1862....	15,485	20,964	....	20,964[1]	
December 31, 1862	20,553	23,267	1,892	25,159	
January 31, 1863	18,139	19,858	1,797	21,655	
February 17, 1863.....	20,997	18,945	1,579	20,524	
March 14, 1863........	......	31,640	1,721	33,361	
April 7, 1863	......	34,342	2,471	36,813	
May 15, 1863..........	......	23,957	2,617	26,574	
June 3, 1863..........	......	19,423	2,617	22,040	
June 23, 1863	......	19,389	2,617	22,006	
July 22, 1863	......	21,735	3,061	24,796	Gen. G. T. Beauregard, from Sept. 24, 1862, to April 20, 1864.
August 1, 1863	20,772	21,120	4,095	25,215	
September 1, 1863.....	26,088	26,411	3,587	29,998	
October 1, 1863	28,151	31,488	3,587	35,073	
November 1, 1863	......	......	......	29,535[2]	
December 1, 1863	27,336	29,778	3,600	33,378	
December 31, 1863	28,347	30,347	3,709	34,056	
January 31, 1864.....	32,068	34,850	3,377	38,227	
February 10, 1864.....	28,792	31,006	3,547	34,553	
Feb. 19, 1864, at Augusta, Ga...........	......	......	......	1,427	
April 10, 1864........	27,463	21,722	10,900	32,622	
April 30, 1864........	24,210	17,394	11,418	28,812	
June 1, 1864	11,284	11,647	1,634	13,281	
June 30, 1864	11,818	12,016	2,262	14,278	Major-Gen. Sam'l Jones,from April 20, 1864, to Oct. 5, 1864.
July 30, 1864....	11,221	11,822	2,157	13,979	
August 31, 1864.......	11 124	12,222	1,660	13,882	
September 30, 1864....	10,993	11,921	1,940	13,861	
October 1, 1864, at Augusta, Ga............	......	......	......	1,695	
October 31, 1864	11,988	13,422	1,613	15,035	Lieut.-Gen. W. J. Hardee, from Oct. 5, 1864, to Feb. 16, 1865.
November 20, 1864....	12,055	13,839	......	13,839	
January 20, 1865	25,290	29,863	......	29,863	
January 31, 1865	24,956	30,062	......	30,062	

[1] Troops serving in Florida not included.   [2] "Effective total" in Department.

IX.—*Names of Vessels, Officers Commanding them, and Armaments in the Attack of the Defences on Roanoke Island, February 7 and 8, 1862, and Operations following at Elizabeth City and Newbern in which many of these Vessels were engaged.*

Name of vessel.	Commanders of vessels.	Armament.
Stars and Stripes ...	Lieut.-Com'g Reed Werden..	4 VIII-in., 1 30-pdr. rifle.
Louisiana	" Alex. Murray..	1 VIII-in., 3 32- pdrs., 1 12-pdr., rifled.
Hetzel..............	" H.K.Davenport	1 IX-in., 1 80-pdr., rifled.
Delaware..........	" L. P. Quacken-bush......	1 IX-in., 1 32-pdr., 1 12-pdr., rifled.
Commodore Perry ..	" C. W. Flusser..	1 100-pdr., 4 IX-in., 1 12-pdr., rifled.
Valley City	" A. C. Chaplin..	4 32-pdrs., 1 12-pdr., rifled.
Underwriter.......	" W. N. Jeffers..	1 VIII-in., 1 80-pdr., rifled ; 1 12-pdr., rifled.
Commodore Barney.	" R. T. Renshaw.	4 IX-in., 1 32-pdr., 1 12-pdr., rifled.
Hunchback	" E. R. Colhoun .	3 IX-in., 1 100-pdr., rifled.
Southfield	" C. F. W. Behm.	3 IX-in., 1 100-pdr., rifled.
Morse........... ..	Acting-Master Peter Hayes..	2 IX-in.
Brincker	" J. E. Giddings	1 30-pdr., rifled.
Lockwood,..........	" G. W. Graves.	1 80-pdr., rifled, 1 12-pdr., rifled.
Whitehead	" French.......	1 IX-in.
Seymour	" Wells	1 30-pdr., 1 12-pdr., rifled.
Ceres.............	" McDiarmid...	1 30-pdr., rifled ; 1 32-pdr.
Putnam	" Hotchkiss....	1 20-pdr., rifled.
Shawshen	" Woodward ...	2 20-pdrs, rifled.
Granite	Master's Mate Boomer	1 32-pdr.

X.—*Names of Commanding Officers and the Batteries of Vessels that engaged the Ram Albemarle, May 5, 1864.*

Mattabesett, flag-ship of Captain Melancton Smith, commanded by Commander John C. Febiger. Battery: 2 100-pounder Parrott rifles, expended 27 solid shot ; 4 IX-inch Dahlgrens, expended 23 solid shot ; 4 24-pounder howitzers, expended 1 shrapnel ; 2 12-pounder howitzers, expended 1 shell. Casualties, 3 killed, 5 wounded.

Sassacus, Commander F. A. Roe. Battery : 2 100-pounder Parrott rifles ; 4 IX-inch Dahlgrens ; 2 24-pounder howitzers ; 2 20-pounder howitzers ; 2 12-pounder howitzers ; expenditure not given. Casualties, 1 killed, 19 wounded.

Wyalusing, Commander W. W. Queen. Battery : 2 100-pounder Parrott rifles, expended 47 solid shot, 28 shell ; 4 IX-inch Dahlgrens, expended 37 solid shot, 33 shell ; 2 24-pounder howitzers, expended 27 shrapnel, 18 shell ; 2 12-pounder howitzers (one rifled). Casualties, 1 killed.

Miami, Acting Volunteer Lieutenant Charles A. French. Battery : 1 100-pounder Parrott rifle, expended 41 solid shot ; 6 IX-inch Dahlgrens, expended 76 solid shot ; 1 24-pounder howitzer.

Whitehead, Acting Ensign G. W. Barrett. Battery : 1 100-pounder Parrott rifle, expended 17 solid shot ; 3 24-pounder howitzers.

Commodore Hull, Acting Master Francis Josselyn. Battery : 2 30-pounder Parott rifles, expended 60 shell ; 4 24-pounder howitzers, expended 24 shell.

Ceres, Acting Master H. H. Foster. Battery : 2 20-pounder Parrott rifles (pivot).

XI.—*List of Ordnance left on Morris Island on the night of its Evacuation, September* 6, 1863.

BATTERY WAGNER.

Two X-inch Columbiads (1 dismounted and broken, 1 serviceable); 1 X-inch mortar, serviceable; 2 VIII-inch shell guns (1 serviceable, 1 injured by shell and carriage disabled); 2 VIII-inch siege howitzers (1 dismounted and broken to pieces); 1 VIII-inch S. C. howitzer, serviceable; 2 32-pounder smooth-bores, serviceable; 1 42-pounder carronade, serviceable; 1 VIII-inch siege mortar, brass, spiked with friction tube two days before evacuation; 3 32-pounder carronades, serviceable; 2 12-pounder howitzers, serviceable.   Total, 17.

BATTERY GREGG.

Two X-inch Columbiads (1 carriage injured and the other serviceable) ; 1 IX-inch Dahlgren, serviceable; 1 X-inch S. C. mortar, serviceable; 2 12-pounder howitzers, serviceable.   Total, 6.

XII.— *Vessels Engaged in the Second Bombardment of Fort Fisher ; their Armament, Ammunition Expended, and Casualties in Action, January* 14 *and* 15, 1865, REAR-ADMIRAL D. D. PORTER, *U. S. Navy, Commanding Fleet.*

LINE NO. 1.

Names of vessels.	Commanders.	Batteries.	Shells expended.	Killed.	Wounded.	Missing.
Brooklyn	Alden	2 100-pdrs., rifled ... 2 60-pdrs., rifled ..... 20 IX-in. shell guns.	Not given.	2	12	0
Mohican	Ammen	1 100-pdr., rifled...... 2 30-pdrs, rifled .... 6 IX-in. shell guns ...	.... 17 419	12	0	0
Tacony...........	Truxtun......	2 XII-in............. 4 IX-in	309 361	0	0	0
Kansas...........	Watmough ...	1 100-pdr., rifled ..... 1 30-pdr., rifled ..... . 2 IX-in. shell guns ...	.... 91 394	0	1	0
Yantic	Harris.... ...	1 100-pdr., rifled ...... 1 30-pdr., rifled ...... 2 IX-in. shell guns ...	.... 23 202	2	2	0
Unadilla..........	Ramsay	1 XI-inch shell gun.... 1 20-pdr., rifled.......	358 45	0	0	0
Huron...........	Selfridge	1 XI-inch shell gun.... 1 30-pdr., rifled	300	0	5	0
Maumee....	Chandler	1 100-pdr., rifled ...... 1 30-pdr., rifled....... 2 32-pdrs............	117 14 206	0	0	0
Pequot	Braine	1 150-pdr., rifled....... 1 30-pdr., rifled 6 32-pdrs	146 33 319	3	5	0

TABLE XII.—*Continued.*

Names of vessels.	Commanders.	Batteries.	Shells expended.	Killed.	Wounded.	Missing.
Pawtuxet.........	Spotts........	1 100-pdr	42			
		1 XI-inch	116	0	0	0
		4 IX-inch shell guns..	305			
Seneca	Sicard........	1 XI-inch shell gun....	222			
		1 20-pdr., rifled	30	0	0	0
		2 100-pdrs., rifled	....			
Pontoosuc	Temple.......	4 IX-inch shell guns...	313	0	7	0
		2 20-pdrs	5			
		1 60-pdr., rifled.......	94			
Nereus	Howell	2 30-pdrs,, rifled	122	3	3	0
		6 32-pdrs	324			

LINE NO. 2.

Minnesota........	Lanman......	1 150-pdr., rifled......	89			
		4 100-pdrs., rifled	....	13	23	0
		1 XI-inch shell gun....	70			
		42 IX-inch shell guns..	1,495			
Colorado	Thatcher.....	1 150-pdr., rifled	....			
		1 XI-inch shell gun....	30	3	14	0
		46 IX-inch shell guns .	756			
Wabash	Smith........	1 150-pdr., rifled	154	0	12	0
		42 IX-inch shell guns..	1,781			
Susquehanna ...∙∙	Godon........	2 150-pdrs., rifled.... .	215	3	15	8
		12 IX-inch shell guns .	643			
Powhatan .....∙	Schenck......	3 100-pdrs., rifled...	Not			
		1 XI-inch shell gun .	given.	3	19	7
		14 IX-inch shell guns				
Juniata ......∙ ∙.	Phelps	1 100.pdr., rifled......	....			
		2 30-pdrs., rifled	238	5	10	0
		6 VIII-inch shell guns.	765			
Shenandoah ∙ ∙...	Ridgley	1 150-pdr., rifled......	....			
		1 30-pdr., rifled.......	30	6	0	5
		2 XI-inch, rifled	287			
Ticonderoga......	Steedman ...	1 30-pdr., rifled	29	1	6	0
		12 IX-inch shell guns..	523			
Vanderbilt	Pickering	2 100-pdrs., rifled.....	18			
		2 30-pdrs., rifled	65	0	0	0
		12 IX-inch shell. guns.	87			
Mackinaw........	Beaumont....	1 XI-inch shell gun....	190	0	2	0
		6 IX-inch shell guns ..	749			
Tuscarora	Frailey........	1 100-pdr., rifled......	53			
		2 30-pdrs., rifled	47	3	12	0
		6 VIII-inch shell guns.	114			

TABLE XII.—*Continued.*

LINE NO. 3.

Names of vessels.	Commanders.	Batteries.	Shells expended.	Killed.	Wounded.	Missing.
Santiago de Cuba.	Glisson.......	1 30-pdr., rifled ...... 2 30-pdrs., rifled ...... 5 32-pdr. shell guns ...	68 25 106	}1	9	0
Fort Jackson......	Sands	1 100-pdr., rifled .... 2 30-pdrs., rifled .... 8 IX-inch shell guns.	Not given.	}1	10	0
Osceola..........	Clitz	1 100-pdr., rifled.. 1 XI-inch shell gun ... 4 IX-inch shell guns ..	175 106 38	}0	0	0
Sassacus.........	Davis	2 100-pdrs., rifled ..... 2 20-pdrs., rifled ...... 4 IX-inch shell guns ..	145 119 98	}0	0	0
Chippewa	Potter........	1 20-pdr., rifled....... 1 IX-inch shell gun...	 74	}0	0	0
Cuyler...........	Caldwell.....	2 32-pdrs., shell guns.. 8 30-pdrs, rifled	6 43	}0	0	0
Maratanza........	Young	1 100-pdr., rifled .... 1 IX-inch shell gun..	Not given.	}0	0	0
Rhode Island	Trenchard....	2 30-pdrs., rifled ...... 1 IX-inch shell gun ... 8 VIII-inch shell guns.	69 94 136	}8	2	0
Monticello	Cushing......	1 100-pdr., rifled ...... 3 30-pdrs., rifled ...... 2 IX-inch shell guns...	115 3 144	}4	4	0
Alabama	Langthorne...	2 30-pdrs., rifled .... 1 IX-inch shell gun.. 6 32-pdrs	Not given.	}0	0	0
Montgomery......	Dunn	1 30-pdr., rifled ...... 1 X-inch shell gun ... 4 VIII-inch shell guns.	192 158 230	}2	4	0
Iosco	Guest	2 100-pdrs., rifled .... 4 IX-inch shell guns ..	200 358	}2	12	0

ARMOR-PLATED VESSELS.

Names of vessels.	Commanders.	Batteries.	Shells expended.	Killed.	Wounded.	Missing.
New Ironsides	Radford	2 150-pdrs., rifled.... 2 60-pdrs., rifled .... 14 XI-in, shell guns.	971	0	0	0
Monadnock.......	Parrott.......	4 XV-inch shell guns....	441	0	0	0
Canonicus........	Belknap	2 XV-inch shell guns....	297	0	3	0
Mahopac	Weaver	2 XV-inch shell guns....	153	0	0	0
Saugus...........	Calhoun......	2 XV-inch shell guns....	212	0	1	0
Malvern (flag-ship)	....	....	....	3	1	0

Vessels in reserve line not given. The total of killed is 74 ; wounded, 289 ; missing, 20. The total of shells thrown from the vessels, from which returns are in the Department, 18,716. The Brooklyn and Susquehanna probably threw 2,000, and ten smaller vessels 1,000, making a probable total of 21,716 during the second bombardment. The number of shells thrown during the first bombardment was probably about 15,000.

INDEX.

Beaumont, Commander, 128

Beauregard, General G. T., proclamation of, concerning blockade at Charleston, 78 et seq., 137

Beauregard, Fort, see Fort Beauregard

Bedell, Lieutenant, 63

Behm, Lieutenant C. F. W., 177, 189

Belknap, Colonel, of Eighty-fifth New York, 197

Belknap, Lieutenant-Commander George E., 100, 156

Belle, the, U. S. tug, 214

Belvidere, the, U. S. transport, 18, 33, 49

Benjamin, J. P., 16 (note)

Berry, Captain, 25

Bertwistle, Ensign, 237

Bienville, the, U. S., 21

Black Warrior, the, 184 et seq.

Blockade, proclamation concerning, 78; blockade running, 146

Blythewood, Mr., plantation of, 37

Bombshell, the, 205 et seq.

Boomer, Master's Mate E., 177

Boston Navy Yard, 7 et seq.

Boston, the, U. S. transport, 46, 49 et seq.

Boun, Lewis, 62

Boutelle, Mr., 18, 36, 91

Bowen, Mr., bar-pilot, 220

Boyden, Master's Mate, 218

Bradford, Colonel, 170

Bradford, Mr., of the Coast Survey, 220

Bragg, General, 236, 240, 242

Braine, Lieutenant D. L., 174

Branch, Colonel John L., his report on abandonment of Rockville, 40, 171

Brannan, General, 70 et seq.

Breese, Captain K. R., 232 et seq., 237

Bridge, Horatio, Chief of Provisions and Clothing Bureau, 3

Brincker, the, 177, 181, 183, 189

Brintnall, Assistant Surgeon, 63

Britannia, the, 210, 229

Brooklyn, the, U. S. steamer, 6, 223, 228

Brown, Colonel, 173

Brown, John, raid of, 1

Brunswick, Ga., 56 et seq.

Bryson of the Lehigh, 146; of the Chippewa, 194

Buchanan, President, favors separation of States, 2

Buckingham, the, 229

Budd, Lieutenant-Commanding P. A., 21, 41; killed, 60, 68

Buist, Dr., 32

Burnside, General A. E., 171, 176, 190

Butler, General B. F., 165 et seq., 168 et seq., 171, 219; at Fort Fisher, 222, 224 (note), et seq.

Campbell's plantation, 54

Canandaigua, the, U. S. vessel, 74, 131, 156

Canonicus, the, U. S. monitor, 156, 221, 229

Case, Commander, 178; at Roanoke Island, 182

Catskill, the, 90 et seq., 96 et seq., 125 et seq., 131 et seq., 146

Cavendy of the Gemsbok, 194

Ceres, the, 177 et seq., 181, 183 et seq., 197, 202 et seq., 205, 209

Chadwick, Ensign, 143

Chaplin, Lieutenant-Commanding J. C., commands the Dai Ching, 155, 177, 189

Preble, Commander George H., 152

Prentiss, Commander G. A., 66 et seq.

Preston, Lieutenant S. W., 102, 138, 218, 221, 233; death of, 237 et seq.

Princess Royal, the, prize steamer, 79, 81

Proclamations: forbidding all intercourse between Confederate and National forces, 35; concerning the blockade at Charleston, 78 et seq.

Pulaski, Fort, see Fort Pulaski.

Putnam, the, 177 et seq., 181, 183, 194

QUACKENBUSH, Commander, 155, 177, 183, 189

Quaker City, the, 79, 81, 218, 223

RALEIGH, the, 211

Ranger, the, 179

Read, battery of, 26

Remey, Lieutenant, 138

"Regulators," 68 et seq.

Relief, the, U. S. store-ship, 7

Renshaw, Lieutenant R. T., 177, 189

Republic, the, 229

Resignations of officers, 4 et seq.

Reynolds, Major John G., 14, 49 et seq.

Rhind, Lieutenant-Commanding A. C., 63, 92, 128, 218, 220 et seq.

Rhoades, Assistant-Surgeon, 58

Rhode Island, the, 218, 228

Richmond, the, U. S. vessel, 7

Ringgold, Captain Cadwalader, 17

Ripley, General, 16 (note), 132 et seq., 135 et seq.

Roanoke Island, 171, 173, 175; map of, 180 et seq.

Roanoke, the U. S. frigate, 7, 33

Robertson, Master, conduct commended, 62

Robeson, Lieutenant T. R., 178

Rockville, desertion of, 39 et seq.

Rodgers, Commander C. R. P., 13, 21, 27; reconnoitres Wassaw Sound, 38; commands advance against Port Royal Ferry, 43 et seq.; in Wassaw Sound, 46; in St. Andrew's Inlet, 50 et seq., 55 et seq.; at Fort Pulaski, 61 et seq., 70; highly commended, 102, 109

Rodgers, Commander George W., of the Catskill, 92 et seq., 125, 127 (note), 128; death of, 131 et seq., 146, 162 (note)

Rodgers, Commander John, 19, 27; makes a reconnoissance on Tybee Island, 35 et seq.; threatens Savannah, 47 et seq.; off Charleston, 91; in Wassaw Sound, 117, 122, 162 (note)

Rogers, Ensign, 150

Rowan, Captain S. C., 128, 137, 146, 165, 172, 177, 179; at Roanoke Island, 182 et seq., 185 et seq.; at Newbern, 189 et seq.

SABINE, the, U. S. frigate, 6, 17

St. Andrew's Inlet, 48 et seq.

St. Augustine, Fla., surrendered to Captain Rodgers, 55 et seq., 59 et seq.

St. Louis, the, U. S. sloop, 6

St. Mary's, Ga., 53

www.ingramcontent.com/pod-product-compliance
Lightning Source LLC
Chambersburg PA
CBHW031944080426
42735CB00007B/256